NEW FLAVOURS *of the*
VIETNAMESE
TABLE

MAI PHAM

Born in Vietnam, Mai Pham moved to the United States with her family in 1975. After a career as a journalist, she opened two Lemon Grass restaurants in California. She now teaches at the Culinary Instit... of A........ ... . food writer.

To my grandmother
huynh thi kien
for teaching me that food is love

And to
trong nguyen
for this and much more

NEW FLAVOURS *of the*
VIETNAMESE
TABLE

PHAM

EBURY PRESS

1 3 5 7 9 10 8 6 4 2

Published in 2008 by Ebury Press, an imprint of Ebury Publishing

Ebury Publishing is a division of the Random House Group

Text © Mai Pham 2007

Mai Pham has asserted her right to be identified as the author of this Work
in accordance with the Copyright, Designs and Patents Act 1988

The Random House Group Limited Reg. No. 954009

Addresses for companies within the Random House Group
can be found at www.randomhouse.co.uk .

A CIP catalogue record for this book is available from the British Library

Design: Estuary English and seagulls.net

Printed and bound in the UK by
CPI Mackays, Chatham ME5 8TD

ISBN 9780091926908

Contents

Acknowledgements

IN THE Vietnamese tradition, all success results from the work, guidance and blessings of *many* people, including those who have passed on. So with the successful completion of this book, I first wish to thank my *ong ba*, or ancestors, for helping me to create and share this book and my parents, Pham Van Xuan and Vo Thi Thom, for instilling in me a passion for food and cooking.

At Lemon Grass Restaurant – the source of much of my joy for the past twelve years – I thank my manager Kate Griffin, along with William Bernard, Thaddeus Winter, David Young, Quyen Ha, Tang Nguyen, Kiet Nguyen, Albert Castorena, Su Hoang, Hoang Ngo, Tuyet Lieu Ngo, Juan Camargo, Andre Douglas and all the wonderful service staff for making our restaurant consistently the best year after year. To our great customers – your laughter, your applause and your loyalty make it all worthwhile.

My deepest gratitude goes to my business partner, Trong Nguyen, whose energy, talent and sharp mind never cease to amaze and inspire me, and to our dynamic management team at World of Good Tastes and La Bou Bakery and Cafés. I'm proud to be working alongside such caring people as Marlene Underwood, Lisa Limcaco, Michael Kyalwazi, Suzanne Ferris, Angie Barrett, Alfonso Ozuna, Bette Chauvin, Trista Harman, Que Tran, Thuyen Nguyen, Huong Nguyen, Caryl Hearn, Maria Lurie and many others.

At HarperCollins, my thanks go to Susan Friedland, who first embraced the concept for this book after reading an article I'd written on *pho*, the Vietnamese beef noodle soup, and to Vanessa Stich, Roberto de Vicq de Cumptich, Betty Lew, David Koral and others for their very excellent work on the manuscript; to Carrie Weinberg and Gypsy Lovett for their publicity efforts; and to my talented agent, Jane Dystel.

In the media, my thanks go to Laurie Ochoa, formerly of the *Los Angeles Times*: Susan Spungen of *Martha Stewart Living*: Michael Bauer, Miriam Morgan and former staff member Mary Ann Mariner of the *San Francisco Chronicle*: and to Martha Holmberg, Joanne Smart and Susie Middleton of *Fine Cooking*, for their keen interest in Vietnamese cuisine and for encouraging me to share my passion with a Western audience.

I'm grateful to Tom and Ae Glasheen for both their friendship and generous help with recipe development; to Minh Xuan Ngo, Lan Ngo, Mai Hoang, Nickolay Kachagin, Tuy Nguyen, Jeff Drescher and Bridget Feighan for their invaluable help with recipe testing; to Nguyen Dinh Xuong for his help with the Vietnamese language and translations; to Helen Burns and Janet Fletcher for their editorial input; to Quoc K. Tran for his meticulous research and to my siblings Phred Pham, Loc Pham and Denise Pham Healy for sharing and tasting recipes as well as answering food and computer questions.

In Vietnam, my gratitude goes to more street-food vendors and cooks than I can possibly name here, folks who've showered me with great good and others who've supported my research over the years.

In Saigon, my sincere *cam on* goes to Pham Thi Ngoc Tinh, Nguyen Doan Cam Van, Nguyen Huu Hoang Trang, Dieu Ho and the Caravelle, New World, Omni and Huong Sen Hotels; in Hue, Nguyen Thi Hanh, Lai Thi Minh Huong of the Huong Giang Hotel and the Morin Hotel; in Hanoi, U.S. Ambassador Pete Peterson and his wife, Vi; U.S. Agricultural Trade Officer Ross Kreamer and his wife, Chris; cultural expert and journalist Huu Ngoc of The Gioi Publishing; Minh Tam, Dam Thanh, Pham Ba Khanh Thinh of Seasons of Hanoi Restaurant; the Nikko, Heritage, Metropole and Golden Key Hotels; in Can Tho and Sapa, the Victoria Hotel; in Danang, the Furama Hotel and in Nha Trang, the Ana Mandara Resort; and in Bangkok, the Amari Watergate, Shangri-La and Indra Regent Hotels.

I'm grateful to Marcia Selva and her staff at Global Spectrum in Washington, D.C., and her associates in Vietnam, including Tran Dinh Song and Hoang Tran Anh and at Trails of IndoChina, Linh Nguyen and John Tue Nguyen, for their help with in-country travel arrangements and for their commitment to making the best of Vietnamese culture more accessible to Westerners.

Thanks to my favourite suppliers and purveyors, including Suong and Nho Pham, and Can and Oanh Pham, who grow the most beautiful Vietnamese herbs this side of the Pacific Ocean. To Jerry and Sidney Mahoney, for finding and bringing to us the best seafood; and to Hemingway Fish, General Produce, Del Monte Meat, Saigon Market, Vinh Phat Market and Wing Wa Market, and to our friends at the Sacramento farmers' markets. When I think about what it all takes to bring the best to the Vietnamese table, I feel extremely grateful to these folks.

At The Culinary Institute of America, my warmest thanks go to Ferdinand Metz, Tim Ryan and Mark Erickson for their support over the years in bringing Vietnamese culinary traditions to a wider professional audience. To the late Catherine Brandel, Toni Sakaguchi, Robert and Cathy Jorin, Ken Woytisek, Lars Kronmark, Robert Danhi, and Bill and Holly Briwa for their friendship and support, and for their dedication to teaching authentic Asian flavours. And last but not least, to Greg Drescher, whose insights, passion and long-standing commitment to the preservation of traditional cultures and cuisines around the world have greatly inspired my work. I share his vision and cherish his love and support.

Introduction

Heaven
Please make the rain fall
So I may have water to drink
So I may plough my rice field
So I may have my bowl of rice
And my fish in great slices.

A Vietnamese farmer's verse

RETURN TO VIETNAM

Vietnam today is a land of peace and action, of old and new. In the lush, emerald-green countryside, women wearing traditional conical hats work diligently to transplant rice seedlings. At a floating market in the Mekong Delta, a couple manoeuvres their boat past competing vendors, hoping to sell out of their juicy crab apples. At pagodas surrounded by lotus-blooming ponds, elderly monks say their prayers as incense smoke swirls above the altar.

On the streets, where freshly painted billboards touting mobile phones stand next to soaring buildings, a driver with a live pig strapped on his motorcycle weaves in and out of traffic, heading to the slaughterhouse.

In recent years, since the opening of Vietnam to the Western world, there's a new sense of excitement. I can feel it each time I return. The streets are more crowded and the rooftops get higher. The market stalls are bursting with new merchandise, from yet more types of rice paper to the latest tennis shoe designs. Clothes are brighter and more colourful, and the smiles seem wider. I love what I see, what I hear and most of all, what I eat.

It's very different from the country that my family and I left more than twenty-five years ago, only days before Saigon fell to Communist rule on 30 April 1975. We'd left with just the clothes on our backs, fighting our way through the pandemonium at the airport before climbing aboard a plane that would fly us to safety. In the distance I could see the artillery smoke surrounding the city. I remembered my frail grandmother back at the house. She stood at the front gate as we said goodbye, crying as I had never seen anyone cry before. She was fearful that we would never see one another again.

Six years ago, I ventured back to Vietnam for the first time. I had two dreams to fulfil – to reunite with my then ninety-six-year-old grandmother and to eat *pho* (rice noodle soup with beef and aromatic herbs), my favourite food on earth, on Vietnamese soil. What unfolded was something much more encompassing, something that would later deeply affect my life. I reconnected with my extended family for the first time in more than two decades. I made peace with my homeland, a country that had seen nothing but war and suffering for almost a century.

During my first trip back I spent most of my time in the Mekong Delta, in my ancestral village of Quoi Son, just being by my grandmother's side, making up for lost time. When I touched her silvery white hair, kissed her pinkish skin and tightly held her bony hands for the first time in more than twenty years, I felt such joy and relief. Not only had she survived, but she thrived. Granted she'd become older and weaker, but there were things about her that hadn't changed, like the wrinkles in her nose when she smiled, the way she laughed and her inquisitive demeanour.

As I walked around her home, the same house where several generations of my family had lived, I noticed that all the furniture, including the family altar, was still there. The picture of my grandfather

– that handsome man with shoulder-length hair – still graced the altar, along with burning incense and offerings of fruit. And the kitchen, it still looked exactly the same. No walls, just a thatched roof supported by large beams. There were two clay stoves and a barbecue pit, all fuelled by the coconut husks gathered from the plantation. It was in this modest kitchen that my grandmother prepared many splendid meals, and it was here that she instilled in me a passion for cooking.

EXPLORING THE LAND AND FOOD

Thanks to that nurturing reconnection, I became more at ease about being back. I started roaming the country, travelling the back roads, from the northern mountainous terrain of Sapa to the southern tip of Ha Tien. It was the first time since the war that I had ventured far outside of my home town of Saigon.

But it wasn't until I savoured my first bowl of *pho* that I finally came to terms with being back. I was so excited as I walked down the narrow alley near our home to find the little soup shop that my sister Denise and I once frequented. It was still there, still packed with hungry diners. For a moment I was taken aback by the noise, the slurping, the yelling of orders, the banging of dishes. The noodle man was there, bare chested, working in front of the steaming soup pot, swinging his copper-wire basket of noodles, dipping them in and out of the hot water.

When my bowl arrived, I felt ecstatic. The noodles were so soft they practically melted. The broth had the buttery beefy flavour I remembered so fondly. Even the chilli sauce tasted like real chilli sauce. I looked up, hoping to see if anyone else around felt the same way, but all I heard was slurping.

In the weeks following, after many bowls of *pho*, I felt very much at home. I could see that the sins of war had been forgiven, that the animosity had dissipated, and that in peacetime, the Vietnamese – both southerners like myself and northerners – were actually friends, not foes.

I spent endless hours at places where I used to eat as a youngster – not at fancy restaurants, but at market stalls, street cafés and wherever I could catch up with home cooks. No matter where I travelled, I found myself lingering in front of stoves, watching the cooks chop and stir. I scrutinized their movements and facial expressions and chronicled as much as I could, both on paper and on film. I ate and chatted with these cooks, sometimes at the very same market stall day after day. Sometimes I even followed them home for more secrets on how to prepare all the dishes that I love, from the best steamed rice rolls to the most fragrant warm soy milk with pandanus leaves.

THE WORLD OF PHO AND NOODLES

Since that first trip, I've gone back to Vietnam every year, to see my grandmother and to further explore the world of Vietnamese noodles and street foods. Each time I returned I ate endless versions of *pho* and immersed myself in all kinds of street and market foods. I also spent a lot of time with my aunts and uncles, learning about our favourite family recipes, dishes my mom used to make for us when we were still living in Saigon.

New Flavours of the Vietnamese Table is a collection of these recipes – dishes that I think are the best that Vietnam has to offer. They include noodles – noodle soups, noodle salads and noodle stir-fries – as well as other favourites. Although many are traditionally cooked and served at market stalls and street corners, they're easily replicated in a home kitchen. In Vietnam, street foods are highly regarded and the people who cook them are considered master chefs. Many have spent a lifetime perfecting one, or at most a few, speciality recipes that are typically packed with flavours. Instead of relying on many courses to create a spectrum of tastes, they must deftly achieve this with just one bowl or plate. It makes sense, then, that if one wants to truly learn great Vietnamese cooking, one focuses on these dishes.

In developing the recipes, I've made every effort to retain and preserve the authenticity of each dish. Where modifications were necessary and appropriate, I've made sure the flavours remain true. Most recipes were given to me by the street vendors whom I was fortunate to work with over the course of my travels. Many have even become new additions to our menu at Lemon Grass Restaurant, much to the delight of our customers. Other recipes came from my mother and aunts and other home cooks. But regardless of the source, all have been tested and can be easily re-created in a home kitchen.

Let me then take you to the parts of Vietnam that I love and share with you all the delectable flavours that I have been so fortunate to experience. Along the way, I'll share glimpses of the local culture and introduce you to the cooks who've enchanted me with the idea that love, life and food – when woven together against the backdrop of family and tradition – are the most beautiful form of human expression.

Mai Pham

Vietnamese Cuisine: An Overview

FROM THE BEGINNING

I once asked my grandmother where she thought Vietnamese cuisine came from. After thinking about it for a few seconds, she started laughing, her hands waving in the air. 'Where else but from our *ong ba* [our ancestors]?' she asked. That's my grandmother for you.

There's no question that Vietnamese cuisine is deeply rooted in the cooking of neighbouring China. A quick look at our history shows that our ancestors came from China, part of a tribal group who migrated south and settled in the northern part of Vietnam about 1500 B.C. Over the centuries, empires rose and fell. By the second century B.C., the Chinese had annexed the country and rigorously imposed their system of government and religion. They introduced ancestor worship and Confucianism and Buddhism, established schools to spread the Chinese script and levied taxes to support a system of mandarin rule. Over time, the Vietnamese began to adopt the food traditions of southern China, including the custom of eating with chopsticks, cooking by stir-frying and steaming and using ingredients such as noodles, soy sauce, ginger and tofu.

Being at a major crossroads of Southeast Asia, Vietnam was continually prone to other foreign influences as well. In the sixteenth century, European explorers started arriving, bringing foods from the New World, such as tomatoes and peanuts. During French rule, which lasted a hundred years from the mid-1800s to the mid-1900s, the Vietnamese learnt to eat butter, yoghurt, the baguette, coffee and vegetables like asparagus and artichokes. In addition, trading and migration between neighbouring Thailand, Cambodia and Laos – all greatly influenced by India – led to the adoption of curries and spices into the local cooking.

But as much as Vietnamese cuisine has borrowed from or been influenced by foreign cultures, it has always managed to retain its unique character. When you look at it closely, what really sets it apart boils down to three main factors: the extensive use of *nuoc mam* (fish sauce) to season almost every dish, the high consumption of *rau thom* (aromatic herbs) and the distinctive style of eating small pieces of meat or seafood wrapped in lettuce or rice paper and dipped in sauce.

These characteristics apply to all three culinary regions of Vietnam, although each has a slightly different approach to cooking. In the rich, fertile south – the rice bowl of the country – the food is particularly vibrant and robust and makes liberal use of garlic, shallots and spices. Southern cooks are partial to sweet and sour flavours and eat more fresh herbs than in any other part of the country. Historically southerners have always been more open to foreign influences and cultures, as evidenced by the popularity of Indian- and French-inspired foods in Saigon. In the former imperial capital of Hue and in the central region where the climate is cooler, the food tends to be spicier and heavier. The preferred noodles are thicker and broths are tinged with bright red chillies. The seat of the Nguyen dynasty from the early 1800s to the mid-1900s, Hue is known for its refined royal cuisine. Royal banquets are said to have included more than fifty dishes, all elaborately and artfully prepared by hand, many in miniature sizes. Today, Hue dishes are often prepared in a similar fashion.

In the harsh, mountainous terrain of the north, the cooking is simple and straightforward, in large part because the region suffered more deprivation from the war than any other region. Dipping sauces are made saltier so they can be eaten with lots of rice. Soups are mostly clear broths with vegetables and only a little meat. Sticky rice is served without the rich mung bean paste and the shredded coconut toppings common in the south.

Despite that, the north has its own great culinary traditions as well. Some of the best dishes originated in this area, including *pho* (rice noodle soup with beef), *cha ca* (grilled fish seasoned with dill) and *bun cha* (grilled pork with rice noodles). In fact, it is these great dishes that have placed Hanoi back on the culinary map in recent years.

FUNDAMENTALS OF VIETNAMESE FLAVOURS

As you read and experiment with the recipes in this book, you'll come away with the impression that Vietnamese cooking isn't about complicated techniques. Rather, it's about securing the freshest possible ingredients and, with minimal handling, combining them in a way that showcases their simple, natural goodness.

Unlike the European approach of blending and harmonizing ingredients, which one sees in slow braises or sauce reductions, the Vietnamese prefer to cook by layering flavours, textures and temperatures so that the ingredients remain separate and distinct. Take *pho bo*, for example. The noodles and broth provide substance and by themselves the flavours are rather delicate. However, when eaten with fresh herbs, chillies and limes, the flavours are immediately transformed, becoming spicy, aromatic and tangy all at the same time.

Picture another scenario at a typical multiple-course family meal: simmered Ginger Chicken, which is fairly well seasoned, is served with a delicately flavoured soup, a steamed vegetable dish, a stir-fry and some steamed unsalted rice. But the meal isn't quite complete without a platter of fresh herbs and a bowl of spicy salty fish dipping sauce to tie together all the flavours. For the cook, the ultimate aim is to present the diner with a feast of contrasts across the entire meal, as well as with each bite.

THE VIETNAMESE PANTRY

To create delicious and authentic Vietnamese food, it's important that you have a firm grasp on the essential ingredients listed below. The building blocks of Vietnamese flavours, they're used to make dipping sauces and season foods. You can use this list as a shopping guide for stocking your Vietnamese pantry. Fish sauce, fresh herbs and rice noodles are so integral to our cuisine that I've provided additional information under separate sections.

You can buy all the ingredients at Asian stores and possibly in well-stocked supermarkets. If you have access to an Asian store but don't live near one, consider buying extra to save for later use. Many items (such as fish sauce and dried rice noodles) have a long shelf life and will last for some time. Fresh ingredients such as vegetables, aromatic roots, meats and seafood should be bought as close to cooking time as possible. In some instances where I think it might be helpful, I've included my favourite brands. However, these preferences will probably change as new products continue to enter the marketplace each year.

Sauces and Spices

Fish sauce *nuoc mam* **(Viet Huong, Flying Lion Phu Quoc, Saigon)**
Almost every Vietnamese dish is seasoned with this quintessential sauce. A liquid extraction made from fermented fish and salt, *nuoc mam* is used to salt and enhance foods and to make dipping sauces. When cooking, start with a small amount and increase as necessary. Wipe the opening of the bottle clean after each use and store on the work top or in the refrigerator. Fish sauce will last almost indefinitely. (For more information, see page 21.)

Bean sauce *tuong hot* **(La Bo De, Dragonfly)**
Made from whole or crushed fermented soya beans, this sharp-tasting
sauce is used to season stir-fries and to make sauces. When used in a
dipping sauce (such as one served with salad rolls – see Rice Paper-
wrapped Salad Rolls, page 105), it's generally cooked with vinegar, puréed
onions and sometimes sticky rice, then garnished with chillies and
ground peanuts. In recent years, a ready-to-serve dipping sauce called
tuong goi cuon (salad roll sauce) has become available in the West under
the brand La Bo De.

Hoisin sauce *sot tuong* **(Koon Chun)**
Made from soya bean purée and five-spice powder, this condiment is
used in dipping sauces, marinades and stir-fries. When used as a
dipping sauce, hoisin is prepared the same way as the bean sauce above.
Many Vietnamese restaurants use this sauce for salad rolls and for
serving with *pho*.

Ground chilli paste *tuong ot toi* **(Rooster)**
An important condiment, this fiery sauce is made with coarsely ground
red chillies, garlic and vinegar. It's used to garnish sauces and noodle and
rice dishes.

Oyster sauce *dau hao* **(Hop Sing Lung, Ng Yup or any higher-priced
brands)**
A thick brown sauce made from oyster extract, salt, sugar and spices,
this seasoning ingredient is used to add savouriness to Chinese-style
dishes. It does a wonderful job of coating meats and seafood, giving
them a shiny, succulent look. When using this sauce, reduce the amount
of salt or fish sauce in the dish, as it can be salty. For a vegetarian
version, try vegetarian mushroom oyster sauce.

Soy sauce *nuoc tuong* (Pearl River Bridge, Kikkoman)
Although not used as extensively as fish sauce, soy sauce is a common
seasoning in vegetarian and stir-fried dishes. Vietnamese cooks make
delicious dipping sauces by combining it with lime juice, garlic and
chillies. (For Soy-lime Dipping Sauce, see page 27.)

Rice and Noodles

Rice *gao*
The Vietnamese prefer *gao thom*, the long-grain jasmine variety, and use
the absorption method to cook rice. For best flavour, serve the rice
promptly after it's finished cooking. Asian stores carry dozens of brands
and the best way to select rice is to just try several and stick to those you
like. (For more information on cooking rice, see page 153.)

Rice, glutinous or sweet *gao nep* (Elephant, Erawan)
Sticky rice is used extensively in desserts and breakfast items. More
dense and starchy than regular rice, it's typically used to make puddings
and fillings for banana leaf-wrapped cakes. Sticky rice is usually soaked
in water overnight, then steamed.

Rice flour *bot gao* (Elephant, Erawan)
Not to be confused with sweet sticky (glutinous) rice flour, this is the
most common starch in Vietnamese cooking. It's made from short-grain
rice and used to make sweet and savoury noodles, crêpes, dumplings
and cakes. When shopping for this item, make sure it's rice flour from
Thailand, not the generic rice flour used in baking.

Rice paper *banh trang* (Kim Tar, Elephant, Erawan)
Rice papers are thin wrappers made from rice flour (sometimes in
combination with tapioca starch), salt and water and are sun-dried on
bamboo trays, which give them their distinctive pattern. They're

available in round, square and triangular shapes. When purchasing rice paper, look for packages with thin, translucent sheets. Avoid the thick, opaque ones. Before using, you must reconstitute dried rice papers in warm water until pliable. They're used to wrap salad rolls and spring rolls (see page 108).

Rice vermicelli *bun* (Thap Chua, GGG)
Sold as rice sticks, these dried small, wiry noodles are used extensively in Vietnamese cuisine to make noodle salads and soups. More fragile than pasta, they need less cooking time. Rinse well in water after cooking and let the noodles become dry and sticky before serving. In Vietnam, these noodles are sold fresh, but in the West (except in a few Asian stores) they're only available dried (see page 124).

Rice sticks *banh pho* (Elephant, Two Ladies, Kim Tar)
These flat, thin dried noodles resemble linguine and are available in several widths – small, medium and large. Also made from rice flour, salt and water, they're used in noodle soups and stir-fries. To expedite the cooking time, these noodles are first soaked in water, then boiled. (For information on cooking rice noodles for *pho* and other dishes, see page 49.)

Other Ingredients
Coconut milk *nuoc cot dua* (Mae Ploy, Chao Koh, Taste of Thai)
Coconut milk is used to enrich curries and desserts. In Vietnam, cooks either make it by squeezing grated coconut with hot water or buy it freshly made at the market. In the West, the canned products are easily available although not quite as good. When buying this product, make sure it is unsweetened (see page 158).

Fragrant herbs *rau thom*

The Vietnamese eat an enormous amount of herbs. A family meal often consists of a table salad (see page 85), which includes lettuce and different varieties of mint and basil. Diners just snip off the sprigs and add to their bowls or plates, creating little salads as they go. Fresh herbs are also used as garnishes and accompaniments to soups, salads, and noodle dishes. For a more detailed list of Vietnamese herbs, see page 39.

Peanuts *dau phong*

An important ingredient in Vietnamese cuisine, peanuts are used in a great variety of dishes. They're typically roasted, then chopped and used to add richness and texture to many noodle salad and rice dishes.

Tamarind pulp *me*

Made from the flesh of tamarind pods, this thick paste is used to add tartness to soups and stir-fried dishes. The seedless pulp is sold as blocks (a liquid concentrate is also available but not as good) and needs to be softened in warm water before it is strained and the juice is added to food. Look for this product in the dried food section of Asian stores.

TECHNIQUES AND APPROACHES

Before proceeding to the kitchen, read through chapter 2 to gain a good grasp of how Vietnamese flavours are combined and how a meal comes together. Having this crucial information will be very helpful once you dive into your first recipe. Also read the recipe thoroughly before cooking and try to visualize the techniques and imagine how the flavours may taste. I've often found that this process can help you become better prepared for the actual cooking.

Fortunately, Vietnamese cuisine isn't, for the most part, complicated. Because it relies so much on dipping sauces and the contrasting of flavours and textures, the cooking techniques are basic – boiling or simmering, stir-frying or frying, steaming and grilling. There is less to do at the stove since much of the creation of flavour happens at the table, where the diner dips this food into that sauce, and eats this with that.

Perhaps one of the most important steps in the kitchen is the pounding of spices with a mortar and pestle to make dipping sauces. This pounding action creates more intense flavours than, say, the blending motion of a food processor. This is particularly important when making salad dressings and dipping sauces because the flavours need to be intense enough to balance other delicate-tasting foods such as steamed rice or steamed vegetables.

Another technique that deserves special attention is the layering of ingredients, especially in noodle dishes and rice dishes with raw herbs and vegetables. As already mentioned, the Vietnamese cook strives to create flavours by layering different yet complementary ingredients and by presenting them in such a way that they remain separate. For this reason, vegetables and meat are often cut into thin slices or strips and are handled with great care so they don't break down during cooking and become too blended and homogeneous.

SPECIAL EQUIPMENT AND TOOLS

Most Vietnamese dishes can be easily prepared with regular pots and pans. However, the following tools will make the job easier and the food will come out tasting and looking better.

For dishes that require frying and stir-frying, a 35 or 40 cm (14 or 16 inch) wok is the most practical for everyday cooking. It's big enough so you can cook quickly without crowding the pan. Plus you can always cook a small amount in a large wok but not vice versa. (You can also use a wok as a steamer by placing a steamer on a rack over boiling water.) You might also consider buying a couple of sizes of nonstick pans and frying pans, especially if you want to make Vietnamese crêpes and pan-seared tofu. For simmering, you can use any medium-sized pot or saucepan.

Claypots are wonderful cooking vessels for preparing deeply flavoured braised dishes. I always have a few different kinds and sizes in my kitchen, and I also use them as serving dishes. (For more information on handling and cooking with claypots, see page 163.)

A Chinese two-tier aluminium steamer is a great tool to have if you do a lot of steaming. I have a 40 cm (16 inch) steamer that I use all the time to steam whole fish and chicken, sticky rice and various rice cakes. (For more information on Chinese steamers, see page 198.)

The Japanese mandoline is another valuable tool. It can cut vegetables into delicate, attractive slices and strips (see page 90). You can achieve these cuts with a knife, but it requires more patience and practice. If you like eating salads as much as I do, consider investing in a mandoline.

For noodle soup recipes, buy a long-handled wire strainer for dunking noodles in boiling water and some large, deep Chinese- or Japanese-style bowls in which to serve them.

However, if you buy only one thing for the Vietnamese kitchen, make it a mortar and pestle (see page 30). A useful tool for making dipping sauces and marinades, the mortar is great for pounding chillies, garlic and herbs.

CREATING A MEAL FROM THIS BOOK

From a menu-planning standpoint, keep in mind that this book consists of two kinds of recipes – street or market foods and home-cooked dishes. In Vietnam, when you're hungry for a certain street food, you go to your favourite vendor and order that speciality. Then, if you want something else, you move to another vendor and eat another speciality and so on, until you're full. What's especially rewarding about hopping from one street café or market kitchen to another is that you get to eat foods prepared by true masters, people who've worked with the same small set of recipes for years, often decades.

To create a similar experience at home, you can offer several dishes at the same time. For example, Sizzling Saigon Crêpes (see page 131) and Vietnamese Spring Rolls (see page 101) make a fun roll-your-own meal since both call for wrapping foods with lettuce and herbs. If you're still hungry you can serve Hue Chicken Salad (see page 83) or one of the many other salads in this book. Recipes in chapters 3, 4 and 5 are particularly appropriate for such casual menus. To a Westerner, these meals are reminiscent of a 'grazing' menu, made up of several appetizer-type dishes as opposed to a more predictable first and second course affair.

If you're interested in serving *pho* or one of the other meal-in-a-bowl soups, you won't need to worry about offering many other dishes. With a generous portion of noodles and the towering plate of herbs that should accompany the dish, *pho* certainly has enough carbohydrates, protein and vegetables to make a satisfying meal in itself. And in the *pho* tradition, one can always finish the meal with delicious Vietnamese Coffee (see page 256) or one of the many sweet drinks, such as Iced Red Bean Pudding with Coconut Milk (see page 243).

For a more home-cooked-style meal, refer to recipes in chapters 6, 7 and 8. A typical Vietnamese family meal consists of two meat or seafood dishes, a vegetable side dish and a soup. Since the foundation of such meals is rice, it's important that it be properly cooked and served steaming hot in generous quantities. For tips on cooking rice, please refer to page 153. Some menu suggestions are also included in the back of this book.

Sauces, Condiments and Herbs

EACH DAY at the crack of dawn, Chi Tuyet (Sister Tuyet) and her cousin arrive at the Ben Thanh Market in Saigon with baskets of rice noodles and crates of herbs and vegetables. For the past fifteen years, they've been coming here to sell their famed *bun thit nuong* (rice noodles with barbecued pork). It's the only dish they offer, but it's a dish that unveils the secrets of Vietnamese cooking.

After she unloads her ingredients and starts the charcoal brazier for the meat, Chi Tuyet begins to uncork her jars of dipping sauces, wiping and lining them up in the front row of the stall. The largest jar contains *nuoc cham* (Vietnamese dipping sauce). The others are filled to the rim with crispy shallots, pickled garlic and cucumbers, fresh chillies, chilli paste, ground peanuts, spring onion oil and dried shrimp. 'This is what drives my business', boasts Chi Tuyet, pointing to the beautiful array of sauces and condiments.

While we speak, Chi Tuyet places the pork skewers on the grill. As the meat sizzles and the charcoals flare, a delicious aroma ascends. It is now mid-morning and the entire food section hums with activity. Cooks are busy ladling soups, barbecuing meats and fulfilling orders. A group of hungry shoppers stops to inspect a steaming pot of soup with crab dumplings. A man carrying a block of ice twice his size tries to squeeze through. Chi Tuyet slips the smoky pork off the skewers and places it on a bed of soft, cool noodles and crunchy herbs and greens. She garnishes the bowl with marinated daikon (a variety of Japnese radish) and carrots, spring onion oil and chopped peanuts.

To eat, I add a generous amount of *nuoc cham* before tossing the noodles a few times. After one bite, I can understand immediately what Chi Tuyet had meant when she said earlier that the success of her food – and her business – depends on these very sauces and toppings. Even though the noodle dish is made with all kinds of ingredients, the flavours don't begin to come together until the final sauce and condiments are added. The sweet and spicy sauce immediately enhances the dish while the spring onion oil gives it savouriness. A sprinkling of roasted peanuts adds richness and nuttiness and a dab of chilli paste gives the dish a fiery finish. Without these toppings, *bun thit nuong* wouldn't be the fabulous dish that it is.

In fact, as I look round at the food stalls around Chi Tuyet, every vendor has the same attractive display of condiments. It seems clear that no matter what is being served, these accompaniments are every bit as important as the main dishes themselves.

This chapter contains the essential dipping sauces and condiments that accompany many of the recipes in this book. Together they make up the most basic component of Vietnamese cuisine. Most are simple and quick to make and can be easily prepared in advance and stored in the refrigerator.

One thing to keep in mind as you're preparing them is the critical role that they play in balancing the flavours of other dishes or the meal as a whole. For example, if a noodle or rice dish calls for spring onion oil or fried shallots, make sure you serve it that way. Otherwise, the dish will lack flavours and not be balanced. To a novice cook, some of the dipping sauces may seem overly seasoned and salty, too sour or even bland (like the Light Vietnamese Dipping Sauce, which is supposed to be delicate so it won't overpower the accompanying rice cakes with prawns dish). Reserve judgement until you have tasted them with other components of the dish.

These principles underscore a recurring theme that makes Vietnamese cooking particularly distinct from other Asian cuisines. Flavours are built on several levels – by layering meat or seafood with starch and fresh herbs, by contrasting the hot with the cool, the soft with the crunchy, and by using dipping sauces and condiments to blend them all together on a plate or in a bowl.

Vietnamese Dipping Sauce
nuoc cham

NUOC CHAM is a must at every Vietnamese table, no matter what is served. You can use this condiment for dipping meat, seafood and vegetables, and for drizzling on rice. When serving it with steamed meats (such as steamed chicken), I often reduce the water by half so the sauce is more concentrated.

You can often determine a family's roots just by looking at and tasting their *nuoc cham*. If it's clear and dotted with chopped chillies, the cook is probably from the central or northern regions, where a simple and straightforward version is preferred. But if it's diluted with water and lime juice and sweetened with sugar, one can surmise that the cook is from the verdant south.

Although it will keep for up to two weeks in the refrigerator, *nuoc cham* is best when freshly made. I prefer the intense flavour of the tiny Thai bird's eye chillies, but any hot chillies will do.

Makes 250 ml (8 fl oz)
3 Thai bird's eye chillies or 1 serrano chilli, or to taste
1 garlic clove, sliced
3 tablespoons sugar
170 ml (5½ fl oz) warm water
1½ tablespoons fresh lime juice
5 tablespoons fish sauce
2 tablespoons finely shredded carrot for garnish (optional)

• Cut the chillies into thin rings. Remove one-third of the chillies and set aside for a garnish. Place the remaining chillies, garlic and sugar in a mortar and pound into a coarse, wet paste. (If you don't have a mortar, just chop with a knife.) Transfer to a small bowl and add the water, lime juice and fish sauce. Stir well to dissolve. Add the reserved chillies and carrots. Set aside for 10 minutes before serving.

NOTE: *Nuoc cham* is very amenable to variations and adaptations. In Vietnam, cooks like to use various vegetables to flavour the sauce, such as thinly sliced marinated daikon and carrots, ginger, spring onion oil or peanuts and even slices of kohlrabi and the core of a white cabbage. Each imparts a distinctive savouriness.

Nuoc Mam, the Quintessential Sauce

Without good fish sauce, the father's daughter will not shine.'
Vietnamese proverb

I HAVE ALWAYS been struck by the above saying. On one level, it points to the Vietnamese view of the universe and how everything is seen from the family's perspective. The implied pronoun — in this case 'she' – is replaced with the 'father's daughter'. On another level, it suggests that without good fish sauce, the quintessential sauce of Vietnamese cuisine, food can never taste good, no matter how talented the cook.

While the saying about the fish sauce may sound a bit exaggerated, it really isn't. At our own home in Saigon we used fish sauce at every meal in two different ways – for making dipping sauce and for seasoning food. Whenever we sat down to the table, there was a bowl of *nuoc cham*, which is the diluted dipping sauce made from *nuoc mam*, the concentrated fish sauce. It wasn't particularly impressive, just a clear, amber-tinted sauce with bits of garlic and chillies, but somehow it often ended up being the highlight of the meal. If one dish was deemed wonderful, the *nuoc cham* would take credit. If an entire meal was spectacular, well, it was the sauce that tied the flavours together.

In our family, my sister Denise was the only person entrusted with the task of making the sauce. Her version was always consistent, a guarantee of a perfect meal. To this day, whenever we get together she's still the *nuoc cham* master.

She usually begins the ritual by crushing garlic cloves. Using a stone mortar and pestle, she pounds them with chillies and sugar until they become a paste. (The sugar eases the process and keeps the chillies from splashing into the eyes.) Then she juices a lime, gently scraping off the pulp to make sure the inner white flesh doesn't get too bruised and make the sauce bitter. The lime juice is then combined with the fish sauce and chilli mixture for an interesting balance of sweet and sour. The prized concoction is now ready to be placed in the middle of the family table.

In Vietnam, the best fish sauce comes from *ca com* or *ca linh*, both of the anchovy family, and are made by small producers like Tran Thien and his wife Kim Sa, whom I met on a trip to Ha Tien, not too far from the fish sauce capital of Phu Quoc Island off the southern coast of Vietnam. Thien grew up helping his father make *nuoc mam* – first for family consumption and later for sale at the local market. In recent years he's decided to expand the family business, hoping to get in on the international market. 'The country is rebounding after all the war years. *Nuoc mam* is now very popular throughout the world and my dream is to make the best product and export it,' he says.

To stay on schedule, Tran works with a local fisherman who brings him fresh *ca com*, highly favoured for its flavour and oil content. Since his house sits right on the river, the boat unloads it at the back door. After rinsing the fish, he transfers them to a tank where they're layered with one-third of the fish weight in salt. The fish are left to ferment in the brine for four months, after which a liquid is collected, drip by drip, and then pumped back into the tank. This simultaneous percolation and fermentation process continues for about eight months, after which it is siphoned and bottled.

The first extraction contains 35 to 38 per cent protein and is sold as *nuoc mam nhi* (premium grade), which commands a considerable price tag. The second and third pressings are made by adding more brine to the same batch of fish and allowing it to ferment for a much shorter cycle.

They're sold as *nuoc mam thuong* (regular fish sauce) and *nuoc mam kho* (cooking fish sauce). The latter pressings have less flavour and are generally used for cooking as opposed to making dipping sauces.

In the West, it's difficult to distinguish premium grades from lesser ones because they're not bound by any labelling standards. In general, the higher-priced bottles containing a lighter-coloured sauce tend to be better. In Vietnam, the premium product is slightly viscous and lighter in colour than the dark brown liquid common in the West. It's best to try several brands and stick with those that you like. I find that Viet Huong, Flying Lion Phu Quoc and Golden Boy (all made in Thailand) are best for dipping sauces and the more pungent products such as Squid, Tiparos and Saigon are better for cooking. But in recent years there's been a deluge of new brands entering the marketplace and I suspect we'll see even more in the near future.

Light Vietnamese Dipping Sauce
nuoc cham lat

ONE OF THE greatest rewards of working in the food business is meeting other great cooks. Pham Thi Ngoc Tinh is one of them. Passionate about the cooking of her native Hue, she's made it her job to preserve it. At her small, family-run Thuong Chi Restaurant in Saigon, she specializes in central regional cooking, reviving recipes that have been forgotten or are no longer cooked.

This is the dipping sauce Tinh prepares to accompany many Hue specialities, such as *banh beo* (Steamed Rice Cakes with Prawns, see page

115). Unlike the all-purpose Vietnamese Dipping Sauce, which is southern in influence, this recipe is delicately flavoured with prawn stock. If you don't have prawn shells, use whole prawns.

> *Makes 315 ml (10 fl oz)*
> **2 handfuls of raw prawn shells**
> **500 ml (16 fl oz) water**
> **3½ tablespoons fish sauce**
> **4 tablespoons sugar**
> **1 teaspoon rice vinegar**
> **1 to 2 Thai bird's eye chillies or ½ serrano chilli, cut into**
> **thin rings**

- Combine the prawn shells and water in a small pan. Bring to the boil, then reduce the heat and simmer for 5 minutes. Strain and set aside to cool.

- Measure out 250 ml (8 fl oz) of the prawn stock and place in a bowl. Add the fish sauce, sugar, vinegar and chillies and stir well. This sauce will keep for up to 2 weeks if refrigerated in a covered jar.

Ginger-lime Dipping Sauce
nuoc mam gung

THIS IS PROBABLY one of my favourite standby sauces. Intensely gingery and spicy, it goes well with foods that have been simply prepared, such as steamed or grilled chicken, meat or seafood. Although

this sauce will keep for up to two weeks, I prefer to make it fresh
because the ginger tends to lose its sharp flavour when held overnight.

Makes about 185 ml (6 fl oz)
1 teaspoon chopped garlic
2 to 3 Thai bird's eye chillies or 1 serrano chilli, chopped
3 tablespoons sugar
3 tablespoons minced ginger
60 ml (2 fl oz) fish sauce
2 tablespoons fresh lime juice
3 tablespoons water

- Place the garlic, chillies, sugar and ginger in a mortar and pound into
a paste. (You can also chop by hand.) Transfer to a small bowl and add
the fish sauce, lime juice and water. Stir well to combine. Set aside for
15 minutes before serving.

Vietnamese Bean Dipping Sauce
tuong goi cuon

UNLIKE THE CLEAR *nuoc cham,* this dipping sauce is quite thick
and used with dishes such as Rice Paper-wrapped Salad Rolls and
Grilled Prawn Paste on Sugarcane (see pages 105 and 142). There are many
versions of this recipe, including one that my mother likes to make with
sticky rice as a thickener. In Hue, the sauce often includes minced pork
and liver.

This recipe is very simple to make and delicious, especially if you can find fermented whole soya beans. You can also embellish it with garlic, chillies and ginger and serve it on grilled fish, chicken and beef. If you can't find soya beans, substitute 75 ml (3 fl oz) hoisin sauce and omit the sugar.

> *Makes 375 ml (12 fl oz)*
> **A handful of fermented whole soya beans (see Glossary**
> **   page 260)**
> **125 ml (4 fl oz) water**
> **75 ml (3 fl oz) unsweetened coconut milk (see page 158)**
> **2 tablespoons rice vinegar**
> **3 tablespoons chopped onion**
> **2 tablespoons sugar**
>
> *For the garnish:*
> **1 tablespoon ground chilli paste, or to taste (see Glossary**
> **   page 259)**
> **1 tablespoon chopped Roasted Peanuts (see page 34)**

- Place the soya beans, water, coconut milk, vinegar, onion and sugar in a blender or food processor and process just until smooth. Transfer the mixture to a saucepan and bring to the boil over moderate heat. (If you don't have a food processor, cook the soya bean mixture first, then beat with a whisk.) Reduce the heat and simmer for about 5 minutes until the sauce thickens enough to coat a spoon. Add a little water if it's too thick. Set aside to cool.

- To serve, transfer to individual sauce bowls and garnish each with chilli paste and chopped peanuts. This sauce will keep for up to 2 weeks if refrigerated in a tight-lidded jar.

Soy-lime Dipping Sauce
nuoc tuong pha

THIS VEGETARIAN dipping sauce can be made with any soy sauce, including the Japanese-style Kikkoman, although the Vietnamese prefer the lighter-bodied Chinese-style products marketed under brands like Kim Lan, Bo De and Pearl River Bridge. Like dipping sauces made with fish sauce, you can embellish this with different aromatics such as ginger and coriander.

Makes about 250 ml (8 fl oz)
1 garlic clove
2 Thai bird's eye chillies
2½ tablespoons sugar
75 ml (3 fl oz) soy sauce, preferably Chinese style
2½ tablespoons fresh lime juice with pulp
60 ml (2 fl oz) water, or to taste

- Place the garlic, chillies and sugar in a mortar and pound into a paste. (You can also chop the garlic and chillies by hand.) Transfer to a small bowl and add the soy sauce, lime juice and water. Stir until well blended. This sauce will keep for up to 3 weeks if stored in the refrigerator in a tight-lidded jar.

Sweet Soy Sauce
with Chillies and Ginger
nuoc tuong den ot

WHENEVER I'M in Saigon, I can't resist going to the Chinatown section
of Cholon to look for Hainan chicken, a steamed chicken dish served
with rice cooked in chicken stock. What makes it particularly
wonderful is this sweet soy dipping sauce thick with chopped ginger
and chilli paste. I've found that it's good on anything steamed, including
steamed vegetables and dumplings, as well as boiled noodles.

Makes 125 ml (4 fl oz)
3 tablespoons sweet soy sauce (see page 36)
2 tablespoons water
I tablespoon minced ginger, preferably young
I teaspoon ground chilli paste (see Glossary page 259)
**2 to 3 Thai bird's eye chillies or I serrano chilli, cut into
thin rings**

- Combine all the ingredients in a small bowl and set aside for 10 minutes
before serving so the flavours are well blended. This sauce will keep for
2 weeks if stored in the refrigerator in a tight-lidded jar.

Chilli-lime Dipping Sauce

nuoc mam chanh

THIS SPICY and limy dipping sauce is guaranteed to add zip to steamed and grilled foods and even salads. If you have a mortar and pestle, put them to work. This is one dish that benefits greatly from the pounding of the fresh chillies.

Be sure to use a fresh lime and gently scrape the segments and pulp into the sauce. For a really authentic touch, add a handful of thinly cut strips of cucumber, about 1 mm ($^1/_{16}$ inch) wide, to the sauce. Serve the sauce with fried or grilled fish or rice.

Makes about 125 ml (4 fl oz)
1 or 2 garlic cloves
3 Thai bird's eye chillies, chopped, or to taste
3 tablespoons sugar
3 tablespoons fish sauce
3 tablespoons freshly squeezed lime juice with some pulp
  and segments
3 tablespoons water

- Place the garlic, chillies and sugar in a mortar and pound into a paste. (You can also chop the chillies and garlic by hand.) Transfer to a small bowl and add the fish sauce, lime juice and pulp and the water, if needed. Set aside for 15 minutes for the flavours to develop. This sauce will keep for up to 2 weeks stored in the refrigerator in a tight-lidded jar.

The Mortar and Pestle

IN THE Vietnamese kitchen, the mortar and pestle are important tools for pulverizing herbs, spices and other ingredients. The pounding imparts a more intense flavour than chopping and mincing. I use a mortar and pestle to make dipping sauces and marinades and to grind roasted peanuts and toasted rice paper. Meatballs and shrimp and fish pastes can also be prepared in a mortar. Although a small food processor can also do the job, it isn't quite the same. Instead of pounding and mashing the ingredients into irregular pieces (which is desired in a Vietnamese dipping sauce), the machine chops and minces in a more uniform fashion.

When using the pestle, pound it freely in an up-and-down motion. Many novices make the mistake of pressing (as opposed to pounding) the pestle into the mortar, which tends to make the job harder and longer. Once in a while, run the pestle in a circular motion against the sides of the mortar to push the ingredients back into the centre.

For grinding spices and herbs, buy a stone – not wooden – pestle and mortar, one that's 15 cm (6 inches) or wider at the rim so the ingredients don't spill out so easily. The stone version, with its rough surfaces, does a better job of pulverizing spices and herbs while the wooden one is more appropriate for pounding soft, fleshy ingredients, such as green papayas.

Spring Onion Oil
mo hanh

I ALWAYS HAVE a small jar of this simple and versatile condiment in my kitchen. It can be used to garnish everything from rice, noodles, soups and salads to grilled meats and is particularly useful for enhancing the savoury flavour of vegetarian dishes. If you refrigerate spring onion oil, bring it to room temperature before serving.

> *Makes 125 ml (4 fl oz)*
> **60 ml (2 fl oz) vegetable oil**
> **5 spring onions, green parts only, cut into thin rings**

- Heat the oil in a small pan over moderate heat. Add the spring onions and stir for 10 seconds. Immediately remove from the heat and transfer the oil with the spring onions to a small bowl. Place in the refrigerator to cool for 10 minutes. (This helps the spring onions stay green.) Remove and set aside at room temperature until ready to serve. This sauce will keep for up to 2 weeks stored in the refrigerator in a tight-lidded jar.

Fried Shallots
hanh phi

LIKE SPRING ONION OIL, fried shallots add a new dimension to savoury dishes. Use this important garnish on noodle dishes and foods that have been simply prepared, like steamed dishes.

When frying the shallots, keep a close eye on them as they can turn from golden to brown in seconds. I remove the shallots from the oil about 10 seconds before I think they're ready because they'll continue to cook from their own heat.

Makes about 45 g (2 oz)
**5 shallots, cut crossways into 2 mm (⅛ inch) thick slices
250 ml (8 fl oz) vegetable oil**

- Spread the shallots out on paper towels and set aside to air-dry for 30 minutes.
- Combine the shallots and oil in a frying pan and bring to a slow boil. Reduce the heat to low and cook for about 15 minutes until the shallots are golden. Stir so the shallots brown evenly.
- Remove with a slotted spoon or strain the oil through a wire-mesh sieve. Transfer the shallots to a plate or tray lined with paper towels. (Discard the oil or save it to use as a cooking oil in stir-fries.) Once cool, the shallots are ready to use. If stored in a jar with a tight lid at room temperature, the shallots will keep for up to 1 week.

Caramel Sauce

nuoc mau

THIS IS ONE of the most important sauces for grilled meats, claypot specialities (see page 163) and other simmered dishes. It adds body and colour to foods while imparting a sweet, smoky flavour.
Be very careful when making this because burnt sugar is extremely hot. To avoid overcooking the sugar, bring the water to the boil before starting the recipe.

makes 125 ml (4 fl oz)
125 g (4½ oz) sugar
75 ml (3 fl oz) boiling water

- Place the sugar in a small, heavy-bottomed saucepan over moderate heat. The sugar will melt and start to caramelize in about 2 to 3 minutes. Stir a few times (the edges will start to brown fast) and let the mixture bubble for about another minute or so until it turns dark brown. Quickly but carefully remove the pan from the heat and slowly stir in the boiling water. Stand back as the mixture might splatter. Set aside to cool. If stored in a tight-lidded jar at room temperature, this sauce will keep for up to 1 month.

Roasted Peanuts
dau phong ran

THE VIETNAMESE LOVE peanuts and eat them in many different ways. They boil them and eat them as snacks and add them to soups and desserts. But the most popular way of preparing peanuts is to roast them and use them as a garnish for noodles, salads and sticky rice. Store-bought peanuts are a substitute, but freshly roasted peanuts are much more flavourful.

> *makes 160 g (5 oz)*
> **160 g (5 oz) raw, shelled peanuts, skins removed**

• Preheat the oven to 170°C/325°F/Gas Mark 3. Place the peanuts on a baking tray and bake for about 20 minutes until golden. Halfway into the baking, gently shake the tray so the peanuts roast evenly. (You can also roast the peanuts in a dry pan over low heat.) Remove and set aside. Use the peanuts whole or coarsely crush them with a mortar and pestle, a food processor or a knife.

Shallot-garlic Marinade
nuoc uop

EVERY VIETNAMESE COOK has his or her favourite version of this marinade. It's used to create the distinctive sweet, smoky flavour of the grilled pork commonly served with noodles. It's also great on lamb, chicken, prawns and tofu.

> **Makes about 185 ml (6 fl oz)**
> **40 g (1½ oz) shallots, coarsely chopped**
> **½ tablespoon coarsely chopped garlic**
> **1 tablespoon fish sauce**
> **1½ teaspoons Caramel Sauce (see page 35) or ½ tablespoon brown sugar**
> **½ tablespoon soy sauce**
> **½ teaspoon salt**
> **1 teaspoon sugar**
> **60 ml (2 fl oz) vegetable oil**

- Place the shallots, garlic, fish sauce, Caramel Sauce, soy sauce, salt, sugar and oil in a food processor and process for about 15 seconds until well blended. (You can also chop the shallots and garlic very finely by hand, then mix them with the remaining ingredients.) Although you can refrigerate this marinade for several days, it's best when freshly made.

Soy Sauce

LIKE FISH SAUCE, soy sauce is an essential ingredient in our cooking, especially in dishes of Chinese origin. One of the world's oldest condiments, soy sauce is made with cooked soya beans, roasted wheat and a mould starter that have been mixed in a briny solution and allowed to ferment. After a period of six months to a year, the liquid is drained and bottled.

The Southeast Asian kitchen is usually stocked with several different kinds of soy sauce, but they generally fit into two main categories – light and dark. Light soy sauce is thinner, saltier and more appropriate for dipping sauces. In this category, you can use the Chinese or Japanese soy sauce brands such as Pearl River Bridge or Kikkoman. Always taste the sauce before using because each brand differs in saltiness and flavour.

In the second category, there are two (but similar) kinds – *dark soy* (also called black soy sauce), which contains molasses and is thick and full-bodied, and *sweet soy sauce*, which is even thicker and sweeter. Both blacken food and are typically used only in small amounts, especially in cooked noodles and braised dishes. For example, *pho xa tieu chau*, a Chinese-style noodle dish, gets its delicious caramelized flavour from drizzling the sweet soy sauce into the hot pan.

Marinated Daikon and Carrots
cu cai ca rot chua

A favourite condiment in our home around Tet (Vietnamese New Year), this is served in much the same way as a vegetable, often accompanying a simmering dish like *thit heo kho* (Aunt Tam's Pork in Claypot, see page 173). Sweet and sour, these crunchy vegetables also make a great garnish for dipping sauces.

Makes about 900 ml (1½ pints)
250 ml (8 fl oz) rice or distilled white wine vinegar
5 tablespoons sugar
900 g (2 lb) small daikon (Japanese radish), peeled, halved
    lengthways and cut across into 1 cm (½ inch) thick slices
2 carrots, peeled and cut into matchstick strips
1½ teaspoons salt

- Combine the vinegar and sugar and bring to the boil. Remove from the heat and set aside to cool.

- Place the radishes, carrots and salt in a bowl and toss several times. Set aside for 20 minutes, then rinse thoroughly. Using your hands, squeeze the vegetables to remove the excess water. Pat dry with paper towels and place in a bowl.

- Add the vinegar mixture and let the vegetables marinate for at least 1 hour before serving. To store, transfer to a tight-lidded jar and refrigerate. The vegetables will keep for up to 3 weeks.

Marinated Chillies
ot ngam giam

SIMPLE TO MAKE, these chillies greatly enhance noodle soups and rice dishes. If you like spicy foods, I'd suggest making extra to have on hand at all times. The blanching keeps the chillies green, and the garlic – even if you don't eat it – adds to the flavour and presentation.

Makes 10 spicy chillies
250 ml (8 fl oz) rice or distilled white wine vinegar
90 g (3½ oz) sugar
2 teaspoons sea salt
10 serrano or jalapeño chillies, cut into 5 mm (¼ inch) rings
10 small garlic cloves (optional)

- Combine the vinegar, sugar and salt in a glass jar large enough to hold all the ingredients. Stir well to dissolve. Set aside.

- Bring a small pot of water to the boil. Using a sieve, dip the chillies and garlic into the boiling water for 5 seconds. Drain completely, then put in the vinegar mixture, pushing the chillies and garlic down so they are fully submerged. Cover and refrigerate for at least 1 day before serving.

Chicken Stock
nuoc dung ga

IN VIETNAMESE COOKING, a good chicken stock is rich but clear, with no salt or seasonings added. A neutral-tasting stock makes it easier for the cook to season and balance the flavours of the final dish.

Makes about 1.75 litres (3 pints)
1.8 kg (4 lb) chicken wings and bones, excess skin and fat removed, rinsed
2 litres (3½ pints) water

- Place the chicken wings and bones in a large stockpot and add the water. Bring to the boil, then reduce the heat to low. Simmer for at least 2 hours, skimming the surface often to remove any foam or impurities that rise to the top.

- Remove the stock from the heat. Let cool, then strain before using. You can refrigerate the stock for up to 1 week or freeze it for future use.

Asian Herbs: For Flavour and for Health

FOR CENTURIES, cultures and cuisines around the world have embraced herbs, not only for their flavours and aromas but also for their medicinal qualities. In Thailand, cooks love to throw cupfuls of basil into their salads, stir-fries and soups, treating them no differently from vegetables. In Laos and Cambodia, herbs are used to garnish and perfume noodle soups, broth soups and salads.

But nowhere do fresh herbs play as important a role as they do in Vietnam, where a typical meal often includes, among other things, a huge platter of table salad piled high with *rau thom*, or aromatic herbs. The selection varies according to the meal. If the table salad accompanies *pho* (rice noodles with beef soup), it will include saw-leaf and Asian basil. If it goes with grilled meats, it will have a generous amount of green and red perilla (see pages 43, 44) and different kinds of mint. To eat, we either tear the greens into small pieces and add them to our bowls or use them to wrap little pieces of meat or seafood and dip in sauce. There is no question that fresh herbs play a critical role at the Vietnamese table.

The high consumption of herbs fulfils both practical and culinary purposes. The traditional Vietnamese diet relies mostly on a huge amount of rice, so herbs (as well as fish sauce) are necessary to make that staple food more palatable. Herbs are also easily available and affordable. Many grow wild, thriving along the edges and banks of wet rice fields. Unlike the Western notion of using herbs in small amounts to season food, the Vietnamese use them as greens. For example, when savouring Grilled Prawn Paste on Sugarcane (see page 142), a single diner can easily consume two to three bunches of fresh herbs, picking the leaves off the sprigs as the meal progresses.

Rau thom is also considered a valuable yin food. Like the Chinese, the Vietnamese believe in the necessary balance of the yin and yang energies. Foods are classified as either *nong* (hot, or yang) or *mat* (cool, or yin). Most starches and proteins constitute the hot energy and, as a rule, must be paired with the cool herbs and vegetables. But beyond this, herbs are also eaten to prevent or cure specific illnesses. For example, the various types of mint and basil are believed to aid digestion and blood circulation and to promote general wellness.

When purchasing herbs, choose the freshest-looking sprigs you can, free of blemishes. Don't wash them until you're ready to use them. Store them in a plastic bag in the refrigerator. (The Vietnamese like to blow air into the bags to prevent the herbs from getting bruised.) Before using, trim to the desired length, then refresh by submerging the whole sprigs in cool water, soaking them for 30 minutes, draining or spinning them dry in a salad spinner.

The following are the most commonly used Vietnamese herbs. Unfortunately, the nomenclature is a bit confusing, since some herbs have more than one English name. To be most accurate, it's best to use their botanical or Vietnamese names. Many are available at Asian stores in larger cities. Mint and *rau ram* are very easy to grow and if you're serious about Vietnamese cuisine, consider planting them. For the best-tasting tender herbs, plant them in bright shade or filtered light and in areas where they can be protected from frost. For more information on growing Asian herbs, Carole Saville's *Exotic Herbs* is one of the best sources I've seen on the topic.

VIETNAMESE HERBS

Asian basil/Thai basil/holy basil/anise basil – *Ocimum basilicum* – *rau que*
To me, this is one of the most seductive herbs in Vietnamese cuisine. Every time I smell a bunch at the produce section of an Asian store, my immediate inclination is to go and get a bowl of *pho*. With pointed oval green leaves and purplish stems and flowers, this beautiful herb is a must when it comes to noodle soups. Delicately scented with liquorice, this popular variety of the Asian basil family is used all over Southeast Asia. The Thais love to toss cupfuls into their stir-fries, soups and curries. They also deep-fry the leaves for garnishes. The Vietnamese prefer them raw, using them in *pho* and in any dishes in which meats are wrapped in lettuce. Don't substitute Italian basil because it's too strong. Use mint instead.

Crab claw herb – *rau cang cua*
Spicy and tart, this rare but delicious herb is commonly used in salads in Vietnam. Delicate and a bit spongy, *rau cang cua* has small green oval leaves that are shiny on the top and pale on the bottom. Often they're sold with heavy flowering tops (hence the name crab claw).

Fish mint/fishscale mint – *Houttuynia cordata* – *rau diep ca*
You will either love or hate this herb. Unlike other herbs, *rau diep ca* doesn't have much of an aroma, but it does have a strong taste. It is sour, almost like sorrel, with fishy undertones. It has dark-green, arrowhead-

shaped leaves with light brown, leggy stems. (This green herb is a cousin of the same *houthuynia* that is used as a decorative ground cover.) In Vietnam, fish mint is served in table salads that accompany grilled meats and fish. It's particularly refreshing and flavourful in Lemongrass Beef on Cool Noodles (see page 135). Substitute mint or Asian basil.

Lemongrass – *Cymbopogon citratus – xa*

This is the main herb used to make marinades for grilled meats. A woody, fibrous pale green stalk, lemongrass imparts a sublime citrusy flavour to foods. It's used in two main ways – finely chopped or pounded into a paste and added to marinades or stir-fries, such as Stir-fried Chicken with Lemongrass and Chillies (see page 164); or cut into 5 to 7.5 cm (2 to 3 inch) pieces and used to infuse broths and curries. Peel the 2 to 3 tough outer layers of the stalk and use only the bottom bulb, about 7.5 to 10 cm (3 to 4 inches) from the base, discarding the fibrous tops.

Mint/spearmint – *Mentha arvensis – rau hung lui*

The most versatile and widely used herb is probably mint, especially the mild-tasting, fuzzy-leafed variety. In Vietnam, mint is harvested when the leaves are tiny, smaller than the size of a penny, and have a slightly more coriander-like than a sharp mint flavour. It's the main herb in table salads and in dishes wrapped in rice paper like Rice Paper-wrapped Salad Rolls (see page 105). Mint is a natural accompaniment to rich foods like pork.

The Vietnamese also eat another type of mint called *rau hung cay*, although not as extensively as *rau hung lui*. Unlike the spearmint variety, *rau hung cay* has thin, paper-like oval leaves with serrated edges. Its mild peppermint taste is preferred in noodle dishes. Substitute spearmint.

Rice paddy herb – *Limnophila aromatica – ngo om*

If you bundle up and chop these darling little herbs, your hands will smell like cumin perfume. Both the long, thin stems and the tiny green leaves about 5 mm (¼ inch) long are used extensively to flavour soups, like Sweet-and-sour Prawn Soup with Fresh Herbs (see page 76). To experience this fragrant herb at its finest, chop and add it to your soup just before serving. *Ngo om* also makes an elegant garnish. Substitute coriander.

Red perilla/*shiso*/beefsteak – *Perilla frutescens* – *rau tia to*
A bit lemony and anise-like, *rau tia to* has purple stems with wide, oval leaves that are deep purple on the bottom and dark green on top. Its fuzzy texture gives a faintly scratchy feel in the throat. The Vietnamese like to shred the leaves and add them to noodles or use in table salads and as wrappers. It is one of the preferred herbs in Sizzling Saigon Crêpes (see page 131) because the strong anise flavour helps to season the mild-tasting rice-flour crêpe. Substitute Asian basil.

Saw-leaf herb/saw-tooth herb/coriander – *Eryngium foetidum* – *ngo gai*
If you saw the saw-leaf herb as a whole plant, you might think twice about eating it. A member of the coriander family, this stiff, thistle-like herb grows in clusters with leaves spreading close to the ground. The dark-green leaves are 7.5 to 10 cm (3 to 4 inches) long with serrated edges (hence the name). They are chewy when raw but quickly soften in hot soups. *Ngo gai* has a refreshing floral and coriander-like aroma. The Vietnamese love to garnish their *pho* with this herb. Substitute coriander or Asian basil.

Pepper leaf, wild betel leaf – *Piper sarmentosum* – *la lot*
This is a relative of the betel leaf. In Vietnam, *la lot* is used as a wrapper for grilled meats and as an aromatic leaf for flavouring soups and stir-fries. When used to season food, it's shredded and added towards the end of the cooking, as in the Spicy Lemongrass Tofu (see page 222). For

wrapping, you can substitute large red perilla leaves or grape leaves. For flavouring foods, substitute Asian basil.

Vietnamese balm/green perilla – *Elsholtzia ciliata* – *rau kinh gioi*
This lesser-known herb also happens to be one of the most flavourful. Also referred to as green perilla because of its resemblance to red perilla, *rau kinh gioi* is a relative of lemon balm, but has a more pronounced lemongrass flavour. *Rau kinh gioi* is a shrubby plant similar to red perilla and has light-green oval leaves with serrated edges. It is used with noodles and in soups but is particularly delicious in Hanoi Rice Noodles with Grilled Pork (see page 136). Substitute red perilla or Asian basil.

Vietnamese coriander – *Polygonum odoratum* – *rau ram*
I love *rau ram*, especially the small tender sprigs that our farmer grows for the restaurant. They're spicy, sharp and flavourful, with the hint of coriander. *Rau ram* has small pointed green leaves, about 2.5 to 4 cm (1 to 1½ inches) long, with brown veins and slightly knobby brown stems. These aromatic leaves are usually eaten raw, in salads such as Hue Chicken Salad (see page 83), and in noodle soups such as Hue Beef Vermicelli Soup (see page 59). *Rau ram* can be easily propagated by placing some stems in water and letting them root. Plant in shade or filtered sun and keep snipping the tops to encourage new growth. Small young leaves have the best flavour. *Rau ram* also makes a great houseplant or hanging plant. Substitute mint or Asian basil.

Noodle Soups and Broths

Oh my beloved
life without you is like
pho without its broth.
Vietnamese song

THE TRAFFIC NOISE gets louder by the minute as motorists and cyclists pour into Hang Giay Street. On the pavement, shoppers are browsing through the neighbourhood fruit stands, looking for the best picks. But the people sitting next to me at this low table are oblivious to all the commotion. Instead, they're anxiously wiping their chopsticks, fiddling with their little dishes of lime and chopped chillies. It's morning in Hanoi, and morning means *pho*, the country's beloved rice noodle soup with beef.

Up until a few years ago, the thought of coming to Hanoi seemed so remote. How could I ever visit a place that brought tragic memories of the war all over again, a city where my father's enemies once ruled?

But after one bite of my noodles, I immediately knew. I had come to taste my favourite food in the city that created it. This particular bowl of *pho* was as soothing and delicious as I had imagined it would be. Unlike the darker broth and the more chewy noodles served in other parts of Vietnam and in the West, the rice noodles here are almost sheer, and the broth is clear, like spring water, yet intensely aromatic of beef marrow bones.

As I slurp my steaming soup, I can't help but flash back to Saigon in the sixties, when my parents used to take my siblings and me to Pho 79. It was a noodle shop like this one, small and run-down, with wobbly tables and squeaky stools. Yet no one ever judged Pho 79 by its looks, only by the enticing beefy aroma that wafted through the air and the crowds that squeezed through the front door each day. Every time we arrived, the place was packed. As soon as we found a party about to leave, we would dash over, waiting inconspicuously for the right moment to seize our table.

Once seated, we felt relieved. My parents would then place their usual order: *pho* with the rare and cooked beef topping and *ca phe sua da* – a delicious coffee drink served with condensed milk and ice. While waiting, we would grab the chopsticks and spoons from an aluminium container and dust them off. Moments later, our soup would arrive. We would bend down and inhale the aroma, as if to verify its authenticity. Invariably, the broth smelled utterly beefy, laced with just-roasted spices. The rice noodles looked velvety and fresh, the edges of the rare beef curled up expectantly in the hot broth. All was well.

Then, our arms and hands would fly across the table, all reaching for the lime, basil, saw-leaf herbs and fresh chillies to garnish our bowls.

Even though our family first discovered *pho* in Saigon, the dish actually originated in Hanoi, following the French occupation in the latter 1800s. The Vietnamese, who valued cows and buffaloes as indispensable beasts of burden, didn't eat red meat, preferring instead pork, chicken and seafood. When the French arrived, however, many Vietnamese, especially those belonging to the upper classes, began to share the French affection for beef. Dishes made with *boeuf* began appearing at the markets and in restaurants, and in time, red meat became part of the Vietnamese diet.

How this actually led to the creation of *pho* remains a debate. Some scholars believe the dish parallels the history of Vietnam, harbouring both a Chinese and a French connection. It was the French, they theorize, who introduced the idea of using bones and lesser cuts of beef to make the broth. (After all, in a society that wasted nothing, what was one to do with all the bones carved from *biftecks*?) In fact, they believe the dish was first created when Vietnamese cooks learnt to make *pot-au-feu* for their French masters. The name *pho* – pronounced '*fuh*' – might have even come from the French word *feu*, for fire.

Others argue that while the French popularized beef, it was actually the Chinese who created *pho*, as evidenced by its use of noodles and ginger. According to Huu Ngoc, a Hanoi-based scholar who's written extensively about the local culture and cuisine for more than five decades, historical records suggest that the soup is related to two ancient dishes called *chao pho* and *luc pho*, which translate into soup with *pho* and beef with *pho*. The word *pho*, he says, was probably a mispronunciation of *phan*, as in the Chinese phrase *nguu nguc phan*, which means rice paste soup with beef.

Regardless of the origin, the Vietnamese were quick to interject their own ideas. Using ingredients inspired by their foreign rulers, they customized *pho* by adding *nuoc mam* (fish sauce), the defining ingredient.

In the 1930s, in part spurred on by nationalistic sentiments, some Hanoi scholars wrote passionately about *pho*, crediting it not only as a food that provided the necessary nutrients in one convenient bowl, but a food that symbolically freed the people who created and ate it. At last, the Vietnamese were free to express themselves, if only through their *pho*.

The infectious enthusiasm for the dish spread south in 1954, when the country was partitioned. The north fell under Communist control and almost a million northerners fled, taking with them a dream of a new life in the democratic south and a love of *pho*.

Pho took the south by storm. My mother, a southerner who had just moved from her village to Saigon, had never seen or heard of the soup until the late fifties. At the time my mother and her contemporaries slurped on *hu tieu*, a Chinese-style rice noodle soup made with pork. But when she first tasted *pho*, she became an instant convert. From then on, whenever she and my father could afford it, which was about once a month, they would treat themselves to this new delicacy.

When *pho* migrated south, it was embellished. Reflecting the abundance of its new surroundings, it was served with more meat, more noodles, more broth. Southerners demanded richer and livelier flavours and discernible textures. They started adding bean sprouts and herbs, such as saw-leaf and basil. But it didn't stop there. Garnishes such as lime wedges, fresh chillies, chilli sauce and *tuong*, or bean sauce, were added, giving the dish a new character. As in the north, it quickly became a favourite, but only after it had been modified to reflect southern taste and mentality.

In 1975, when my family and I first arrived in the United States, following the fall of Saigon, one of the foods we missed most desperately was *pho*. We ate *pho* whenever we could, even though the versions of the soup we found lacked the distinctive herbs and complex flavour of real *pho*. To us, a steaming bowl of *pho* was a welcome thought. A taste of home, it warmed our spirit and gave us the comfort and solace needed during our first difficult years in America.

Fortunately, over the years, immigrant families such as ourselves have readjusted and rebuilt our lives. And somehow, in the midst of all this transformation, *pho* – which followed us through tumultuous times and journeys – has become a big part of our everyday life. Authentic recipes have been dusted off, preserved and cooked with great fervour.

And so, as I'm slurping my bowl of *pho* in Hanoi, I can't help but ponder the parallels of this great soup and my own life. It's comforting to know that wherever I happen to be, whether it's in Vietnam or California, *pho* will always be there, ready to nourish and sustain me.

There are several key things to keep in mind as you prepare *pho* and other noodle soups. First, *pho* takes time to prepare and it's best that you don't get distracted by trying to cook too many other dishes when making this special soup. It's really best eaten by itself.

Second, focus on the noodles. Unlike pasta, rice noodles are very delicate and require special attention to come out right. Follow the instructions on preparing the noodles and make sure they're absolutely hot before ladling the broth on top.

For the recipes in this chapter, it helps to have the proper kitchen tools and the correct size bowls. If you love noodle soups as I do, invest in a good, heavy-bottomed soup pot, a long-handled wire strainer for cooking noodles and some big, deep 1 litre (32 fl oz) soup bowls. It's absolutely critical to have bowls large enough to accommodate a generous amount of broth to keep the noodles hot throughout the meal. Nothing is worse than lukewarm noodle soup.

And lastly, pay attention to the garnishes. What gives *pho* its distinctive qualities are the last-minute additions of the paper-thin onions, the fresh herbs, the lime wedges and the chillies.

PREPARING NOODLES FOR PHO

For *pho*, use dried rice noodles, the white, translucent linguine-type noodles sold as *banh pho*, or rice sticks. They come in 400 or 450 g (14 or 16 oz) bags and are available in small, medium and wide. For *pho*, buy the small, 2 mm ($\frac{1}{16}$ inch) width noodles.

To use, first soak the noodles in cold water for 30 minutes, then drain. Bring a big pot of water to a rolling boil. When you're ready to serve (not before), place the noodles, one portion at a time, into a sieve and lower it into the boiling water. Using chopsticks or a long spoon, stir so the noodles untangle and cook evenly. Blanch just until they're soft but still chewy, about 10 to 20 seconds depending on the thickness. Drain completely, then transfer to a preheated bowl. Cook the remaining noodles the same way. The bowls are now ready to be assembled. (If you're cooking for several people, you may also cook the noodles all at once by adding them directly to the pot of boiling water. Just make sure to serve them immediately.)

If you're able to buy fresh *pho* noodles, which are now becoming increasingly available, omit the soaking but blanch them in boiling water.

Vietnamese 'Pho' Rice Noodle Soup with Beef
Pho bo

THIS BELOVED noodle soup is a complete meal in itself and is best served for breakfast or lunch on a weekend. Because the simmering takes at least two hours, I like to prepare the broth a day ahead of time and keep it in the refrigerator, where it will last for three days. Many cookery books call for it to be made with oxtail bones, but I prefer marrow bones and beef chuck, which is what *pho* cooks in Vietnam use. A good *pho* broth needs to be clear, not muddy and dark, and certainly fragrant with beef, anise and ginger.

You can serve this soup with several toppings, but the easiest ones to prepare at home are cooked and raw beef. If you're pressed for time, refer to the recipe on page 55 for a quick version that uses store-bought stock.

To use broth that has been made in advance, bring it to the boil, then add fresh ginger to refresh it. Come serving time, get friends or family to help cook the noodles and assemble the bowls. Make sure that the broth is boiling hot and the bowls preheated. Allow about 1 part noodles to 3 parts broth for each bowl.

Serves 6 as a main dish

For the broth:
2.25 kg (5 lb) beef marrow or knuckle bones
900 g (2 lb) beef chuck, cut into 2 pieces
2 x 7.5 cm (3 inch) pieces of ginger, cut in half lengthways
    and lightly bruised with the flat side of a knife, lightly
    charred (see page 53)
2 onions, peeled and charred (see page 53)
60 ml (2 fl oz) fish sauce
75 g (3 oz) rock sugar or 3 tablespoons sugar
10 whole star anise, lightly toasted in a dry pan
6 whole cloves, lightly toasted in a dry pan
1 tablespoon sea salt

For the noodle assembly:
450 g (1 lb) dried 1 mm (1/16 inch) wide rice sticks, soaked,
    cooked and drained (see page 49)
150 g (5 oz) beef sirloin, slightly frozen, then sliced paper-
    thin across the grain

- In a large stockpot, bring 5.5 litres (9 pints) water to the boil. Place the bones and beef chuck in a second pan and add water to cover. Bring to the boil and boil vigorously for 5 minutes. Using tongs, carefully transfer the bones and beef to the first pot of boiling water. Discard the water in which the meat cooked. (This cleans the bones and meat and reduces the impurities that can cloud the broth.) When the water returns to the boil, reduce the heat to a simmer. Skim the surface often to remove any foam or fat. Add the charred ginger and onions, fish sauce and sugar. Simmer for about 40 minutes until the beef chuck is tender. Remove one piece and submerge in cool water for 10 minutes to prevent the meat from darkening and drying out. Drain, then cut into thin slices and set aside. Let the other piece of beef chuck continue to cook in the simmering broth.

- When the broth has been simmering for about 1½ hours altogether, wrap the star anise and cloves in a spice bag (or piece of muslin) and add to the broth. Let infuse for about 30 minutes until the broth is fragrant. Remove and discard both the spice bag and onions. Add the salt and continue to simmer, skimming as necessary, until you're ready to assemble the dish. The broth needs to cook for at least 2 hours. (The broth will taste salty but will be balanced once the noodles and accompaniments are added.) Leave the remaining chuck and bones to simmer in the pot while you assemble the bowls.

- To serve, place the cooked noodles in preheated bowls. (If the noodles are not hot, reheat them in a microwave or dip them briefly in boiling water to prevent them from cooling the soup down.) Place a few slices of the beef chuck and the raw sirloin on the noodles. Bring the broth to a rolling boil; ladle about 2 to 3 big ladlefuls into each bowl. The broth will cook the raw beef instantly. Garnish with onion, spring onions and coriander. Serve immediately, inviting guests to garnish the bowls with bean sprouts, herbs, chillies, lime juice and black pepper.

How to Char Ginger and Onions

TO CHAR GINGER, hold the piece with tongs directly over an open flame or place it directly on a medium-hot electric burner. While turning, char for about 3 to 4 minutes until the edges are slightly blackened and the ginger is fragrant. Char the onions in the same way. Peel and discard the blackened skins of the ginger and onions, then rinse and add to the broth.

How to Enjoy Pho at a Restaurant

IN VIETNAM, *pho* is mostly restaurant food. Although it can be prepared at home, most people prefer the ritual of going out to a noisy soup shop, where they can slurp their favourite soup while chitchatting and gossiping. Fortunately, *pho* shops are now springing up in the West too. The best way to choose a *pho* shop is to find one that is busy (higher turnover usually means fresher ingredients) and one that serves all the proper garnishes. Personally, I would not patronize a soup shop that does not, at the very least, offer fresh Asian basil (and preferably saw-leaf herb).

Eating *pho* is an art in itself and the following guidelines are designed to help you better appreciate this wonderful dish.

1. When ordering *pho*, beware. It comes in many sizes, from small to *xe lua* or 'train' size, which can feed two or three. Unless you're super-hungry, go for the medium bowl.

2. You can choose individual or combination toppings, from rare to well-done beef, to brisket and meatballs, even tripe, tendon and so on. If you're not sure, try the *pho tai nam*, the rare and well-done combination.

3. Eat *pho* while it's piping hot. If you wait for it to cool down, the noodles will expand and become soggy, and the dish will taste bland. (Some connoisseurs don't even talk while they eat their *pho*, preferring to save serious chatting for later.)

4. Begin by adding bean sprouts, fresh chillies and a little squeeze of lime. Using your fingers, pluck the Asian basil leaves from their sprigs and, if available, shred the saw-leaf herbs and add them to the soup. Add them little by little, eating as you go. (If you put them in all at once, the broth will cool too fast and the herbs will overcook and lose their bright flavours.) Chilli sauce and hoisin sauce are traditional condiments, but I avoid them because, to my taste, they mask the flavour of *pho*.

5. Push the garnishings into the hot broth and gently turn the noodles.

6. With spoon in one hand and chopsticks in the other, pull the noodles out of the broth and eat, alternatively slurping the broth. It's perfectly acceptable to be seen with clumps of noodles dangling from your mouth, eyes squinting from the steam.

7. The broth is served in large amounts to keep the noodles warm and to help season the dish. It's not meant to be consumed in its entirety. But if you're in the mood, it's not considered rude to tip the bowl and slurp down every last drop.

Consider finishing the meal with Vietnamese Coffee (see page 256) with condensed milk and ice. Brewed in individual filters at the table, it's sweet, delicious and very strong. If you're planning a busy day, get one. It will keep you buzzing for a while.

Quick Pho
pho nhanh

WHENEVER I NEED a quick fix for a *pho* craving, I resort to this recipe. Although nothing can compare to the made-from-scratch version, this is also very good. The key is to come up with a flavourful broth, scented with the prerequisite charred ginger and star anise, and then to serve the dish with all the necessary herbs and garnishings. The only commercial stock that I've found at the supermarket that would work is chicken, not beef, since the latter is too dark for this recipe. If you have access to an Asian store, you might want to look for canned *pho* stock. It's quite good, although it contains MSG. Even though this recipe is made with chicken broth, you can serve either a chicken or beef topping with it.

Serves 6 as a main dish

For the broth:
6 whole star anise, lightly toasted in a dry pan for
    2 minutes
6 whole cloves, lightly toasted in a dry pan for 2 minutes
1 teaspoon whole black peppercorns
1.75 litres (3 pints) store-bought reduced-salt chicken
    stock
500 ml (16 fl oz) water
7.5 cm (3 inch) piece of ginger, cut in half lengthways,
    lightly bruised with the flat side of a knife and charred
    (see page 53)
1 small onion, charred (see page 53)
3 tablespoons fish sauce

1 tablespoon sugar
¼ teaspoon salt
2 chicken thighs or breasts (about 625 g/20 oz)

For the noodle assembly:
450 g (1 lb) dried 1 mm (⅟₁₆ inch) wide rice sticks, cooked
    (see page 49)
⅛ onion, sliced paper-thin
2 spring onions, cut into thin rings
3 tablespoons finely chopped coriander

For the garnish:
225 g (8 oz) bean sprouts
10 sprigs of Asian basil
12 saw-leaf herb leaves (optional)
3 Thai bird's eye chillies or 1 serrano chilli, cut into thin
    rings
1 lime, cut into 6 wedges
Freshly ground black pepper

- Place the star anise, cloves and peppercorns in a spice bag (or a piece of muslin); set aside.

- Place the chicken stock, water, charred ginger and onion, fish sauce, sugar, salt and spice bag in a large pot and bring to the boil. Add the chicken and cook for 5 minutes. Reduce the heat and simmer for about 15 minutes until the chicken is done. Remove the chicken and set aside to cool. Let the broth continue to simmer. When the chicken is cool enough to handle, hand-shred into 1 cm (½ inch) thick strips. Set aside until ready to serve.

- To serve, place the cooked noodles in preheated bowls. (If the noodles are not hot, reheat in a microwave or dip briefly in boiling water.) Add to each bowl a few slices of onion and some shredded chicken. Ladle a generous amount of boiling broth on top. Add spring onions and coriander. Invite guests to garnish their bowls with bean sprouts, fresh herbs, chillies, squeezes of lime juice and black pepper.

Vietnamese Rice Noodle Soup with Chicken
pho ga

WHENEVER I'M IN Saigon, I love going to the noodle shops on Pasteur Street and getting my fill of chicken *pho*. The choice of toppings is almost endless – breast meat, leg meat, thigh meat, wings and giblets, and all with or without the skin. And, if you get there early, you can order a side dish of immature (unlaid) chicken eggs.

This recipe is also delicious without any exotic parts of the chicken. Use a good-quality bird and take care not to let the broth boil too vigorously or it will get cloudy.

Serves 6

For the broth:
6 whole star anise, lightly toasted in a dry pan for
    2 minutes
6 whole cloves, lightly toasted in a dry pan for 2 minutes

1 teaspoon whole black peppercorns

1.35 kg (3 lb) chicken wings and bones, skin removed

1 whole chicken (about
    1.5 kg/3½ lb), split in half

10 cm (4 inch) piece of ginger, cut in half lengthways,
    lightly bruised with the flat side of a knife, charred (see
    page 53)

2 onions, peeled and charred (see page 53)

60 ml (2 fl oz) fish sauce

2 tablespoons sugar

1 tablespoon sea salt

For the noodle assembly:

450 g (1 lb) dried 1 mm (⅟₁₆ inch) wide rice sticks, cooked
    (see page 124)

½ onion, sliced paper-thin

3 spring onions, cut into thin rings

20 g (¾ oz) chopped coriander

For the garnish:

450 g (1 lb) bean sprouts

20 sprigs of Asian basil

12 saw-leaf herb leaves (optional)

3 Thai bird's eye chillies or 1 serrano chilli, thinly sliced

1 lime, cut into 6 wedges

Freshly ground black pepper

- Place the star anise, cloves and peppercorns in a spice bag; set aside.
- In a large stockpot, bring 4 litres (7 pints) water to a rolling boil. Add the chicken wings and bones and the chicken halves. Boil vigorously for

3 minutes, then reduce the heat to a simmer. Skim the surface as necessary to remove any fat or foam. Add the charred ginger, onions, fish sauce, sugar and salt. Cook for about ½ hour until the chicken is just done. Remove the chicken (but not the chicken wings and bones) and set aside to cool.

- Add the spice bag to the pot and cook the broth for a total of 1½ hours. Remove and discard the spice bag. Reduce the heat to very low.

- Remove the skin from the chicken and discard. Hand-shred half of it into bite-sized strips. (Save the other half for another use, like chicken salad. You don't need much to garnish *pho*, but you do need a whole chicken to make a good broth.)

- To serve, place the cooked noodles in preheated bowls. (If the noodles are not hot, reheat in a microwave or dip briefly in boiling water.) Place some onion and shredded chicken on top. Bring the broth back to a rolling boil, then ladle into each bowl. Top with spring onions and coriander. Invite guests to garnish their bowls with bean sprouts, fresh herbs, chillies, squeezes of lime juice and black pepper.

Hue Beef Vermicelli Soup
bun bo Hue

IN HUE, there's no question that this dish – not *pho* – is the most popular noodle soup. It is heartier, made with both pork and beef and lots of chillies and lemongrass. For the best flavour, prepare the aromatics and float them in the broth right at the end. The preferred noodles for this dish are not the rice sticks used in *pho*, but a fat, round rice vermicelli similar to spaghetti. Recent brands from China actually label them as noodles for *bun bo Hue*. If you can't find them, use the smaller noodles called *bun* (rice vermicelli, see page 124).

Makes 6 servings

For the broth:
3 lemongrass stalks, bottom white parts only
1.35 kg (3 lb) pork bones
700 g (1½ lb) boneless pork leg, cut in 2 pieces
700 g (1½ lb) beef shank, cut in 2 pieces
3 tablespoons fish sauce
1 teaspoon salt
2 tablespoons sugar
1 teaspoon shrimp sauce
   (see Glossary page 265)
2 tablespoons vegetable oil
2 teaspoons annatto seeds
   (optional, see Glossary page 257)
1 teaspoon minced shallot
1 teaspoon dried chilli flakes

For the noodle assembly:
450 g (1 lb) dried fat rice vermicelli (like spaghetti),
   cooked for about 10 minutes until soft, drained and
   rinsed (see page 124)
½ onion, sliced paper-thin
15 g (¾ oz) chopped coriander
2 spring onions, cut into
   thin rings

For the garnish:
**2 handfuls of *rau ram* (Vietnamese coriander leaves),
  coarsely chopped**
**150 g (5 oz) very thinly shredded cabbage, soaked in cold
  water and drained (optional)**
I lime, cut into 6 wedges
4 Thai bird's eye chillies, chopped

- Peel the tough outer layers of the lemongrass and discard. Finely chop enough for 2 tablespoons and set aside. Using the flat side of a knife, lightly bruise the remaining stalks. Cut into 7.5 cm (3 inch) pieces; set aside.

- Place the pork bones, pork leg and beef shank in a large pot. Add water to cover, bring to the boil, then drain. Return the bones, pork and beef to the pot and add 2.65 litres (4½ pints) fresh water. Add the lemongrass stalks. Bring to the boil, then reduce the heat to a simmer. Cook for about I hour until the meat is tender but still firm. Skim the surface to remove any foam or fat that rises to the top.

- With a slotted spoon, remove I piece of the pork leg and I piece of the beef shank and submerge in cool water for 10 minutes to keep them from turning dark. Remove from the water and trim any excess fat or chewy parts from the shank and pork. Slice both meats into thin bite-sized strips; set aside. Allow the remaining meat to simmer in the broth.

- Add the fish sauce, salt, sugar and shrimp sauce to the broth and continue to simmer.

- Heat the oil in a small saucepan over moderate heat. Remove the pan from the heat and add the annatto seeds, if using. Let them foam for 30 seconds, then strain the oil into another pan (or remove the seeds with a slotted spoon). Heat the annatto oil over moderate heat and add the shallot, chilli flakes and reserved chopped lemongrass. Stir for about 10 seconds until fragrant. Remove from the heat immediately and add to the broth.

- To serve, divide the cooked noodles evenly among preheated bowls. (If the noodles are not hot, reheat in a microwave oven or blanch in boiling water.) Top with a few strips of pork and beef shank. Ladle a generous amount of hot broth on top and garnish with sliced onion, coriander and spring onions. Serve with *rau ram*, cabbage, if desired, lime wedges and chillies on the side.

Rice Noodles with Prawn Dumpling Soup
bun rieu

A SPECIALITY of the north, this soup is traditionally made with *cua dong* (rice field crabs), which are prized for their delicate sweet flavour. Vietnamese cooks use a mortar and pestle to pound them lightly before making dumplings. This version calls for prawns, although cooked crabmeat would be lovely, too. I like to make this soup when tomatoes are at their peak.

Serves 6

For the dumplings:
110 g (4 oz) raw prawns, peeled, deveined and patted dry
110 g (4 oz) minced pork or minced chicken

½ teaspoon white pepper
½ teaspoon salt
2 teaspoons fish sauce
I egg
3 tablespoons finely chopped onion

For the broth:
I tablespoon vegetable oil
I tablespoon minced shallot
I teaspoon chopped garlic
I teaspoon ground dried chillies
3 tablespoons fish sauce
4 ripe tomatoes, quartered
1.25 litres (2 pints) fresh Chicken Stock (see page 38) or
    store-bought reduced-salt chicken stock
500 ml (16 fl oz) water
I teaspoon *ruoc* (shrimp paste), see Glossary page 265
¼ teaspoon sea salt
I teaspoon fresh lime juice

For the noodle assembly:
450 g (I lb) dried *bun* (rice vermicelli or rice sticks),
    cooked 3 to 4 minutes, drained and rinsed (see page
    124)
2 spring onions, cut into thin rings
15 g (¾ oz) chopped coriander

For the garnish:
150 g (5 oz) thinly shredded white cabbage, soaked in cold
    water for 30 minutes and drained
225 g (8 oz) bean sprouts

25 g (1 oz) Asian basil or *rau ram* leaves
2 Thai bird's eye chillies or 1 serrano chilli, chopped
1 lime, cut into 6 thin wedges

- To make the dumplings, place the prawns, pork, white pepper, salt, fish sauce, egg and onion in a food processor and pulse for about 15 seconds until the mixture becomes a lumpy paste. (Do not overmix or the dumplings will be tough.) You can also mince all the ingredients by hand. Transfer to a bowl until ready to use.

- To make the broth, heat the oil in a pan over moderate heat. Add the shallot and garlic and stir for about 20 seconds until fragrant. Add the chillies, fish sauce and tomatoes and stir for 1 minute. Add the chicken stock, water, shrimp paste, salt and lime juice and bring to the boil. Reduce the heat to a simmer.

- Scoop up a heaped tablespoon of the prawn mixture and slip it into the broth. Make all the dumplings this way. Cook for about 10 minutes until the dumplings rise to the surface and are cooked.

- To serve, place the cooked noodles in preheated bowls. Ladle a generous amount of boiling broth into each bowl and top with several dumplings. Garnish with spring onions and coriander. Serve immediately with cabbage, bean sprouts, basil, chillies and lime wedges on the side.

My Tho Noodle Soup
hu tieu My Tho

WHENEVER I VISIT my grandmother in the Mekong Delta, I always stop at one of the noodle shops near the ferry station for a bowl of *hu tieu My Tho*. Named after the capital of Tien Giang province, this dish is a cousin of Chinese egg noodle soup but is made with rice noodles and poached, rather than barbecued, pork.

Serves 6
1 recipe **Noodle Broth** (see page 66)
450 g (1 lb) pork shoulder
1 tablespoon vegetable oil
1 shallot, minced
1 garlic clove, minced
150 g (5 oz) minced cooked pork
1 teaspoon fish sauce

For the noodle assembly:
450 g (1 lb) dried large 2 mm (⅛ inch) wide rice sticks, cooked (see page 49), drained and rinsed
12 medium raw prawns, peeled, deveined and cooked
¼ onion, sliced paper-thin
2 tablespoons Chinese-style preserved cabbage (optional, see Glossary page 263)
2 spring onions, cut into thin rings
15 g (¾ oz) chopped coriander

For the garnish:
90 g (3½ oz) bean sprouts
3 Thai bird's eye chillies, sliced
1 lime, cut into 6 wedges

- Bring the broth to a simmer in a large pot, then add the pork shoulder and cook for 30 to 40 minutes until done. (The meat should still be firm for better slicing.) Remove the pork and submerge in cool water for about 15 minutes to keep the meat from turning dark. Remove, cut into thin slices and set aside. Continue to simmer the broth until ready to serve.

- In a frying pan, heat the oil over moderate heat. Add the shallot and garlic and stir for about 20 seconds until fragrant. Add the minced pork and fish sauce and stir well. Set aside until ready to use.

- To assemble, bring the broth back to a vigorous boil. Place some of the cooked noodles in each preheated soup bowl. Top with 1 tablespoon of the minced pork mixture, a few slices of the pork shoulder and 2 prawns. Ladle a generous amount of hot broth into each bowl. Top with sliced onion, a teaspoon of the preserved cabbage, if desired, and some spring onions and coriander. Invite guests to garnish their bowls with bean sprouts, chillies and a squeeze of lime.

Noodle Broth
nuoc leo

TO A VIETNAMESE COOK, the most important thing about making broth is that it must be clear. So when making this, simmer the broth uncovered and do not let it boil vigorously. You can use this all-purpose stock for any noodle soup, be it with egg noodles or rice noodles. The dried toasted squid imparts a distinctive savouriness.

> ***Makes 2.65 litres (4½ pints)***
> **3.5 litres (6 pints) water**
> **2.25 kg (5 lb) pork and/or chicken bones**
> **I small dried squid (see Glossary page 265), lightly toasted on a grill or in a dry pan**
> **75 ml (3 fl oz) soy sauce, preferably light**
> **Salt to taste**

• Place the water in a soup pot and bring to a rolling boil. Add the bones and squid. Reduce the heat to low and simmer for at least 2 hours, skimming often to remove any foam and impurities that rise to the top. Thirty minutes before the end of the cooking time, stir in the soy sauce and salt. Strain the broth before using.

Rice Soup with Chicken and Ginger
chao ga

RICE SOUP is one of the simplest and most satisfying dishes you can make. It can be served plain, with just a scattering of spring onions, or it can be more sumptuous as in this recipe. If you're pressed for time, use store-bought chicken stock and cooked chicken to garnish it. For an authentic meal, serve this with Hue Chicken Salad (see page 83). While it may sound strange to pair hot soup with cold salad, the combination actually works.

You can use any rice, but the long-grain jasmine variety is best for this recipe. The toasting of the rice prior to cooking it in the broth gives the soup its nutty flavour. This is also great with minced beef, pork or tofu.

> **Serves 4 to 6**
> **1.75 litres (3 pints) water**
> **½ whole chicken, excess fat trimmed**
> **¼ teaspoon sea salt**
> **2 teaspoons vegetable oil**
> **I garlic clove, sliced**
> **100 g (4 oz) rice, preferably long-grain jasmine, rinsed and**
>   **drained**
> **I tablespoon fish sauce**
> **I tablespoon minced ginger**
> **2 spring onions, cut into thin rings**
> **4 sprigs of coriander, thinly sliced**
> **2 tablespoons Fried Shallots (optional, see page 32)**
> **Freshly ground white or black pepper**

- Bring the water to a rolling boil in a large soup pot. Add the chicken and salt. Reduce the heat and simmer the liquid. Skim any foam or fat that rises to the surface.

- Place the oil, garlic and rice in a frying pan over moderate heat. Stir gently for 3 to 4 minutes until the grains start to turn opaque.

- Add the rice to the soup pot. Cook for about 25 minutes total, until the chicken is just done. Remove the chicken and set aside to cool.

Add the fish sauce and ginger to the soup. Let the rice continue to cook for about 30 minutes until the kernels open and are tender.

- Remove the skin from the chicken and shred the meat into bite-sized strips.

- When ready to serve, ladle the soup into preheated soup bowls and garnish each with chicken, spring onions, coriander, shallots and pepper. Serve immediately.

Curry Noodle Soup with Chicken
bun cari

MY MOTHER OFTEN prepared this dish during Tet, or Vietnamese Lunar New Year, as part of a banquet offering to our ancestors. It's basically a curry made with extra broth, which is then poured over rice noodles and vegetables. When serving, make sure the curry is piping hot so the noodles and vegetables, which are served at room temperature, won't turn the whole dish tepid.

Serves 4
1 tablespoon vegetable oil
2 garlic cloves, minced
1 teaspoon ground chilli paste (see Glossary page 259)
3 tablespoons curry powder, Vietnamese Three Golden
    Bells brand if you can find it
225 g (8 oz) boneless, skinless chicken thighs, sliced into
    bite-sized strips

375 ml (12 fl oz) unsweetened coconut milk
1 litre (1¾ pints) homemade Chicken Stock (see page 38)
   or store-bought reduced-salt chicken stock
¼ teaspoon ground turmeric
3 tablespoons fish sauce
1 tablespoon sugar
A handful of *rau ram* (Vietnamese coriander), leaves only
2 handfuls of shredded romaine lettuce
90 g (3½ oz) bean sprouts
450 g (1 lb) dried *bun* (small rice vermicelli or rice sticks),
   cooked 4 to 5 minutes, rinsed and drained (see page 124)
3 tablespoons chopped coriander
2 spring onions, cut into thin rings

For the garnish:
1 lime, cut into 4 wedges
4 Thai bird's eye chillies or 2 serrano chillies, cut into thin
   rings (optional)

- Heat the oil in a medium pan over moderate heat. Add the garlic and stir for about 10 seconds until fragrant. Add the chilli paste, curry powder and chicken and stir-fry for 1 minute. Add the coconut milk, chicken stock, turmeric, fish sauce and sugar. Bring to the boil, then reduce the heat to a simmer.

- Divide the *rau ram*, lettuce and bean sprouts among 4 preheated soup bowls. Divide the cooked noodles among the bowls. Bring the curry to a rolling boil, then ladle a generous amount of stock with some of the chicken over the noodles. Garnish each bowl with coriander and spring onions. Serve immediately with the lime wedges and the optional chillies on the side.

Roast Duck and Egg Noodle Soup

·mi vit tim

THIS HEARTY SOUP is one of my favourite winter meals, especially on Sundays, when often all I want is something simple and comforting. If you have access to good Chinese barbecued duck this is very quick to prepare. If you don't, any roast duck or chicken will work. I've called for fresh Chinese-style egg noodles (see page 125), but you can use any kind, including instant ramen noodles.

Serves 4
1 tablespoon vegetable oil
1 shallot, thinly sliced
900 ml (1½ pints) Noodle Broth (see page 66) or store-bought reduced-salt chicken stock
250 ml (8 fl oz) water
1 tablespoon soy sauce
½ teaspoon five-spice powder
2 teaspoons sugar
2.5 cm (1 inch) piece of ginger, peeled and cut in half lengthways
½ teaspoon salt, or to taste
450 g (1 lb) fresh egg noodles, cooked until soft but still firm, 3 to 4 minutes
150 g (5 oz) baby bok choy or any Asian mustard greens, cut diagonally into 5 cm (2 inch) pieces and blanched in boiling water for 20 seconds
½ Chinese-style roast duck, boned and sliced into bite-sized pieces

2 tablespoons chopped coriander
2 spring onions, cut into thin rings
¼ recipe Marinated Chillies (see page 37) or 2 to 3 Thai
   bird's eye chillies or ½ serrano chilli, chopped

- Heat the oil in a pan over moderate heat. Add the shallot and stir for
  about 20 seconds until fragrant. Add the broth, water, soy sauce, five-
  spice powder, sugar, ginger and salt and bring to the boil. Reduce the
  heat and simmer the mixture for 10 minutes.

- Divide the cooked noodles evenly among 4 preheated soup bowls. (If
  the noodles are not hot, reheat in a microwave oven or blanch briefly
  in boiling water.) Top with bok choy and some duck slices. Bring the
  broth to a rolling boil. Ladle a generous amount into each bowl and
  garnish with coriander and spring onions. Serve with the Marinated
  Chillies or fresh chillies on the side.

Noodle Soup with Meatballs
hu tieu bo vien

SOMETHING OF A Chinese version of *pho*, this soup is a popular dish in
our neighbourhood and in the Chinatown section of Saigon. The broth
is made by simmering pork and beef bones along with meatballs, tripe,
brisket and other cuts of beef. The meatballs and meat are served as a
topping and are often dipped in hoisin sauce and chilli sauce. However,
I prefer the delicate flavours of the toppings and do not serve any sauce
with this dish.

The best noodles for this soup are the thin, wiry rice vermicelli (also sold under the Thai name *sen mee*), but you can also use the more common rice sticks used for *pho*.

Serves 4

For the meatballs:
325 g (11 oz) beef chuck, cubed
1 tablespoon chopped shallot
1 tablespoon fish sauce

For the broth:
900 ml (1½ pints) store-bought beef stock
1 litre (1¾ pints) water
1½ teaspoons five-spice powder
5 cm (2 inch) piece of ginger, peeled and bruised with the
    flat side of a knife
2 tablespoons soy sauce
1 tablespoon sugar

For the noodle assembly:
225 g (8 oz) bean sprouts, blanched
325 g (11 oz) dried small rice sticks, cooked, drained and
    rinsed (see page 49)
5 romaine lettuce leaves, each cut into thirds
150 g (5 oz) beef sirloin, thinly sliced
2 spring onions, cut into thin rings
15 g (¾ oz) chopped coriander
3 tablespoons Fried Shallots, see page 32 (optional)

For the garnish:
10 sprigs of Asian basil
4 lime wedges
4 Thai bird's eye chillies or another fresh chilli, chopped

- Combine the beef with the shallot and fish sauce. Place in a food processor and process into a smooth paste. Remove and mould into meatballs, each about 1.5 cm (⅔ inch) in diameter. Set aside.

- In a pan, combine the beef stock, water, five-spice powder, ginger, soy sauce and sugar and bring to the boil. Add the meatballs and reduce the heat. Skim the top to remove any foam or impurities. Simmer for about 10 minutes until the meatballs are cooked through. Remove and set aside until ready to serve.

- To serve, bring the broth to a rolling boil. Divide the bean sprouts and cooked rice noodles among 4 preheated soup bowls. (If the noodles are not hot, reheat in a microwave oven or blanch briefly in boiling water.) Place a few pieces of romaine, a few slices of sirloin and meatballs on top of the noodles. Pour the hot broth over the noodles and garnish with spring onions, coriander and Fried Shallots, if desired. Invite guests to add basil leaves, squeezes of lime juice and chillies to their bowls before eating.

Chicken and Cellophane Noodle Soup

mien ga

AS A KID, I loved just sucking on these soft, transparent noodles, also known as bean threads or glass noodles. Even though they come dried and wiry, they cook up plump and succulent and can easily double in size. Eat the soup soon after it's cooked because the noodles can absorb nearly all the broth if left in the bowl too long.

Serves 4
1 tablespoon vegetable oil
1 garlic clove, thinly sliced
1 shallot, thinly sliced
1.25 litres (2 pints) fresh Chicken Stock (see page 38) or store-bought reduced-salt chicken stock
500 ml (16 fl oz) water
225 g (8 oz) boneless, skinless chicken breast
50 g (2 oz) cellophane noodles, soaked in water for 30 minutes, drained and cut into 30 cm (12 inch) strands
4 dried wood-ear mushrooms, soaked in hot water for 30 minutes, woody stems discarded and cut into 2 or 3 pieces, if large
1½ tablespoons fish sauce
2 teaspoons sugar
2 handfuls of chopped baby bok choy or spinach
2 spring onions, cut into thin rings
3 tablespoons chopped coriander
Freshly ground black pepper

- Heat the oil in a large pan over moderate heat. Add the garlic and shallot and stir for about 20 seconds until fragrant. Add the chicken stock and water and bring to the boil. Add the chicken breast and cook for 8 to 10 minutes until just done. Remove and set aside to cool.

- Add the cellophane noodles, mushrooms, fish sauce and sugar. Reduce the heat to a simmer and cook for 5 minutes. Stir in the bok choy.

- Hand-shred the chicken into bite-sized strips. Using chopsticks or tongs, divide the noodles among 4 preheated bowls and ladle broth over them. Place some chicken on top, then garnish with the spring onions, coriander and black pepper. Serve immediately.

Sweet-and-sour Prawn Soup with Fresh Herbs
canh chua tom

UNLIKE NOODLE SOUPS, this *canh*, or clear broth soup, is meant to be eaten with other foods. At our home, my mom often served this with a savoury dish like Aunt Tam's Pork in Claypot (see page 173). Traditionally this is made with catfish, but any seafood works nicely, as does chicken or tofu. Make sure to add the herbs right before serving to get the most flavour and aroma. Taro stem (see Glossary, page 267), prized for its sponge-like texture, gives this soup an interesting dimension, but it's equally delicious without it. For this recipe, I prefer to use Costa Rican pineapple, which is similar to the sweet and crunchy Vietnamese variety.

Serves 4

1 tablespoon vegetable oil

1 teaspoon minced garlic

½ teaspoon ground chilli paste (see Glossary page 259)

900 ml (1½ pints) fresh Chicken Stock (see page 38) or
store-bought reduced-salt chicken stock

250 ml (8 fl oz) water

1 tablespoon fish sauce,
or to taste

1 tablespoon sugar

2 tablespoons tamarind pulp, soaked in 75 ml (3 fl oz)
water for 30 minutes, then pushed through a sieve,
solids discarded

20 cm (8 inch) piece of taro stem, peeled and cut
diagonally into 1 cm (½ inch) slices (optional, see
Glossary page 267)

2 plum tomatoes, cut into
2.5 cm (1 inch) cubes

2 tablespoons fresh lime juice

150 g (5 oz) raw prawns, peeled and deveined

¼ fresh pineapple, cut into thin bite-sized chunks

2 tablespoons Fried Shallots (see page 32)

90 g (3½ oz) bean sprouts

2 tablespoons rice paddy herb (see page 42) or coriander,
chopped

2 tablespoons Asian basil leaves, chopped

2 Thai bird's eye chillies, chopped, or to taste

- Heat the oil in a large saucepan over moderate heat. Add the garlic and
chilli paste and stir for about 10 seconds until fragrant. Add the chicken

stock, water, fish sauce, sugar, tamarind, taro slices, if using, tomatoes and lime juice and bring to the boil. Reduce the heat and simmer for 5 minutes. Add the prawns and pineapple and cook for about 2 minutes until the prawns are just done. Remove from the heat.

- Stir in the Fried Shallots, bean sprouts, rice paddy herb, basil and chillies. Transfer the soup to a tureen and serve immediately.

Cabbage Soup with Prawn Dumplings
canh cai

THE VIETNAMESE HAVE an affinity for making dumplings out of all kinds of meat and seafood, moulding them into different shapes and sizes and adding them to soups, stews and even sandwiches. As a child, I loved helping my mother make this soup and watching the dumplings rise to the top as they cooked. This soup and a well-seasoned seafood dish like Caramelized Garlic Prawns (see page 200) make a satisfying meal.

Serves 6
110 g (4 oz) raw prawns, peeled, deveined and minced
3 dried black mushrooms (shiitake), soaked in water for
   30 minutes, stemmed and chopped
50 g (2 oz) finely chopped onion
4 teaspoons fish sauce
¼ teaspoon freshly ground black pepper

½ tablespoon vegetable oil

I shallot, minced

I garlic clove, minced

I litre (1¾ pints) fresh Chicken Stock (see page 38) or
   store-bought reduced-salt chicken stock

250 ml (8 fl oz) water

½ cabbage, cut crossways into 5 mm (¼ inch) wide slices

Salt and freshly ground black pepper to taste

I spring onion, cut into thin rings

3 sprigs of coriander, thinly sliced

- Combine the prawns, mushrooms, onion, 2 teaspoons of the fish sauce
  and all of the black pepper in a bowl. Mash with a fork until well
  blended and sticky. Set aside.

- Heat the oil in a medium pan over moderate heat. Add the shallot and
  garlic and stir for about 10 seconds until fragrant. Add the chicken
  stock, water and the remaining 2 teaspoons fish sauce. Bring to the boil,
  then reduce the heat slightly to maintain a simmer.

- Scoop a heaped tablespoon of the prawn mixture and drop it into the
  soup. Make more dumplings this way and add to the liquid. Cook,
  skimming the surface as needed, for about 10 minutes until the
  dumplings float to the top and are cooked through. Add the cabbage
  and cook for 2 minutes. Season with salt and pepper, garnish with spring
  onion and coriander and serve immediately.

Tofu, Tomato and Chive Soup
canh dau hu he

THIS NORTHERN SOUP is typical of how *canh* (clear broth) is prepared in Vietnam. It calls for chicken stock and simple ingredients. You can use any vegetables you like, from root vegetables to leafy greens. By itself, the soup may taste bland, but at the Vietnamese table, a clear broth is designed to balance the entire meal. You will want to serve this with other main dishes, such as Caramelized Garlic Prawns (see page 200) or Ginger Chicken (see page 161).

Serves 4
1 tablespoon vegetable oil
2 shallots, sliced
1.25 litres (2 pints) fresh Chicken Stock (see page 38) or
    store-bought reduced-salt chicken stock
1 tablespoon fish sauce
175 g (6 oz) soft or medium tofu, drained and cut into
    2.5 cm (1 inch) cubes
2 ripe tomatoes, cut into
    thin wedges
2 small bunches of chives, ends trimmed and cut into
    7.5 cm (3 inch) lengths
8 sprigs of coriander, cut into 5 cm (2 inch) lengths

- Heat the oil in a soup pan over moderate heat. Add the shallots and stir for about 10 seconds until fragrant. Add the chicken stock, fish sauce, tofu and tomatoes and bring to the boil. Reduce the heat to a simmer and cook for about 5 minutes. Add the chives and coriander and simmer for 1 minute. Remove the pan from the heat, transfer to a soup tureen or bowl and serve immediately.

Salads and Snacks

Come back to Hue if you so yearn
Back to the Perfume River
For her water runs deep
For she loves you still
Back to the Ngu Mountains
For the birds have flown home
Waiting for you still.
Vietnamese song

BY NIGHTFALL, the banks of the Perfume River are like steamed rice cakes – soft, wet and puffy, and under the yellow moon they reflect a shimmering glow. In the distance, I see small boats drifting, the silhouettes of thin women standing at one end pushing their long oars back and forth.

As in other parts of Vietnam, December is unpredictable. Sun and heat easily succumb to rain and cold. Tonight, though, it's somewhere in between – a blessing, I suppose – as it allows me to sit on the terrace listening to the waves lapping against the edge of the bank.

'When it's cold, it's so cold that your bones shrink,' says Nguyen Thi Hanh, chef of the Huong Giang, a historic hotel with the most captivating view of the river. Tonight she'll personally cook me a traditional Hue dinner including *ga bop* (the local version of chicken salad) which is very characteristic of Vietnamese salads in general. 'I want to make sure you're getting correctly prepared Hue food,' says Chi Hanh, or Sister Hanh, while gently folding the *rau ram* (Vietnamese coriander) into the salad. 'Most people just throw the ingredients together and that's wrong.'

The first step, she explains, is to hand-shred the chicken while it's still warm and massage it with lime juice and paper-thin slices of onions. The meat should be about the size of an index finger or it may dry out, and the onions must be harvested young so they're more sweet than pungent. Chi Hanh says that adding one aromatic at a time keeps the flavours separate, as opposed to having them all blended in the dressing.

Chi Hanh's meticulous and perfectionist demeanour is typical of cooks from the central region. Known for their strong will and passion, they're particularly proud of the royal cuisine, which flourished during the reign of the Nguyen Dynasty from the early 1800s to the mid-1900s.

Take the case of the chicken salad: in the south, it contains cabbage, but Hue cooks wouldn't even think of adding it, for fear it would dilute the flavours and ruin the dish. As a result, *ga bop* is made with just chicken, onions and a generous amount of herbs. In the true royal cuisine tradition, many salads are not tossed in the kitchen, but arranged in attractive piles so their colours and textures can be appreciated before they're mixed at the table.

Chi Hanh learnt to cook from an aunt who had worked at a palace kitchen, and prefers to serve her salads the traditional way. 'I'm afraid that if we don't preserve *com vua* [royal cuisine] the young generation will never know it and that would be sad,' she says. In an effort to uphold the Hue traditions, Chi Hanh joins a handful of local chefs in staging events like royal dinners and cooking classes and working with visiting chefs and food writers like me.

Her *ga bop* is succulent, the herbs are tender and fragrant and the dressing is so tart it puckers my entire mouth. The dish is simple, yet so complex. In many ways, it's like the people of Hue themselves. Despite the devastating war years and the economic hardships, the people here remain proud and hopeful. Many have so little in terms of material comfort, yet they speak with such conviction and passion – about their music, their poetry and about something as simple as their *ga bop*.

This chapter includes both salad and appetizer-type recipes. In Vietnam, they're served either as part of a meal or, more often, as a snack. The salads share one thing in common: they are tossed in a dressing with no or very little oil, making them low in fat. Limey and highly seasoned, these salads are often served as a savoury dish and eaten with rice. In fact, you can make a whole light meal by serving several of these salads and appetizers together.

Hue Chicken Salad
ga bop

THE TWO MOST critical ingredients in this recipe are the chicken, which must be juicy and cooked just right, and the *rau ram*, which must be used liberally. The technique for cooking the chicken is based on the Chinese method of submerging a whole bird in boiling water. This simple method produces moist, succulent chicken every single time. In Hue, *ga bop* is served as a snack with beer or as a side dish to *chao ga* (chicken rice soup). To me it's delicious served any way, even with just a bowl of steamed rice!

Serves 4

Sea salt

½ whole chicken, thigh and leg scored for faster cooking

½ teaspoon black peppercorns, lightly toasted in a pan and ground or ½ teaspoon freshly ground black pepper

2 teaspoons sugar

2½ tablespoons fresh lime juice

1 small onion, sliced paper-thin and rinsed

2 Thai bird's eye chillies or 1 serrano chilli, chopped, or to taste (optional)

20 g (¾ oz) *rau ram* (Vietnamese coriander) leaves or mint leaves

½ tablespoon vegetable oil

4 butterhead lettuce leaves, preferably inner leaves

- Fill a large pot with 1.75 litres (3 pints) water, add 1 teaspoon sea salt and bring to a vigorous boil. Add the chicken and bring the water back to the boil. Reduce the heat and simmer for 10 minutes. Turn off the heat, cover the pot and let the chicken sit in the covered pot for 20 minutes. Remove the chicken and set aside to cool.

- Remove and discard the skin and bones from the chicken. Hand-shred the meat into 5 mm (¼ inch) thick strips and place in a bowl.

- Add the black pepper, 1 teaspoon salt and all the sugar and gently massage into the chicken. Add the lime juice, sliced onion, chillies, *rau ram* and oil and toss gently.

- To serve, line a serving plate with the lettuce leaves and place the chicken salad on top.

Table Salad
rau song

IN VIETNAM, a table salad is used in two main ways – as an accompaniment to meals in which little pieces of meat and seafood are wrapped in the lettuce and eaten with the fingers, and as an all-purpose salad. When eaten as a salad, diners tear off a piece of lettuce with some herbs and add to their bowls of rice or noodles, or fold the leaves and herbs into little packets to dip into a sauce. A nice table salad can include any combination of *rau ram*, Asian basil, red and green perilla and slices of starfruit or green bananas. For detailed descriptions of favoured Vietnamese herbs, see page 39.

Serves 6
1 red- or green-leaf lettuce, leaves separated, washed and drained
½ cucumber, thinly sliced
180 g (6 oz) bean sprouts
5 or 6 sprigs each of mint, Asian basil, *rau ram* and red and green perilla or any herb combination

- Arrange the lettuce in an attractive manner on one side of a large platter. Place the cucumber, bean sprouts and herbs on the other side. Place the platter in the centre of the table and serve.

NOTE: If a table salad accompanies a grilled meat dish, you can also serve pre-soaked rice papers (see page 108) on the side. Just layer some lettuce in between the rice sheets so they don't stick. Or let the guests wet the rice sheets themselves by soaking them in a bowl of warm water at the table.

Cucumber Salad
dua leo ngam giam

THE VIETNAMESE LOVE cucumber and use it as an all-purpose vegetable. Sometimes the cucumbers are just cut into thin rounds and served plain; other times they're dressed in a sweet-and-sour dressing like this one. This refreshing salad goes well with grilled and steamed meats and seafood. It's even great with a bowl of fried rice. For interesting variations, sprinkle different herbs on top.

Serves 4
60 ml (2 fl oz) rice or distilled white wine vinegar
1 tablespoon fresh lime juice
3 tablespoons sugar
½ teaspoon salt
6 pickling cucumbers or gherkins, halved and cut into
**   2 mm (⅛ inch) thick slices**
2 shallots, thinly sliced
½ serrano or other fresh chilli, sliced (optional)
6 sprigs of coriander, chopped

- Combine the vinegar, lime juice, sugar and salt in a bowl. Stir well and add the cucumbers, shallots, chilli, if using, and coriander. Set aside to stand for 15 minutes, then transfer to a bowl to serve.

Roasted Aubergines with Spring Onion Oil
ca tim nuong

IN SAIGON, where there are literally thousands of small family-run restaurants, it's very hard for one to stand out from the rest. Yet Ba Ca Doi manages to do just that. Owner Hoang Thi Tuc, who has been cooking for more than forty years, and her daughter Dinh Thi Huong offer a changing menu each day. This dish is one of their best. For the most authentic flavour, roast the aubergines over charcoals. If you can get small, slender aubergines, about 15 cm (6 inches) or shorter, serve them whole, with the stems and caps intact.

Serves 4
450 g (1 lb) slender, dark purple Asian aubergines
2 tablespoons vegetable oil
2 spring onions, sliced into thin rings
2 Thai bird's eye chillies, chopped, or to taste
1 tablespoon fish sauce
Pinch of salt

- Using tongs, place the aubergines on a hot charcoal barbecue or gas burner. (You can also place them directly on an electric stove over moderate heat.) Roast the aubergines for about 3 to 4 minutes, turning for even charring, until soft on the outside but still firm on the inside. Remove and let cool.

- When cool enough to handle, hold the aubergines by the cap under slow-running water and peel from top to bottom. Pat dry. Place in a wide bowl. If using larger aubergines, cut each one crossways into 7.5 cm (3 inch) long pieces. Pull each piece into two strips. If using very small aubergines, leave them whole.

- Heat the oil in a frying pan over moderate heat. Add the spring onions and stir quickly for about 20 seconds. They should foam upon contact and become fragrant. Remove the pan from the heat and add the chillies, fish sauce and salt. Stir, then pour the spring onion oil over the aubergines. Toss gently and transfer to a serving plate. Serve warm or at room temperature.

Banana Blossom Salad
with Chicken
goi bap chuoi ga

MY REDISCOVERY OF the banana blossom happened in a peculiar way. I was meandering through an orchard behind a house on stilts, where I was staying in Vinh Long – a magical place perched over a small tributary in the Mekong Delta. It was dusk, but appeared much darker because of the big shady trees. All of a sudden, I nearly bumped into a football-looking thing with red flaps and what looked like teeth. I was terrified until I realized that it was just a banana blossom hanging from a large stem, the tiny bananas peeking between the bracts. Since that day, I have been enamoured of this fruit.

Banana blossoms are enjoyed throughout Asia, from Burma to Laos to the Philippines. In Vietnam, *bap chuoi* is used primarily in salads and as a soup garnish. It doesn't taste anything like a banana, but does create a tannic sensation in the mouth similar to the feel or the taste of unripe persimmons, which somehow nicely complements the flavours of fish sauce, chillies and lime. In this recipe, only the petals, or bracts, are used. (Some recipes call for the small fruits to be boiled before being tossed into a salad.)

If you don't have banana blossom, substitute white cabbage. You can also turn this into a delicious vegetarian dish by substituting tofu for the chicken and soy sauce for the fish sauce.

Serves 4
1 garlic clove
2 to 3 Thai bird's eye chillies or 1 serrano chilli
2 tablespoons sugar
3½ tablespoons fresh lime juice
2 tablespoons water
2 tablespoons fish sauce
1 medium banana blossom, about 275 g (10 oz)
225 g (8 oz) cooked chicken, shredded into bite-sized pieces
½ cucumber, seeded and cut into thin strips
¼ onion, sliced paper-thin lengthways
30 g (1 oz) *rau ram* (Vietnamese coriander) or Asian basil leaves, cut in half
2 tablespoons Fried Shallots (see page 32)
2 tablespoons chopped Roasted Peanuts (see page 34)

- Place the garlic, chillies and sugar in a mortar and pound into a paste. Transfer to a small bowl and combine with 3 tablespoons of the lime juice, the water and fish sauce. Stir well and set the dressing aside.

- Peel the two or three tougher outer layers of the banana blossom and discard. Remove the bottom core. Using a Japanese mandoline or a sharp knife, slice the blossom crossways into 1 mm (1/16 inch) thick pieces. Rinse well and place in a bowl. Add cold water to cover and stir in the remaining ½ tablespoon lime juice. Let stand for 15 minutes. Remove the shredded blossom (but leave the banana pieces that have sunk to the bottom) and drain in a colander. Pat dry with paper towels.

- Place the chicken in a bowl and add half the dressing. Set aside to marinate for 10 minutes. Add the banana blossom, cucumber, onion, *rau ram*, shallots and half the peanuts. Add the remaining dressing and toss gently. Transfer the salad to a serving plate, garnish with the remaining peanuts and serve.

The Japanese Mandoline

IN THE VIETNAMESE kitchen, the *dao bao* is an indispensable tool. Similar to a large peeler, this knife is used to thinly slice banana blossom, carrots, cabbage, cucumber and other vegetables and is especially useful for making salads. I've found that the Japanese mandoline, which is available at Asian stores and cookware shops, can do basically the same job and is perhaps easier to handle. If you like Asian salads, it is a valuable kitchen tool to have.

Pomelo and Barbecued Prawn Salad

goi buoi

In this salad, the pomelo – which is more fragrant and sweeter than its cousin the grapefruit – greatly enhances the smokiness of barbecued prawns. If you can't find pomelo, substitute grapefruit, and if the one you have is especially tart, use a little less than is called for below.

Serves 4

16 medium prawns, peeled and deveined
1 teaspoon minced shallot
1 teaspoon fish sauce
1 teaspoon soy sauce
½ teaspoon sugar
2 tablespoons vegetable oil
4 x 20 cm (8 inch) bamboo skewers, soaked in hot water
    for 30 minutes and drained
50 g (2 oz) matchstick carrot strips, soaked in ice water
    for 30 minutes and drained
50 g (2 oz) matchstick cucumber strips, soaked in ice
    water for 30 minutes and drained
150 g (5 oz) pomelo segments, separated into bite-sized
    pieces
60 ml (2 fl oz) Vietnamese Dipping Sauce (see page 19)
20 Asian basil leaves, coarsely chopped
1 tablespoon chopped coriander
1 Thai bird's eye chilli, chopped
2 tablespoons chopped Roasted Peanuts (see page 34)

- Combine the prawns, shallot, fish sauce, soy sauce, sugar and oil in a bowl. Set aside to marinate for 20 minutes.

- Thread 4 prawns on each skewer. Barbecue or grill for about 2 to 3 minutes until the prawns are just done. Set aside.

- Place the carrot, cucumber, pomelo, dipping sauce, basil, coriander, chilli and peanuts in a large bowl and toss gently. Remove the prawns from the skewers, add them to the salad and gently toss a few times. Transfer to a serving plate and serve.

Hanoi Squid Salad
goi muc Hanoi

WHEN I FIRST tasted this delightful dish at the Seasons of Hanoi Restaurant, I knew I had found my favourite squid salad. One of the first upscale restaurants to open after the economic and trade reform policies in the early 1990s, Seasons is known for its efforts in reviving the cooking traditions of the north.

In this recipe, the Asian celery – which is more aromatic than the regular variety – adds a distinctive flavour and crunch. If you can't find it, use regular celery or fennel, but slice it thin.

Serves 4
450 g (1 lb) fresh or frozen cleaned or whole squid, preferably small
2.5 cm (1 inch) piece of ginger, peeled and cut into thin slivers (about 1 tablespoon)

75 ml (3 fl oz) Chilli-lime Dipping Sauce (see page 29)
I shallot, thinly sliced
I Thai bird's eye chilli or ½ serrano chilli, or to taste,
chopped
I or 2 bunches of Asian celery, chewy bottom discarded,
stalks cut into thin matchsticks, soaked in cold water
for 30 minutes and drained
½ cucumber, cut into thin matchsticks, soaked in cold
water for 30 minutes and drained
20 g (¾ oz) Asian basil leaves, cut in half

- To clean a whole squid, pull the tentacles from the tube section. Trim off the tentacles by carefully cutting them right above the eyes. Save the tentacles and discard the bottom part. Pull the thin backbone from the body and discard. Cut the tube into rings about 1 cm (½ inch) thick. Rinse well, making sure the inside of the squid rings is clean.

- Bring a pot of water to a rolling boil. Place the squid in a sieve and dip it into the hot water for about 5 seconds, depending on the thickness, just until the squid plumps up. Drain completely and place in a bowl. Add the ginger and the sauce and set aside for 5 minutes. Add the shallot, chilli, celery, cucumber and basil leaves and toss gently. Transfer to a serving plate.

Lotus Stem Salad

goi ngo sen

LOTUS STEMS LOOK like long, thin spears of asparagus but don't taste anything like them. In Vietnam, they're prized for their crunchy texture and for their ability to absorb sauces. In the West, you can find lotus stems (labelled lotus rootlets) packed in brine in jars. It you can't find the stems, try lotus roots, which are readily available fresh at Asian stores. They're like jícama (see Glossary page 261), crunchy and white, with a beautiful lace-like pattern on the inside. Peel and thinly slice the tuber, then soak in cold water with a little lemon juice.

Serves 4

1 garlic clove, minced

1 Thai bird's eye chilli or ½ serrano chilli, chopped

1½ tablespoons fish sauce

2 tablespoons fresh lime juice

1½ tablespoons sugar

225 g (8 oz) jar of lotus stems, drained, or 1 cup thinly sliced lotus root

½ cucumber, seeded, cut into thin strips, soaked in cold water for 30 minutes and drained

110 g (4 oz) deveined prawns, cooked, peeled and cut in half lengthways

20 g (¾ oz) *rau ram* (Vietnamese coriander) or Asian basil leaves

2 tablespoons Fried Shallots, optional (see page 32)

3 tablespoons chopped Roasted Peanuts (see page 34)

3 sprigs of coriander, cut into 5 cm (2 inch) lengths

- Combine the garlic, chilli, fish sauce, lime juice and sugar in a bowl and stir well. Set the dressing aside.

- Cut the lotus stems diagonally into 5 cm (2 inch) pieces. Place in a bowl and cover generously with water. Using bamboo chopsticks (like the disposable ones at Chinese restaurants), stir the water continuously for 2 to 3 minutes. (The rough surface of the chopsticks will catch the fibres.) Remove the fibres that are wrapped around the chopsticks and discard. Drain the lotus stems and add to the dressing. Toss several times and set aside to marinate for 10 minutes.

- Add the cucumber, prawns, *rau ram*, shallots, if using, and peanuts and toss gently. Transfer the salad to a serving plate, garnish with the coriander and serve.

The Lotus

THE LOTUS IS a beloved plant in Asia, symbolizing purity, perfection and beauty. Every part of the plant is eaten or used. The beautiful white and pink flowers grace temple shrines and family altars. The stamens are made into an aromatic tea, which some believe works like a mild sleep enhancer. The seeds are dried, then boiled and made into sweets or added to puddings and cakes. The large round leaves are used to wrap sticky rice and other foods for steaming.

The lotus has long stems connecting the main plant to its many leaves and flowers. In Vietnam, these stems are peeled, sliced and added to soups and salads. At the base of the plant are clusters of bulbous roots that taste like jícama or water chestnuts. When the tubers are sliced crossways, you can see the beautiful lacy patterns within. Lotus roots are believed to help purify the blood. The Vietnamese and Chinese love them in braised dishes and soups.

Cabbage Salad with Prawns and Pork
goi tom thit

IN VIETNAM, the most popular salad happens to be one of the easiest to make. In this traditional version, the pork and prawns are simply poached, then added to paper-thin slices of cabbage, carrots, cucumbers and *rau ram* and tossed in a lime-based dressing. You can make this with any meat combination (chicken would be great, too), or you can omit the meat and serve it as a side salad. For best results, use a Japanese mandoline for slicing the vegetables.

Serves 4
¼ onion, sliced paper-thin and rinsed
2 or 3 Thai bird's eye chillies, cut into thin rings (optional)
1 tablespoon fish sauce
3 tablespoons fresh lime juice
½ teaspoon salt
3 tablespoons sugar
3 tablespoons water
¼ head of green cabbage
½ carrot, peeled

½ **cucumber, halved crossways**
110 g (4 oz) cooked prawns
110 g (4 oz) cooked pork shoulder or chicken, cut into thin
bite-sized strips
10 g (½ oz) *rau ram* leaves (Vietnamese coriander, see
page 44)
5 sprigs of coriander, chopped
3 tablespoons Fried Shallots, optional (see page 32)
3 tablespoons chopped Roasted Peanuts (see page 34)

- Combine the onion, chillies, if using, fish sauce, lime juice, salt, sugar and water in a large bowl. Set the dressing aside until ready to use.

- Using a Japanese mandoline, shred the cabbage into 1 mm (¹⁄₁₆ inch) thick pieces. (You can also cut it by hand.) Place the cabbage in a large bowl and cover with cold water. Cut the carrot into long matchsticks and add to the bowl to soak for 30 minutes. Cut the cucumber on the diagonal into 2 mm (⅛ inch) thick slices and set aside.

- Add the prawns and pork to the dressing and marinate for 5 minutes. Remove the cabbage and carrot from the water and spin dry. Add to the bowl of prawns and pork, along with the cucumber, *rau ram*, coriander, shallots, if using, and half of the peanuts. Toss gently and transfer to a serving plate. Garnish with the remaining peanuts and serve immediately.

Green Mango Salad with Barbecued Beef

goi xoai voi bo

ONE OF THE most memorable dishes I have had in Saigon in recent years is this tangy green mango salad. The crunchy ribbons of sour mango juxtapose nicely against the smoky barbecued beef. Green mangoes are a special type grown to be eaten when they're green and tart. If you can't find them at Asian stores, substitute Granny Smith apples.

Serves 6

2 tablespoons minced lemongrass
½ tablespoon finely chopped shallot
2 teaspoons fish sauce
I teaspoon soy sauce
I teaspoon sugar
225 g (8 oz) tender beef steak, sliced against the grain
   into 5 mm (¼ inch) thick strips
I green mango, about 450 g (I lb), peeled and cut into thin
   2.5 by 7.5 cm (I by 3 inch) rectangular pieces
75 ml (3 fl oz) Chilli-lime Dipping Sauce (see page 29)
I tablespoon chopped coriander
15 g (¾ oz) Asian basil leaves, cut into thirds
2 tablespoons Fried Shallots (see page 32)
2 tablespoons whole Roasted Peanuts (see page 34)

• Combine the lemongrass, shallot, fish sauce, soy sauce and sugar in a bowl and stir well. Add the beef and marinate for 20 minutes.

- Cook the beef on a grill over a barbecue or sear in an oiled frying pan over high heat for about 1 to 2 minutes until just done.

- In a serving bowl combine the mango with the chilli-lime sauce and toss gently. Add the beef, coriander, basil, shallots and peanuts. Toss gently and serve.

Beef Wrapped in Pepper Leaves
bo nuong la lot

LA LOT (PEPPER LEAF) is used extensively in Vietnam, as an aromatic leaf in stir-fries and soups and as a wrapper. A member of the wild betel family, it has shiny, dark green heart-shaped leaves. If you can't find them, substitute red perilla or *shiso* (see page 43) or grape leaves.

This dish is part of *bo bay mon* (Beef in Seven Ways), a popular special meal, featuring multiple beef courses. To enjoy this dish, serve it as an appetizer or as a topping for Rice Noodles with Fresh Herbs (see page 133).

These rolls are typically barbecued over hot coals. However, I prefer to cook them in a pan because the *la lot* leaves available in the West are too mature and burn more easily when cooked on a barbecue.

Serves 4
4 tablespoons vegetable oil
1½ teaspoons minced garlic
½ onion, chopped
2 tablespoons finely chopped lemongrass
3 tablespoons chopped Roasted Peanuts (see page 34)

I teaspoon ground turmeric

2 teaspoons sugar

2 teaspoons fish sauce

¼ teaspoon salt

225 g (8 oz) coarsely minced beef

30 large *la lot* (pepper leaves, see page 43) or red perilla
   or grape leaves

4 x 15 or 20 cm (6 or 8 inch) bamboo skewers

Table Salad (see page 85), for serving

Vietnamese Dipping Sauce (see page 19), for serving

- Heat 2 tablespoons of the oil in a pan over moderate heat. Add the
  garlic and onion and stir for about 2 minutes until softened. Transfer to
  a bowl. Add the lemongrass, peanuts, turmeric, sugar, fish sauce, salt and
  minced beef. Mix with a fork for about 2 to 3 minutes until well
  blended and sticky. Set aside for 30 minutes.

- To make the rolls, place 1 heaped tablespoon of the meat mixture in
  the centre of a pepper leaf. Using your fingers, shape the meat into a
  cylinder about 5 cm (2 inches) long and 2.5 cm (1 inch) wide. Wrap the
  leaf around the meat but leave the sides open. (If necessary, use 2
  leaves.) When done, place the roll seam side down. Make the remaining
  rolls in the same way.

- Thread 5 rolls onto each bamboo skewer, positioning the rolls so they
  touch one another at the seams. Set aside until ready to cook.

- Heat the remaining 2 tablespoons oil in a large nonstick frying pan over
  a low heat. (Make sure the pan is large enough to accommodate the
  skewers. If not, shorten the skewers.) Add the beef rolls and cook for
  about 5 to 7 minutes total until the meat is done. Do not overcrowd
  the pan. Reduce the heat as necessary to keep the leaves from charring.

- Transfer the skewers to a platter. Remove the skewers and serve the rolls with Table Salad and Vietnamese Dipping Sauce.

Vietnamese Spring Rolls
cha gio

CALLED *NEM RAN* in Hanoi and *cha gio* in Saigon, these crispy rolls are most memorable when served the traditional way – wrapped in lettuce leaves with fresh herbs and then dipped in a sauce and eaten with the fingers. They can be enjoyed as an appetizer or as a meal when served as a topping on Rice Noodles with Fresh Herbs (see page 133).

Cha gio is best when it's made with pork and crab and wrapped in thin rice paper, which is now becoming easier to find. (Previously, many of the imported rice papers were too thick and often cooked up too chewy.) If you can't find the thin rice sheets, try the frozen wheat-flour spring roll wrappers (see Glossary page 265). (Use an egg wash to seal the edges of the rolls.) They aren't as flavourful but are easy to use and cook up quite nicely.

These rolls can be made in advance and cooked halfway. Just before serving, finish them off in a preheated 170°C/325°F/Gas Mark 3 oven for about 15 minutes.

Makes 30 rolls

For the filling:
2 eggs
2 tablespoons fish sauce

½ tablespoon minced garlic

¼ teaspoon sea salt

2 teaspoons plus 3 tablespoons sugar

½ teaspoon ground black pepper

50 g (2 oz) bean threads (cellophane noodles), soaked in
    hot water for 30 minutes, drained and cut into 5 cm
    (2 inch) pieces

5 or 6 dried wood-ear mushrooms, soaked in hot water
    for 30 minutes, drained, chewy stems trimmed and
    finely chopped

100 g (4 oz) minced onion, squeezed gently to remove
    excess liquid

1 taro root, peeled and finely grated or 155 g (5 oz)
    carrots, grated

3 spring onions, cut into thin rings

150 g (5 oz) cooked crabmeat, picked clean or coarsely
    chopped raw prawns

10 oz (275 g) minced pork

1.75 litres (3 pints) warm water

30 x 15 or 20 cm (6 or 8 inch) dried rice paper rounds, plus
    extras

Vegetable oil, for frying

Vietnamese Dipping Sauce (see page 19), for serving

Table Salad (see page 85), for serving

• Make the filling: beat the eggs, fish sauce, garlic, salt, 2 teaspoons sugar
and black pepper together in a large bowl. Add the bean threads,
mushrooms, onion, taro root, spring onions, crabmeat and pork. Using a
fork, gently mix until the ingredients are well blended.

- Fill a large bowl with the warm water. Add the remaining 3 tablespoons sugar to the water and stir to dissolve. (This helps the rice paper turn golden when fried.) Dip a rice paper into the water and turn to moisten the sheet completely. Lay the rice sheet on a damp kitchen towel. Wet another rice paper sheet and place it beside the first. (This allows you to work with one sheet while the second sets.) Place 1 heaped tablespoon of the filling on the bottom third of the sheet. Using your fingers, gently shape into a small cylinder. Lift the bottom edge over the filling, then fold in both sides. Roll into a small cylinder, about 1.5 cm (⅔ inch) wide and 5 cm (2 inches) long. Place seam side down. (If you're using the wheat-flour spring roll wrappers, brush a little egg wash on the edges to seal.) Do not stack the rolls. Continue to make the rolls with the remaining filling and paper in this way. If a wrapper has a tear, reinforce it by patching it with a small piece of dampened rice paper.

- Pour about 4 cm (1½ inches) of vegetable oil into a large frying pan and heat to about 180°C (350°F). Test the temperature by carefully placing a spring roll in it. If the oil foams but not too vigorously upon contact, it is hot enough. Add the rolls without crowding and fry for about 5 to 6 minutes until evenly golden. (Cook in batches, if necessary.) Remove and drain on paper towels. Serve the spring rolls immediately with the dipping sauce and table salad.

Vietnamese Sandwich
banh mi thit

THERE MUST BE thousands of sandwich stands all over Vietnam, but the sandwiches that always stand out in my mind are the *banh mi* at the market in Hoi An. The vendor starts by first heating a small baguette on the charcoal brazier hidden underneath his wooden cart. Then he adds a delicious sauce made from ground pork followed by thinly sliced pork and *cha lua*, a dense pork sausage sold at Vietnamese markets. To finish, he garnishes the filling with fresh herbs and marinated vegetables. One bite into his sandwich and I'm in heaven.

This recipe is based on that delicious sandwich. Try to find a very airy baguette and do serve it with the marinated vegetables. Without them, this sandwich wouldn't be Vietnamese.

Serves 4
2 tablespoons vegetable oil
1 tablespoon chopped garlic
1½ teaspoons five-spice powder
½ teaspoon ground dried chilli or to taste
1 tablespoon soy sauce
2 teaspoons sugar
155 g (5 oz) minced pork
4 x 15 cm (6 inch) baguette pieces
155 g (5 oz) cooked pork shoulder, thinly sliced
110 g (4 oz) *cha lua* (Vietnamese sausage) or ham, thinly sliced
¼ recipe Marinated Daikon and Carrots (see page 36)
⅓ cucumber, seeded, cut into 5 mm (¼ inch) strips

8 sprigs of coriander
1 serrano or jalapeño chilli, thinly sliced on the diagonal
Salt and pepper

- Heat the oil in a medium frying pan over moderate heat. Add the garlic, five-spice powder, dried chilli, soy sauce and sugar and stir for about 10 seconds until fragrant. Add the minced pork and stir a few times. Reduce the heat and cook for about 3 to 4 minutes until the meat is done. Remove from the heat and set aside.

- Reheat the baguette in a 150°C/300°F/Gas Mark 2 oven for about 5 minutes so that the outside is warm and crusty. Cut each baguette in half lengthways without separating. Spread 2 to 3 tablespoons of the minced pork mixture (including pan juices) on the bread. Add a quarter of the pork slices and a quarter of the pork sausage, making sure the meat is evenly spread on the bread. Garnish the sandwich with marinated vegetables, cucumber, coriander and chilli along with some salt and pepper.

Rice Paper-wrapped Salad Rolls
goi cuon

TO ME, this is one of Vietnam's greatest culinary treasures. Made with poached prawns, pork and fresh mint, *goi cuon* are wrapped in rice paper and dipped in a sauce. Similar to a salad that has been rolled up, these are usually eaten as a snack, although they also make a lovely lunch.

The key is to roll these tightly and that requires practice. You can substitute chicken or beef, or tofu and mushrooms for the filling. Grilled fish, such as salmon, also works well. Traditionally *goi cuon* are served whole, but I like cutting them into smaller pieces because they're easier to serve and share. Notice I call for untrimmed pork because the dish benefits from a little fat. In Vietnam, these rolls are traditionally served with a heavier bean sauce, but you can also serve them with the lighter Vietnamese Bean Dipping Sauce (see page 25), which I prefer.

Serves 6 to 8 as an appetizer
155 g (5 oz) pork shoulder, untrimmed, cut into two pieces
12 medium raw prawns, unpeeled
110 g (4 oz) *bun* (rice vermicelli or rice sticks), boiled for
    5 minutes, rinsed and drained (see page 124)
90 g (3½ oz) bean sprouts
10 g (½ oz) mint leaves
1 small head red-leaf lettuce, leaves separated and
    washed
8 x 30 cm (12 inch) dried rice papers, round, plus extras
125 ml (4 fl oz) Vietnamese Bean Dipping Sauce (see page
    25), for serving

- Cook the pork in boiling salted water for about 30 minutes until it's done but still firm enough for slicing.

- While the pork is cooking, bring another small pot of water to a boil. Add the prawns and cook for about 3 minutes until they turn pink. Rinse under running water and set aside to drain. When cool enough to handle, peel, devein and cut in half lengthways. Refresh in cold water and set aside.

- Remove the pork from the heat and drain. When it's cool enough to handle, slice into thin slices, about 2.5 by 6 cm (1 by 2½ inches). Place on a small plate and set aside.

- Set up a salad roll 'station.' Cover a chopping board with a damp kitchen towel. Fill a large bowl with hot water and place it nearby. (Keep some boiling water handy to add to the bowl.) Arrange the ingredients in the order they will be used: the prawns, pork, rice vermicelli, bean sprouts, mint and lettuce.

- Working with 2 rice paper rounds at a time, dip one, edge first, into the hot water for about 10 seconds and turn it to wet completely. Lay the round down on the towel. Repeat with the second rice paper and place it alongside the first. This allows you to work with one while the second is setting.

- Line the bottom third of the rice paper round with 3 prawn halves, cut side up, and top with 2 slices of pork. Add 1 tablespoon rice vermicelli, 1 tablespoon bean sprouts and 4 to 5 mint leaves. (Arrange the ingredients so the rolls end up being about 13 cm/5 inches long and 2.5 cm/1 inch wide.) Halve a lettuce leaf lengthways along the centre rib. Roll up in one piece and place on the filling. (Trim if it's too long.) While pressing down on the ingredients, lift the bottom edge over the filling, then fold in the two sides. Roll into a cylinder about 4 cm (1½ inches) wide and 10 to 13 cm (4 to 5 inches) long. If the paper feels thick, stop three-quarters of the way and trim the end piece. (Too much rice paper can make the rolls chewy.) Repeat with the remaining rice papers and filling.

- To serve, cut the rolls into 2 or 4 pieces and place them upright on a plate. Serve with the sauce on the side.

Rice Paper

IN VIETNAM, *banh trang* (rice paper) is still made by hand, one sheet at a time. In the village of Trang Bang, about fifty miles north of Saigon, there are several dozen families that specialize in this ancient art. Using the same recipes that have been handed down from one generation to another, they work tirelessly, usually in a small corner of the house near a window. The equipment is very basic – a big pot of simmering water sitting on top of a rice husk–-burning stove.

To make *banh trang*, the rice paper-maker (usually the mother or eldest daughter) ladles a thin layer of rice flour batter on a cloth tightly stretched over the pot. The rice batter is allowed to steam for about 20 seconds after which it's transferred to a bamboo mat to be sun-dried. It is during this process that rice papers take on their beautiful pattern from the weave of the mats. Once fully dried, the rice papers pop loose, creating a succession of faint cracks. The women then trim the sheets into perfect rounds by hand. Finally, they're loaded on a bicycle and taken to the village distribution house. In addition to plain rice papers, *banh trang* are available in different flavours such as coconut, ginger and pandanus (see page 245). Some varieties are made with *bot nep* (glutinous rice flour) and once toasted, they puff up and have a great chewy texture.

Mustard Leaf-wrapped Salad Rolls

cuon diep

THIS BEAUTIFUL DISH epitomizes the elegance and meticulousness of Vietnamese royal cuisine. Similar to other delicacies of Hue (the former imperial capital city), these rolls are filled with prawns and pork, then wrapped with tender Chinese mustard leaves. These add a delicious spicy undertone to the dish, but if you can't find them, substitute romaine lettuce leaves. If you are lucky enough to find *gai choy*, the narrow-stemmed variety of mustard leaf, use it.

Makes 12 rolls or about 4 appetizer servings

12 medium cooked prawns, peeled and deveined
2 tablespoons vegetable oil
1 teaspoon minced garlic
½ teaspoon ground chilli paste (see Glossary page 259)
3 tablespoons peanut butter
60 ml (2 fl oz) hoisin sauce (see Glossary page 261)
2 tablespoons fermented whole soya beans (optional, see Glossary page 260)
2 tablespoons rice vinegar
3 tablespoons water
12 Chinese mustard leaves
12 tablespoons cooked *bun* (rice vermicelli, see page 124)
90 g (3½ oz) bean sprouts
24 Asian basil leaves

**150 g (5 oz) cooked pork shoulder, cut into 4 cm x 2.5 cm
x 2 mm (1½ x 1 x ⅛ inch) slices**
**12 spring onions plus extras, blanched in hot water for
5 seconds, drained**

For the garnish:
**2 Thai bird's eye chillies or ½ serrano chilli, finely chopped
(optional)**
2 tablespoons ground Roasted Peanuts (see page 34)

- For the sauce, mince 6 of the prawns. Heat the oil in a small pan over moderate heat. Add the garlic and minced prawns and stir for about 20 seconds until fragrant. Add the chilli paste, peanut butter, hoisin sauce, fermented soya beans, rice vinegar and water. Stir to blend in the ingredients, then reduce the heat. Simmer for about 4 to 5 minutes until the sauce is slightly thickened. (Add more water if necessary.) Set aside until ready to serve.

- To make the rolls, cut the remaining prawns in half lengthways. Place a mustard leaf on a chopping board, with the bottom stem pointing at you and the smooth side facing down. Place 1 tablespoon rice vermicelli on the leaf, followed by 4 or 5 bean sprouts, 2 basil leaves, 1 pork slice and 1 prawn half. Roll the leaves into a small cylinder, about 1.5 cm (⅔ inch) wide. Run the spring onion around the roll twice, then tie into a knot. Repeat until all the rolls are made.

- Trim the ends so the rolls are all the same length. Garnish the dipping sauce with chillies and peanuts, then serve on the side with the rolls. *Cuon diep* can be made in advance and refrigerated until ready to serve.

Hanoi Prawn Cakes
banh tom

IN HANOI, a popular weekend outing is to head out to West Lake and eat *banh tom* (prawn cakes) at one of the many outdoor cafés along the water. There must be at least a dozen restaurants featuring the same *banh tom* – all in full view of the sunset and the ancient pagoda towers nearby.

This dish is usually made with small unpeeled prawns that cook up very crisp and moist. To eat, you wrap the prawn cakes with the herbs and lettuce, then dip in a sauce. Because it's hard to find such small prawns, I've substituted medium prawns. For a more elegant twist, serve these cakes on a small bed of baby greens and herbs. It makes a beautiful and delicious appetizer.

Makes 20 cakes

60 g (2½ oz) plain flour
60 g (2½ oz) rice flour
½ teaspoon baking powder
2 teaspoons sugar
½ teaspoon salt
½ teaspoon freshly ground black pepper
2 spring onions, cut into thin rings
250 ml (8 fl oz) water
325 g (11 oz) sweet potatoes, peeled, cut into thin
    matchstick strips
225 g (8 oz) prawns, peeled, deveined and cut into 1 cm
    (½ inch) pieces
Vegetable oil for frying

Table Salad (see page 85), for serving
Vietnamese Dipping Sauce (see page 19), for serving

- In a bowl, combine the flour, rice flour, baking powder, sugar, salt, pepper, spring onions and water. Set aside for 10 minutes. Fold in the sweet potatoes and prawns. Do not overmix.

- Heat 2.5 cm (1 inch) of oil in a medium frying pan until it reaches about 170°C (330°F) on a deep-fat thermometer. Place 2 heaped tablespoons prawn batter in the middle of a flat metal spatula. Pat the batter down slightly to form a loose, irregular cake about 5 mm (¼ inch) thick.

- Gently push the cake into the hot oil. Fry the cake for about 2 to 3 minutes, turning it over once, until evenly brown and cooked. Drain on paper towels. Repeat with the remaining batter, cooking only 3 or 4 cakes at a time. Keep the cakes warm in a preheated low oven until ready to serve.

- To eat, place a piece of the prawn cake and some herbs on a lettuce leaf from the Table Salad. Fold into a packet, dip into the sauce and eat.

Rice Noodles, Cakes and Rolls

IT'S HARD TO be in Hue without coming here to Quan Ba Do (Mrs. Red's Restaurant), probably the country's most famous place for *banh beo*, a local speciality of steamed rice cakes served with shredded prawns.

'Come on in!' shouts Nguyen Thi Mai, as some friends and I climb out of our vehicle. Ba Mai, or Mrs Mai as she's called, eagerly points us to a table up front, the red shawl on her head slipping as she excitedly pulls out the chairs. Around here, she's considered a master of *banh beo*, a dish that she learnt from her mother, who first sold them at the market more than fifty years ago. (The restaurant was named after her mother, who was always seen wearing a red shawl.)

Several years ago, Ba Mai and her sister decided to open a restaurant at home so they could work together under one roof and still be able to care for their eighty-year-old mother. Every day, while the children frolic on the nearby divan, the women toil in the kitchen, preparing endless batches of *banh beo*.

Knowing that we're hungry, Ba Mai fires up the stove and starts to load the steamer with tiny ramekins. She vigorously stirs the rice flour batter – one moment moving left, another moving right – the sloshing sounds thumping and echoing from the huge vat. 'You have to constantly stir because the rice flour loves to settle at the bottom,' she explains while ladling a tiny amount into the dishes.

Ba Mai says a good *banh beo* should fit perfectly in the mouth, not be so thick and intrusive that it throws off the balance of the toppings. That's why she only puts two tablespoons of batter in each dish. 'You have to start with good *bot gao* [rice flour] and you have to have an excellent sauce,' she says.

The whole process begins early each morning when she hauls two large pails of rice to a nearby mill. The rice, which was soaked overnight to soften and slightly ferment, is then ground into a smooth paste. Once mixed with water, it can be made into *banh beo*, or any of the many noodle products eaten throughout the country. In fact, most Vietnamese rice noodles are prepared this way.

I can see why Ba Mai is so proud of her *banh beo*. When they emerge from the steamer, they look translucent, silkier and shinier than those that I make at my restaurant. The intense heat around the rim of the dish has made the edges puff up, creating a little crater in the centre for the delicious sauce to collect.

Watching her makes me think of how my own mother used to make these rice cakes. In the southern part of Vietnam, cooks often use coconut milk to enrich the batter. Sometimes, when my mother didn't have enough round dishes, she would use porcelain spoons, creating cakes that looked like fat ears.

In our home, my mother turned the cakes out before serving them. But in keeping with Hue traditions, Ba Mai serves them in the ramekins, with the shredded prawn and pork cracklings on top. To eat, I drizzle over some *nuoc cham*, then loosen the cake with a long-handled spoon. The *banh beo* practically melts in my mouth and the prawns, probably still jumping this morning, have a sweet, almost buttery flavour.

By now a few kids are swarming around us, totally in awe of our presence. 'Don't you have this food over there in the U.S.?' asks one little girl while trying to peek through the lens of my camera.

'Yes, we do, but it's not quite the same,' I reply. How could it be the same, I'm wondering, if you take this *banh beo* dish outside of this home? As I'm pondering the idea, I can see Ba Mai loading more dishes into the steamer rack. She's mumbling something about lunch for her mother upstairs. Her sister, while holding a baby in one arm, adds more firewood to the stove.

Steamed Rice Cakes with Prawns
banh beo tom chay

BASED ON A recipe from Mrs Red's Restaurant, these delicious little rice cakes can be made in advance and reheated. You can serve them as an appetizer or as a main course. You will need a large two-tier steamer, either aluminium or bamboo, and at least one dozen shallow dishes, about 7.5 to 10 cm (3 to 4 inches) in diameter. Cook the first dozen cakes, remove them, then reuse the dishes for the next batch. Or, if you have a lot of dishes, serve the cakes in their moulds, as it's done in Hue.

Serves 4 as a main dish (about 48 little cakes)

For the batter:
350 g (12 oz) rice flour
690 ml (23 fl oz) water
½ teaspoon salt

For the topping:
110 g (4 oz) cooked prawns, peeled and deveined
1 tablespoon vegetable oil
1 shallot, finely minced
½ teaspoon fish sauce
½ teaspoon sugar
Pinch of salt
75 ml (3 fl oz) Spring Onion Oil (see page 31)

For the garnish:
315 ml (10 fl oz) Light Vietnamese Dipping Sauce (see
    page 23)

- Make the batter: Whisk the rice flour, water and salt in a bowl and set aside for at least 30 minutes.

- Make the topping: Place the prawns in a food processor and pulse until finely shredded. Alternatively, pound the prawns using a mortar and pestle.

- Heat the oil in a small nonstick pan over moderate heat. Add the shallot and stir for about 1 minute until fragrant. Reduce the heat, add the shredded prawns and stir for 5 to 6 minutes until the mixture is dry and fragrant. Add the fish sauce, sugar and salt. Stir for another minute. Transfer to a bowl and set aside until ready to use.

- Fill the steamer pan halfway with water and bring to the boil. Arrange as many ramekins as will fit on the two steamer racks. Stir the rice batter well, then ladle 1½ to 2 tablespoons batter into each dish. Carefully place the racks on the pan. Cover and steam for about 4 to 5 minutes until the rice cakes are white and shiny. Remove and set aside to cool.

- To turn the cakes out, dip the tip of a small knife in water and run it along the edge of each dish. Transfer the cakes to a plate. Arrange in a circular pattern, with one slightly touching the next. Rinse and wipe the dishes clean and continue to make rice cakes until the batter is finished.

- To serve, sprinkle each cake with ½ teaspoon Spring Onion Oil and ½ teaspoon shredded prawns. Invite guests to drizzle the dipping sauce on each cake before eating.

Rice Rolls with Prawns and Wood-ear Mushrooms
banh cuon chao

NEXT TO *PHO*, this is my all-time favourite dish. Made with thin, almost transparent rice sheets wrapped around pork or prawns and mushrooms, these delicious rolls are eaten all over Vietnam. There are two basic versions – one is stuffed, as in this recipe, and the other is the plain, unstuffed rice sheet served with *cha lua* (pork sausage). I love both versions, but the former is more sumptuous.

The best way to prepare this dish is to recruit a helper: one person makes the rice sheet and the other stuffs it while it's still warm and easy to work with. Traditionally, the sheets are steamed in a special pot (see page 123), but in this simplified version, they're cooked in a nonstick pan. I recommend trying the pan version first, then moving on to the steamed method. Make sure the pan is just moderately hot and that the amount of batter is consistent with each sheet. *Banh cuon* can be made in advance, refrigerated, and reheated in a microwave oven.

The addition of the potato flour strengthens the batter and helps it cook better in a pan.

Serves 4 as a main dish (28 rolls)

For the batter:
265 g (9½ oz) rice flour
80 g (3 oz) potato flour
810 ml (27 fl oz) water
½ teaspoon salt
1 tablespoon vegetable oil
   plus extra for cooking and oiling the baking tray

For the filling:
1½ tablespoons vegetable oil
3 tablespoons minced shallots
½ onion, minced
3 tablespoons dried wood-ear mushrooms, soaked in
   warm water for 30 minutes, drained, chewy centres
   removed and finely chopped
225 g (8 oz) minced raw prawns or minced pork
½ tablespoon fish sauce
1 teaspoon sugar
¼ teaspoon white pepper

For the garnish:
270 g (10 oz) bean sprouts, blanched in boiling water for
   10 seconds
20 g (¾ oz) green perilla (see page 44) or red perilla (see
   page 43) or mint leaves, cut in thirds

20 g (¾ oz) Asian basil leaves, cut in thirds
20 g (¾ oz) Fried Shallots (see page 32)
315 ml (10 fl oz) Light Vietnamese Dipping Sauce (see page 23)

- Make the batter: Combine the rice flour, potato flour, water, salt and 1 tablespoon oil in a bowl and whisk until smooth. (The batter will be thin and watery.) Strain to remove any lumps and let stand for 30 minutes.

- Make the filling: Place the 1½ tablespoons oil in a frying pan and heat over moderate heat. Add the shallots and stir for 10 seconds. Add the onion and mushrooms and cook for 3 to 4 minutes until the onion bits are translucent and soft. Add the prawns, fish sauce, sugar and white pepper and stir for 2 to 3 minutes until the prawns turn pink. Transfer to a bowl and set aside.

- Oil a baking tray and place it near the stove. Heat ½ teaspoon oil in a 20 cm (8 inch) nonstick pan over low heat. Use a paper towel or brush to distribute the oil evenly. Stir the batter thoroughly and ladle 2½ tablespoons into the pan. Quickly swirl the pan so the batter completely covers the surface. The batter should set immediately upon contact. If it sizzles and develops bubbles beyond the edges, reduce the heat slightly and start again. Cover and cook for 30 to 40 seconds until the rice sheet pulls away from the pan. Invert the pan over the oiled baking tray and tap lightly to loosen the rice sheet. Rice flour settles to the bottom readily so it's important to stir the batter vigorously before making each rice sheet. Also allow the pan to reheat for at least 1 minute before making a new rice sheet. Repeat until you have used up the batter. Do not stack the sheets. (After you get the hang of it, you may want to use two pans to expedite the process.) Let the rice sheets cool for 30 seconds, then proceed to stuff them.

- To make the rolls, make a 2.5 cm (1 inch) fold from the bottom of the rice sheet and neatly place 1½ teaspoons filling on top. Fold the sides over and roll into a cylinder about 6 cm (2½ inches) long and 1.5 cm (⅔ inch) wide. *Banh cuon* can be made in advance up to this point and stored in the refrigerator for 2 days.

- To serve, divide the rice rolls among 4 plates. (You can reheat them in a microwave at this point until just warm, not hot.) Top each plate with one-quarter of the bean sprouts and herbs, then garnish with Fried Shallots. Invite guests to drizzle several tablespoons of sauce on top before eating.

Rice Rolls – the Traditional Steamed Method
banh cuon hap

THIS VERSION IS based on an ancient recipe that calls for ladling a thin rice batter on a piece of cloth stretched tightly over a *banh cuon* pot. Prior to owning this special pot, which is essentially a tall pot with a hoop and a pointed lid, I devised my own pot, which works quite well. (See How to Make a Rice Roll Pot on page 123.)

Steamed rice rolls are much more moist and silky than those made in a pan. This recipe may appear daunting but once you're set up, it's really quite simple – and the results are absolutely delicious. As with the previous recipe, find a helper to stuff the rice rolls.

Serves 4 as a main dish (about 28 rolls)

For the batter:
350 g (12 oz) rice flour
625 ml (20 fl oz) water
2 teaspoons vegetable oil
½ teaspoon salt

For the filling:
2 tablespoons vegetable oil, plus extra for oiling the
    baking tray
3 tablespoons minced shallots
½ onion, minced
3 tablespoons dried wood-ear mushrooms, soaked in
    warm water for 30 minutes, drained, chewy centres
    removed and finely chopped
225 g (8 oz) minced prawns or pork
½ tablespoon fish sauce
1 teaspoon sugar
¼ teaspoon white pepper

For the garnish:
270 g (10 oz) bean sprouts, blanched in boiling water for
    10 seconds
20 g (¾ oz) coarsely chopped mint leaves
20 g (¾ oz) coarsely chopped Asian basil leaves
20 g (¾ oz) Fried Shallots (see page 32)
315 ml (10 fl oz) Light Vietnamese Dipping Sauce (see
    page 23)

- Make the batter: Combine the rice flour, water, 2 teaspoons oil and salt in a bowl and whisk until smooth. (The batter will be thin and watery.) Strain to remove any lumps and let stand for at least 30 minutes.

- Make the filling: Heat the 2 tablespoons oil in a frying pan over moderate heat. Add the shallots and stir for 20 seconds. Add the onion and mushrooms and stir for 3 to 4 minutes until the onion is soft. Add the prawns, fish sauce, sugar and pepper and cook for 2 to 3 minutes until the prawns turn pink. Transfer to a bowl and set aside.

- Bring the homemade rice roll pot (make sure it's been filled halfway with water) to the boil. (If you're using the traditional *banh cuon* pot, prepare the pot and the hoop attachment in a similar fashion.) Oil the baking tray and place it near the stove along with the filling.

- Stir the batter well before making each rice sheet. Using a shallow ladle, spoon 2 tablespoons batter onto the centre of the cloth. Using the bottom of the ladle, spread the batter to make a 15 cm (6 inch) wide round sheet. (Work quickly and try not to put pressure on the cloth.) Cover and steam for about 40 seconds until the sheet is translucent. Uncover. (Be very careful removing the lid as the steam is very hot.) Hold a thin spatula at a 45-degree angle and push gently against the side of the rice sheet. When about 1 cm (½ inch) has gathered on the spatula, lift the sheet off in a steady motion and transfer to the oiled baking tray. (Do not stack the sheets.) Gently scrape the cloth clean and repeat. After cooking several rice sheets, tighten the cloth by pulling on the sides. Refill the pot with hot water as necessary by pouring it through one of the slits in the cloth.

- Let the rice sheet cool for 30 seconds. To stuff the rice rolls, make a 2.5 cm (1 inch) fold from the bottom edge of the rice sheet. Neatly place 1½ teaspoons filling on top of this double layer. Fold the sides over and roll into a cylinder about 6 cm (2½ inches) long and 1.5 cm

(⅔ inch) wide. *Banh cuon* can be made in advance up to this point and stored in the refrigerator for 2 days. Before serving, reheat in a microwave oven until just warm, not hot.

- To serve, divide the rolls among 4 plates. Top each plate with one-quarter of the bean sprouts, mint and basil, and shallots. Invite guests to drizzle the sauce on top.

How to Make a Rice Roll Pot

PROBABLY THE MOST important thing about making a rice roll pot is to find a soup pot that is 25.5 to 28 cm (10 to 11 inches) wide with a dome-style lid. It should have a protruding rolled rim to help secure a string in place. You will also need a round piece of smooth cloth (cotton or cotton blend is fine) at least 10 cm (4 inches) wider than the pot; some heavyweight kitchen string; and a long thin metal spatula, about 30 cm (12 inches) or longer, or a non-serrated carving or slicing knife. You will also need a shallow ladle for pouring the batter.

Fill the soup pot halfway with water. Then, with someone helping you, stretch the cloth across the top with drum-like tightness. Secure with 2 or 3 loops of string and tie into a knot. Pull the sides of the cloth again to stretch it as tight as possible. Using a very sharp paring knife or a razor blade, make three 2.5 cm (1 inch) long slits crossways in the cloth, about 2.5 cm (1 inch) from the edge. These incisions help distribute the steam for cooking the rice sheets and provide an opening for replenishing the water. Your rice roll pot is now ready for action.

Vietnamese Noodles

IN VIETNAMESE CUISINE, rice and noodles are the heart of every meal. For most families, dinner is built around rice, but at breakfast and lunch the preferred starch is often noodles. The following noodles are the ones most commonly used. With the exception of egg noodles and cellophane noodles, all are made with rice flour.

Choosing the right noodles to buy can be tricky. For example, *bun* and *banh pho* are distinctly different, yet both are sold in the West under the same 'rice stick' label. When purchasing noodles, make sure you know the correct kind and size.

Rice Vermicelli (also known as rice sticks) *bun*

Bun is a popular type of noodle used extensively in Vietnamese cuisine. It resembles vermicelli and comes in two sizes – small or thin, which is used in salads and room-temperature dishes, and a fatter, wider size (similar to spaghetti and larger), which is preferred in soups. *Bun* is used in dishes like Hanoi Rice Noodles with Grilled Pork (see page 136) and in the filling for Rice Paper-wrapped Salad Rolls (see page 105). Dried *bun* is readily available, and now some Asian stores carry it fresh. There are many brands, but the most consistent one I've found is Bun Thap Chua from China. It has the right thickness and, similar to the fresh *bun* in Vietnam, takes on a 'bouncy' feel when cooked.

To cook *bun*, boil for about 4 to 5 minutes until the noodles are white and softened but still resilient, drain, rinse immediately in cold water and drain completely before serving. (See Rice Noodles with Fresh Herbs, page 133.)

In Vietnam, there's another similar rice noodle called *banh hoi*. These fresh thin (almost hair-like) noodles are sold in small skeins. They're delicious when served with grilled pork.

Rice Noodles (also known as rice sticks) *banh pho*

Banh pho is a flat rice noodle that resembles linguine. It's used in soups such as *pho* as well as in stir-fries. It's also the same noodle used in Thai cuisine to make *pad Thai*. Many Asian stores now stock both the dried and fresh varieties.

To prepare dried rice noodles for stir-fries, soak in cold water for 15 minutes. Then rinse and drain completely before adding to the pan. This technique helps remove the excess starch, thus preventing stir-fried noodles from getting gummy. If using fresh noodles, just add them directly to the pan. For instructions on how to prepare these noodles for soups such as *pho*, see page 49.

Egg Noodles *mi*

Mi is made with wheat flour and eggs and is used in recipes of Chinese origin. Firmer and denser than rice noodles, it comes in various widths. *Mi* is easily available fresh. If using in soup, boil the noodles for about 1 to 2 minutes, depending on their size. If using the thicker chow mein–style noodles in stir-fries, cook for about 2 to 3 minutes, then drain. Toss in a little oil to prevent sticking.

Bean Thread Noodles or Cellophane Noodles *mein*

Also known as glass noodles, cellophane noodles are made from mung bean starch. Available only in dried form and in various widths, these noodles are stiff and wiry and should be soaked in warm water for about 30 minutes before being used. Although they look fragile, *mien* are actually quite sturdy and can absorb a lot of water. They're used in many soups, salads and stir-fried dishes. Cellophane noodles will take anything from 1 to 5 minutes to cook, depending on their size. For a superb example of how to use them, see Coriander Prawns in Claypot, page 198.

Fresh Rice Noodles
banh pho tuoi

SIMPLE AND FUN to make, these noodles are great for stir-fry dishes such as Wok-seared Noodles with Chicken and Mushrooms (see page 129). They're much more delicate than dried noodles, so try to stir them gently and be careful not to overcook. These are best eaten right away. You will need the rice roll pot for this recipe (see page 123).

Makes about 900 g (2 lb)
525 g (1 lb 3 oz) rice flour
875 ml (28 fl oz) water
1 tablespoon vegetable oil plus extra for stacking and oiling the baking tray
½ teaspoon salt

• Place the rice flour, water, 1 tablespoon oil and salt in a bowl and whisk well. Strain to remove any lumps. Let stand for 30 minutes.

- Prepare the rice roll pot as directed on page 123. Bring the water to the boil over moderate heat. Oil a baking tray.

- Stir the batter well before making each rice sheet. Ladle about 3 tablespoons batter onto the cloth, spreading it so the rice sheet is about 15 cm (6 inches) wide. Cover and steam for about 1 minute until the rice sheet becomes translucent and is done. (Be very careful removing the lid as the steam is very hot.) Hold a thin spatula or knife at a 45-degree angle, then push gently against the side of the rice sheet. When about 1 cm (½ inch) has gathered on the spatula, lift the sheet off the cloth in a steady motion and transfer to the oiled baking tray. (You should be able to easily lift and peel the rice sheet. If not, the rice sheet needs to steam longer or the heat isn't high enough.) Brush each sheet with a little oil before stacking it. Scrape the cloth clean and repeat until the batter is finished. After several rice sheets, tighten the cloth by pulling on the sides. Refill the pot with hot water as necessary by pouring it through one of the slits in the cloth.

- Cut the rice sheets into 2.5 cm (1 inch) or wider noodles. If not using right away, cover with clingfilm.

Spring Onion Noodles
mi kho hanh

IT SEEMS LIKE there's a version of this noodle dish everywhere in Asia. Originally from China, it calls for tossing fresh egg noodles with oil that's been infused with spring onions. It can be served as a snack by itself or as a wonderful accompaniment to grilled meats such as

Barbecued Five-spice Chicken (see page 167) or crab dishes such as Salt-and-pepper Crab with Ginger (see page 188).

> ***Serves 4 as a side dish***
> **1 bunch of spring onions**
> **3 tablespoons vegetable oil**
> **2 shallots, thinly sliced**
> **2 tablespoons soy sauce or**
> **to taste**
> **Pinch of salt**
> **450 g (1 lb) fresh egg noodles, boiled for 2 to 3 minutes,**
> **rinsed and drained**

- Remove the white part of the spring onions and cut into thin rings. Cut the green part into 5 cm (2 inch) lengths and set aside.

- Heat the oil in a large nonstick frying pan over moderate heat. Add the shallots and the white and green parts of the spring onions. Stir for about 1 minute until fragrant. Add the soy sauce, salt and noodles. Stir gently, being careful not to break the noodles. Turn several times so the noodles are coated evenly with the oil and are thoroughly heated. Transfer to a serving plate and serve immediately.

Wok-seared Noodles with Chicken and Mushrooms
pho ap chao

THE TERM *ap chao* means 'pressed into the pan'. Traditionally, that's how these noodles were made – seared until they became charred and stuck to the pan. This dish is probably a version of the Chinese *char kway tiow*, rice noodles stir-fried with soy sauce and spices, which is eaten all over Asia. In this recipe, the addition of fresh herbs and fish sauce gives it a Vietnamese touch.

Serves 4

150 g (5 oz) boneless, skinless chicken, cut into bite-sized strips

1 teaspoon cornflour

2 tablespoons water

3 tablespoons vegetable oil

1 tablespoon coarsely chopped Thai bird's eye chillies, or to taste

1 tablespoon chopped garlic

50 g (2 oz) Asian basil or sweet basil

10 dried black mushrooms (shiitake), soaked in warm water for 30 minutes, drained and halved if large

½ tablespoon fish sauce, or to taste

1 tablespoon oyster sauce

75 ml (3 fl oz) fresh Chicken Stock (see page 38), store-bought reduced-salt chicken stock or water

325 g (11 oz) dried 5 mm (¼ inch) wide rice sticks (*banh pho*), cooked, drained and rinsed (see page 124) or 450 g (1 lb) fresh rice noodles

1 tablespoon dark soy sauce (see page 36) or regular soy
    sauce
150 g (5 oz) Chinese mustard greens or bok choy, sliced on
    the diagonal into 5 cm (2 inch) pieces, blanched in
    boiling water for 1 minute and drained
125 ml (4 fl oz) Soy-lime Dipping Sauce (see page 27)

- Combine the chicken, cornflour and water and toss to coat the meat evenly. Set aside to marinate for 10 minutes.

- Heat 1 tablespoon oil in a large nonstick frying pan over moderate heat. Add the chillies and garlic and stir for about 10 seconds until fragrant. Roughly tear half of the basil leaves and add to the pan. Stir in the mushrooms and chicken and cook for about 2 minutes until the meat turns white. Add the fish sauce, oyster sauce and chicken stock. Cook for another minute, transfer to a bowl and keep warm.

- Wipe the pan clean and heat the remaining 2 tablespoons oil over moderate heat. Add the noodles and soy sauce. Cook for 3 to 4 minutes until the noodles are brown and heated through. (If using fresh noodles, don't stir too much.) Add the Chinese mustard greens, the remaining basil and the cooked chicken (along with its juices) and stir gently so all the ingredients heat through. Transfer to a platter and serve immediately with the dipping sauce.

Sizzling Saigon Crêpes
banh xeo

IN SAIGON, there's a small restaurant in the Dinh Cong Trang area that specializes in this dish. Upon arrival at this jam-packed outdoor eatery, guests are greeted by the smells and sounds of *banh xeo* sizzling on a bank of charcoal braziers. To eat, diners tear off a piece of the crêpe, then wrap it with lettuce and herbs and dip it in a sauce. For a more authentic flavour, substitute mustard greens for the lettuce in the accompanying Table Salad. Traditionally, this dish is made with pork and prawns, but other fillings would work nicely, including chicken, tofu and vegetables, or other seafood.

In the summer, instead of a barbecue, set up an outdoor stove, assemble the necessary ingredients and let your guests take turns cooking the crêpes. It's a lot of fun and a good way to eat since you can enjoy the crêpes just as they come out of the pan. You will need a 30 cm (12 inch) nonstick frying pan for this recipe. If you need to use a smaller one, decrease the portion of batter accordingly.

Makes 4 large crêpes

For the batter:
350 g (12 oz) rice flour
125 ml (4 fl oz) unsweetened coconut milk
575 ml (19 fl oz) water
1½ teaspoons ground turmeric
1 teaspoon sugar
½ teaspoon salt
½ teaspoon curry powder, Vietnamese Golden Bells brand
     if you can find it
3 spring onions, cut into thin rings

For the filling:
4 tablespoons vegetable oil
¼ onion, thinly sliced
110 g (4 oz) pork shoulder or chicken breast, thinly sliced
12 medium raw prawns, peeled and deveined
360 g (12 oz) bean sprouts
180 g (6 oz) sliced button mushrooms, lightly sautéed, drained

For the accompaniments:
250 ml (8 fl oz) Vietnamese Dipping Sauce (see page 19)
Table Salad (see page 85)

- Make the batter: Place the rice flour, coconut milk, water, turmeric, sugar, salt, curry powder and spring onions in a bowl and stir well to blend. Set aside.

- Make the filling: Heat 1 tablespoon of the oil in a large nonstick frying pan over high heat. Add one-quarter each of the onion, the pork and the prawns and stir for about 15 seconds until fragrant. Whisk the batter well and ladle about 170 ml (5½ fl oz) into the pan. Swirl so the batter completely covers the surface. Neatly pile about a quarter of the bean sprouts and mushrooms on one side of the crêpe, closer to the centre than to the edge. Reduce the heat slightly, cover the pan and cook for about 5 minutes until the edges pull away from the sides of the pan. Reduce the heat to low. Uncover and cook for another 2 to 3 minutes until the crêpe is crisp and the chicken and prawns are done. Slip a spatula under the crêpe to check on the bottom of the crêpe. If it's not brown, cook for another minute or two.

- Lift the side of the crêpe without the bean sprouts and mushrooms and fold it over the covered side of the crêpe. Using a spatula, gently slide the crêpe onto a large plate. Wipe the pan clean and make the remaining crêpes in the same way. Be sure to oil the pan before beginning the next crêpe.

- To serve, place the crêpes, Vietnamese Dipping Sauce and Table Salad on the table. To eat, tear a piece of the *banh xeo* and wrap with lettuce or mustard leaves and herbs. Roll into a packet, then dip into the sauce and eat.

NOTE: In Hue, this dish is called *banh khoai* (happy pancakes). The crêpes are smaller, about 15 cm (6 inches) in diameter, and are served with a heavier sauce of fermented soya beans. If you want to try this version, use a small pan and reduce the amount of ingredients accordingly. When the crêpe is half-done, drizzle beaten egg around the edges and serve open or folded, with the same accompaniments.

Rice Noodles with Fresh Herbs
bun voi rau thom

IF THERE'S ONE dish that exemplifies just how flavours and textures are contrasted in Vietnamese cuisine, it would have to be *bun*. Made with small rice vermicelli layered on a bed of shredded fresh herbs and greens, it can be served with a variety of meat or seafood toppings. In Vietnam, *bun* is usually a meal in itself but it certainly can be served in smaller, appetizer-sized portions.

To create a complete *bun* meal, make this recipe and serve it with a topping (see the following two recipes.) Make sure that the noodles are completely dry before assembling the bowls. Otherwise, the noodles will not adequately soak up the sauce.

> **Makes 4 main-course servings with toppings**
> **325 g (11 oz) small dried rice vermicelli (*bun*)**
> **90 g (3½ oz) shredded red- or green-leaf lettuce**
> **135 g (4½ oz) bean sprouts**
> **⅓ cucumber, seeded and**
>   **cut into matchsticks**
> **20 g (¾ oz) green or red perilla leaves, fish mint (see pages**
>   **44, 43 and 41) or mint leaves, cut into thirds**
> **20 g (¾ oz) Asian basil leaves, cut into thirds**

- Bring a large pot of water to a rolling boil. Add the rice vermicelli and stir gently to loosen them. Cook for about 4 minutes until the noodles are white and soft but still slightly resilient. Drain and rinse under cold running water. Gently fluff the noodles and set them aside for at least 30 minutes. The noodles should be dry and sticky before serving.

- Gently toss together the lettuce, bean sprouts, cucumber, perilla and basil leaves. Divide the salad mixture among 4 bowls. Top each with one-quarter of the rice noodles. The bowls are now ready for the topping.

NOTE: Ideally, *bun* should not be refrigerated because the noodles become dry and stiff. However, if you need to, store the noodles and greens separately. Just before serving, reheat the noodles (preferably in a microwave oven) just until slightly warm. This will help them become soft and a little sticky again.

Lemongrass Beef on Cool Noodles

bun bo xao

The last time I was in Saigon, I went back to the lively Cho Vuon Chuoi market near our house. I was so excited to find the same stall that my mother used to take me to for noodles. The lady who once fed me had retired and her daughter had taken over. After squeezing myself onto a low bench in front of the hot charcoal stove, I found myself indulging in a delectable bowl of noodles with beef that had just come off a sizzling pan. These days, this dish remains a favourite, both for lunch and for a light dinner. For a delicious variation, try it with prawns or pork.

Serves 4
Rice Noodles with Fresh Herbs (see page 133), ready for serving in noodle bowls

For the topping:
325 g (11 oz) beef sirloin or another tender cut, thinly sliced into bite-sized strips
2 tablespoons minced lemongrass
2 tablespoons oyster sauce
1 tablespoon fish sauce
3 tablespoons vegetable oil
2 garlic cloves, minced
¼ red onion, thinly sliced lengthways

For the garnish:
2 tablespoons Spring Onion Oil (see page 31)
4 tablespoons chopped Roasted Peanuts (see page 34)
250 ml (8 fl oz) Vietnamese Dipping Sauce (see page 19)

- Combine the beef, lemongrass, oyster sauce and fish sauce in a bowl and let the meat marinate for 20 minutes.

- Heat the oil in a large frying pan over high heat. Add the garlic and stir for about 20 seconds until fragrant. Add the red onion and stir for 1 minute, then add the meat. Stir and cook for 3 to 4 minutes until the meat is cooked and the onion is soft.

- To serve, divide the beef topping among the 4 prepared noodle bowls. Garnish each bowl with ½ tablespoon Spring Onion Oil, 1 tablespoon peanuts and about 60 ml (2 fl oz) dipping sauce. Toss several times before eating.

Hanoi Rice Noodles with Grilled Pork
bun cha Hanoi

IN HANOI, if you arrive at Bun Cha Hang Manh a little after noon, chances are you'll have a tough time finding a seat. That's because this restaurant is known to have the best *bun cha* (noodles with grilled pork) in the city. Nguyen Doan Cam Van, a well-regarded television cookery teacher in Vietnam and advocate of northern regional cooking, says locals are quite particular about how *bun cha* should be eaten. Some soak the grilled pork slices and pork patties in the dipping sauce before adding them to their noodles. Others prefer to experience each ingredient with clarity and distinction, dipping and eating each item one by one.

Serves 4
2 spring onions, sliced into thin rings
1 shallot, minced
1 tablespoon fish sauce
1½ teaspoons Caramel Sauce (see page 33) or 1 teaspoon
    brown sugar
¼ teaspoon salt
½ teaspoon freshly ground black pepper
1 tablespoon vegetable oil
225 g (8 oz) pork shoulder, sliced thin across the grain
225 g (8 oz) minced pork
40 g (1½ oz) chopped onions

For the accompaniments:
325 g (11 oz) small, dried bun (rice vermicelli), cooked for
    about 4 to 5 minutes until soft but still firm, rinsed and
    drained (see page 124)
Table Salad (see page 85)
500 ml (16 fl oz) Vietnamese Dipping Sauce (see page 19)

• Combine the spring onions, shallot, fish sauce, Caramel Sauce, salt and pepper in a bowl and stir to blend. Divide the marinade equally between 2 bowls. Add the oil and sliced pork to one bowl and toss to evenly coat the meat. Let marinate for 20 minutes. In the second bowl, add the minced pork and onions and mix well. Shape the minced pork into patties about 5 cm (2 inches) wide and 1 cm (½ inch) thick. Set aside until ready to cook.

- Set the dining table with a platter of noodles and the Table Salad. Divide the dipping sauce among 4 small bowls. Provide each guest with a bowl of sauce and another bowl.

- Preheat a barbecue or grill to high heat. Grill the pork slices and pork patties until the meat is done and the edges are nicely charred on both sides. (You can also cook the pork in a frying pan.) Transfer to a serving plate.

- To eat, place a few slices of pork and pork patties in the bowls of dipping sauce and let them marinate for a few minutes. Invite guests to serve themselves by placing the noodles, herbs and lettuce and meat in their bowls and drizzling some sauce on top.

Rice Noodle Stir-fry with Pork
pho xao

THIS DISH IS especially wonderful if you can make the fresh rice sheets on page 126 or purchase the similar *chow fun* noodle sheets at an Asian store. For stir-fries like this one, I like to cut the noodle sheets into 2.5 cm (1 inch) wide ribbons. If you can't find these fresh noodles, use dried rice sticks or even fresh egg noodles.

Serves 4
½ tablespoon cornflour
2 tablespoons water

225 g (8 oz) pork shoulder or beef flank, excess fat
   trimmed, cut into 2 mm (⅛ inch) thick slices
3 tablespoons vegetable oil
450 g (I lb) fresh rice noodle sheets, cut into 2.5 cm
   (I inch) wide strips, or 325 g (II oz) dried *banh pho* (rice
   sticks, see page 125), preferably 5 mm (¼ inch) or wider,
   cooked for 3 to 4 minutes, rinsed and drained
2 tablespoons sweet soy sauce (see page 36)
¼ onion, cut into wedges
I½ tablespoons fermented whole soya beans (see Glossary
   page 260)
2 teaspoons minced garlic
2 tablespoons oyster sauce
I teaspoon sugar
I teaspoon fish sauce
I teaspoon soy sauce
75 ml (3 fl oz) fresh Chicken Stock (see page 38) or store-
   bought reduced-salt chicken stock
325 g (II oz) Chinese broccoli or regular broccoli, bottom
   stems discarded, cut on the diagonal into 5 cm (2 inch)
   pieces and blanched in boiling water for 20 seconds
5 sprigs of coriander, cut into 5 cm (2 inch) lengths
I25 ml (4 fl oz) Soy-lime Dipping Sauce (see page 27)

- Combine the cornflour and water in a small bowl and mix well. Add the pork and toss to coat the meat evenly. Set aside until ready to use.

- Heat I½ tablespoons of the oil in a large nonstick frying pan over moderate heat. Add the noodles, stirring slightly to loosen them. Drizzle the sweet soy sauce over the noodles, turning them 2 or 3 times to help absorb the sauce. Stir gently for about 2 to 3 minutes until they're hot and the edges are slightly brown. (If using dried noodles, cook a little longer. If the pan is a little dry, sprinkle in 2 to 3 tablespoons water.) Transfer the noodles to a platter and keep warm.

- Wipe the pan clean. Heat the remaining 1½ tablespoons oil in the pan over moderate heat. Add the onion wedges, soya beans and garlic and stir for about 20 seconds until fragrant. Add the pork and cook for 2 minutes. Add the oyster sauce, sugar, fish sauce, soy sauce and stock and stir for 30 seconds. Add the Chinese broccoli. Cover and cook for 2 to 3 minutes until the ingredients are thoroughly hot. Add the reserved noodles to the pan and stir for about 2 minutes until thoroughly hot. Transfer to a platter, then garnish with the coriander sprigs and serve immediately with the dipping sauce on the side.

Noodle Pillows with Chicken and Prawns
mi xao don

IN VIETNAM, street vendors cook these noodles in a wok with a lot of oil, which creates a very crisp and airy pillow. This version is much lighter, but just as delicious. For best flavour, use the fresh egg noodles sold in Asian stores or in the produce sections of some supermarkets. The dried egg noodles will also work.

Serves 4
½ **tablespoon cornflour**
2 **tablespoons water**

110 g (4 oz) skinless, boneless chicken breast, cut into thin
  bite-sized strips
4 tablespoons vegetable oil
450 g (1 lb) fresh egg noodles, cooked, or 225 g (8 oz) dried
  egg noodles, boiled for 3 to 4 minutes, depending on
  the thickness, drained
2 teaspoons minced ginger
1 teaspoon minced garlic
1 to 2 teaspoons fermented black beans (see Glossary
  page 260), rinsed
½ teaspoon dried chilli flakes
12 dried black mushrooms (shiitake), soaked in warm
  water for 30 minutes, drained, stemmed and halved
110 g (4 oz) raw prawns, peeled and deveined
2 tablespoons oyster sauce
1 tablespoon soy sauce
1 small carrot, peeled, cut on the diagonal into thin slices
  and blanched in boiling water for about 30 seconds
¼ onion, thinly sliced lengthways
150 g (5 oz) baby bok choy, cut on the diagonal into 1 cm
  (½ inch) pieces and blanched in hot water for 10 seconds
75 ml (3 fl oz) fresh Chicken Stock (see page 38) or store-
  bought reduced-salt chicken stock
2 tablespoons rice wine or
  dry sherry
5 sprigs of coriander, cut into 5 cm (2 inch) lengths

- Combine the cornflour and water in a bowl and stir well. Add the chicken and toss to coat the meat evenly.
- Heat 2 tablespoons of the oil in a large nonstick frying pan over

moderate heat. Divide the noodles into 4 equal piles and transfer to the pan. Press gently on the noodles to create a flat round pillow. Cook for 3 to 4 minutes on each side until the noodles are golden and crisp around the edges. Add more oil if necessary. Drain on paper towels and keep warm.

- Heat the remaining 2 tablespoons oil in a wok or large frying pan. Add the ginger, garlic, black beans and chilli flakes and stir for about 10 seconds until fragrant. Add the chicken and black mushrooms and cook for 2 minutes. Add the prawns, oyster sauce and soy sauce and stir a few times. Add the carrot, onion, bok choy and chicken stock. Cook for another 2 minutes until the sauce is slightly thickened and the vegetables are thoroughly hot. Splash the pan with rice wine and remove it from the heat.

- To serve, place one noodle pillow on each of 4 plates and top with the chicken and prawn stir-fry. Garnish with the coriander and serve.

Grilled Prawn Paste on Sugarcane
chao tom

THIS FABULOUS DISH is both delicious and beautiful. Eaten throughout Vietnam, it's made with a prawn paste wrapped around sugarcane, which is then grilled. This recipe calls for pork fat, which tenderizes and enriches the paste. Traditional cooks like my mom insist that once the pork fat is poached, it should cool down completely before being folded into the paste. That way, speckles of the translucent fat will still show through the cooked paste. (The best fat to use is fresh bacon, not the white chewy stuff from pork shoulder.)

To properly enjoy this dish, tear off a piece of the prawn paste, then wrap it in lettuce with some herbs before dipping in a sauce. And when the prawn paste is all eaten, chew on the sugarcane and enjoy its sweet, smoky juice. You can use either tinned sugarcane or fresh cane, which is more fragrant but a bit harder to find and handle. The tinned sugarcane is packed in water and holds up well on the grill.

You will need a steamer for this recipe. *Chao tom* makes a lovely appetizer, but the Vietnamese typically serve it as the main dish, with a big table salad and plenty of rice vermicelli on the side.

Makes 24 pieces or 4 main-dish servings
50 g (2 oz) piece of pork fat or I egg white
2 teaspoons vegetable oil
40 g (1½ oz) chopped onion, drained of excess water
3 shallots, minced
I tablespoon fish sauce
¼ teaspoon sea salt
I tablespoon sugar
I teaspoon minced garlic
½ teaspoon ground white pepper
2 tablespoons cornflour
½ teaspoon baking powder
450 g (I lb) raw medium prawns, peeled, deveined and
  patted extremely dry
2 spring onions, chopped
625 g (20 oz) tin 10 cm (4 inch) long sugarcane, drained

For the accompaniments:
225 g (8 oz) small dried *bun* (rice vermicelli), cooked (see
  page 124)

Table Salad (see page 85)
Vietnamese Bean Dipping Sauce (see page 25) or
Vietnamese Dipping Sauce (see page 19)

- If using pork fat, bring a small saucepan of water to the boil. Add the pork fat and cook for 2 to 3 minutes just until the edges turn translucent. Remove the pan from the heat and drain the pork on paper towels. Coarsely chop the fat and set aside. If using egg white, start with the next step.

- Heat the oil in a small saucepan over moderate heat. Add the onion and shallots and sauté for about 1 minute until slightly wilted. Transfer the onion mixture (not the juice) to a bowl and add the fish sauce, salt, sugar, garlic, white pepper, cornflour, baking powder and pork fat or egg white. Add the prawns and toss well.

- Transfer the prawn mixture to a food processor and process until almost smooth but still lumpy. Transfer the paste to a bowl, scraping the work bowl clean. Stir in the spring onions. (If the paste is not cold, refrigerate at this point to stiffen it.)

- Quarter the sugarcane pieces lengthways, or halve them if they're small. Wet your hands with cold water. Place 2 tablespoons of the prawn paste in the middle of your palm. Place a piece of the sugarcane on top and mould the paste around it. The paste should be about 5 mm (¼ inch) thick and about 6 cm (2½ inches) long. Gently press the paste against the stick so that the edges are sealed. Set the prawn stick aside on an oiled plate. Repeat with the remaining sugarcane and paste.

- Oil a steamer basket and place the sugarcane sticks in a single layer. (If necessary, steam in several batches.) Steam for 2 to 3 minutes until the prawn paste turns pink. You can make this dish in advance up to this point. To finish, grill or barbecue the prawn sticks until the paste is hot inside and slightly charred around the edges. Serve immediately with Table Salad, rice vermicelli and dipping sauce.

Bean Thread Noodles with Crab
mien xao cua

MIEN XAO CUA is a very special dish, especially if you can see how it's prepared at one of the seafood restaurants on Dinh Tien Hoang Street in Saigon. The kitchens are located in front and diners can watch the cooks turn and toss the transparent noodles while adding big handfuls of fresh, chunky crabmeat. After watching the cooks, it's impossible not to order at least one plate!

If you can't get crabmeat, use prawns. It won't be as decadent, but will be delicious just the same. Bean threads vary and some can absorb more liquid than others. If they seem dry in the pan, add more stock.

Serves 4
3 tablespoons vegetable oil
3 shallots, thinly sliced
2 garlic cloves, minced
175 g (6 oz) cooked crabmeat or 325 g (11 oz) raw prawns, peeled and deveined
2 tablespoons oyster sauce
1 tablespoon soy sauce
110 g (4 oz) dried bean threads (cellophane noodles, see page 125), soaked in warm water for 30 minutes, drained and cut into 30 cm (12 inch) pieces
A handful of dried wood-ear mushrooms, soaked in warm water for 30 minutes, chewy centres removed and cut in half or thirds
375 ml (12 fl oz) fresh Chicken Stock (see page 38), store-bought reduced-salt chicken stock or water

1 carrot, peeled, cut into
   matchstick strips, blanched for 30 seconds and drained
3 spring onions, cut into 5 cm (2 inch) lengths
6 sprigs of coriander, cut into 2.5 cm (1 inch) lengths
Freshly ground black pepper

- In a large nonstick frying pan, heat 1 tablespoon of the vegetable oil over moderate heat. Add half the shallots and garlic and stir for about 20 seconds until fragrant. Add the crabmeat and cook for 2 minutes. Transfer to a plate and keep warm.

- Heat the remaining 2 tablespoons oil in another frying pan over moderate heat. Stir in the remaining shallots and garlic. When fragrant, add the oyster sauce, soy sauce, bean threads, mushrooms and chicken stock. Stir a few times, then reduce the heat. Cover and cook for 5 to 7 minutes until the noodles are soft and have absorbed almost all of the sauce.

- Add the carrot strips and crabmeat. Cook for about 2 minutes until the carrots are just hot. (If the pan is dry, sprinkle with 2 or 3 tablespoons Chicken Stock.) Stir in the spring onions and toss gently several times. Transfer to a serving plate and garnish with the coriander and black pepper.

Hanoi Grilled Fish with Rice Noodles and Fresh Herbs
cha ca Hanoi

EVERY TIME I enter Cha Ca La Vong, a tiny landmark restaurant in Hanoi, I know I'm in for a special treat. Owned by the same family for several generations, it serves only one dish – *cha ca*, which comes to the table on a small charcoal brazier. To enjoy the dish, one adds the just-cooked fish and wilted dill to the rice noodles and herbs and eats it with *mam tom* (a pungent sauce made from shrimp sauce and pineapple) or Vietnamese dipping sauce, which I much prefer.

Chef and owner Ngo Thi Tinh, who claims it was her grandmother who first popularized this dish, marinates *ca lang*, a local fish from the Red River in *me*, a souring agent made from fermented rice. In this adaptation, I call for catfish and yoghurt instead but any firm-fleshed fish will work.

Serves 4

For the marinade:
4 cm (1½ inch) piece of galangal (see Glossary page 261)
    or 1 teaspoon galangal powder
2 tablespoons plain yoghurt
2 teaspoons ground turmeric
2 teaspoons sugar
2 teaspoons rice vinegar
1 teaspoon shrimp sauce
    (see Glossary page 265)
1½ teaspoons salt

700 g (1½ lb) catfish fillets, cut into 7.5 cm (3 inch) chunks
325 g (11 oz) small dried *bun* (rice vermicelli), boiled for
    4 to 5 minutes, rinsed and drained (see page 124)
1½ heads red-leaf lettuce, torn into bite-sized pieces
2 bunches of Asian basil or mint leaves, preferably tender
    leaves only
4 spring onions, cut into 5 cm (2 inch) lengths
2 bunches of fresh dill, bottom tough stems removed and
    cut into 2.5 cm (1 inch) lengths
80 g (3 oz) whole Roasted Peanuts (see page 34)
125 ml (4 fl oz) Vietnamese Dipping Sauce (see page 19)
2 tablespoons vegetable oil and extra oil for grilling

- Make the marinade: Peel the galangal and cut into thin slices. Pound in a mortar until mushy. Using your fingers, squeeze the pulverized galangal to extract as much juice as you can from the pulp. You should have about 1 tablespoon. (You can also use a Japanese ginger grater.)

- In a large bowl, combine the galangal juice, yoghurt, turmeric, sugar, rice vinegar, shrimp sauce and salt. Add the catfish and toss to evenly coat the fish. Set aside to marinate for 30 minutes.

- Before cooking the fish, set the dining table with a plate of rice vermicelli and a platter of lettuce and Asian basil. Combine the spring onions and dill and put on a plate. Put the peanuts and dipping sauce in separate bowls. Provide each guest with a small bowl and chopsticks.

- Start a charcoal fire or preheat a gas grill to high. Grill the catfish pieces for about 2 minutes on each side, just until halfway done. (The fish will finish cooking at the table.) Transfer the fish to a plate and keep warm.

- To serve, place a portable gas or electric stove in the middle of the dining table. Heat the oil in a small frying pan over moderate heat. Add some catfish pieces, but do not crowd the pan, and a generous amount (a cupful) of dill and spring onions. Using chopsticks or a long-handled spoon, stir gently until the fish is hot and the dill and spring onions wilted. Invite the guests to assemble their own condiments by placing some noodles, lettuce and herbs in their bowls. Top with the catfish, herbs, peanuts and sauce. When the catfish has all been eaten, cook another batch.

NOTE: If you don't have a table-top stove, finish the dish in the kitchen. Heat the oil in a frying pan until hot. Add the fish pieces and dill and spring onions and stir for 2 to 3 minutes until the fish pieces are cooked through. Do not crowd the pan; cook in batches if necessary. Transfer to a platter and serve immediately.

Rice Dishes with Poultry and Meat

AROUND TET (Vietnamese New Year), a whole chicken is a prized food. Symbolizing abundance and prosperity, it sits prominently on the ancestor worship altar, along with the flowers, candles and incense sticks. Since Tet combines the spirit of Christmas, New Year and everyone's birthday (a person is considered one year older on this day) all in one, our family goes to great lengths to welcome our ancestors into our home.

Raised in a traditional Vietnamese home, I was taught that our ancestors are as important as, if not more important than, living members of the family. Because their presence and blessings are considered critical to our well-being, we involve them in our everyday life, remembering them through daily offerings of food and prayers and inviting them to join us for important celebrations.

We were taught that by connecting with them, our purpose in life would become clearer. We were told that every deed and action affects the whole family – including those who have passed on. A good deed makes them happy and proud and therefore eager to watch over us. On the other hand, a misdeed is considered an act of dishonour, a serious offence to the family lineage. Growing up with such taboos and belief systems, I never once dared jeopardize that tradition or embarrass the family in any way.

So, on the first day of Tet, we prepare a sumptuous meal to *ruoc ong ba* (welcome back the ancestors). Besides the whole chicken, we cook dozens of other enticing dishes such as Caramelized Garlic Prawns (see page 200) and a traditional pork stew with hard-boiled eggs called *thit kho dua*. For dessert, we serve *che khoai mon* (Coconut Sticky Rice Pudding with Taro, see page 247), and fresh fruits like watermelon and tangerines. A small portion of each dish is then placed as an offering on the altar.

When we light the incense and say our prayers, the spirits are invoked and the ancestors begin their journey back to Earth. In our prayers, we thank them for watching over us and giving us good luck and health. It is only after these prayers that we can begin to eat.

Then, on the third day of Tet, when the ancestors get ready to depart, we prepare another extravagant send-off meal, this time with different dishes and wine. Towards the end of the ritual, we all go outside and gather around our parents and watch as they dutifully burn beautifully decorated paper tunics and clothes and even symbolic paper money – items which our ancestors will need in Heaven. And once our ancestors are gone, we go back to our own lives but with the lingering thoughts of Tet and a strong reminder that we must, as always, live up to their expectations.

One of the things you'll notice as you cook from this chapter is that, with the exception of steamed dishes and Chinese-style stir-fries, a typical, traditional Vietnamese meat recipe will call for few, if any, vegetables. Vietnamese cooks believe that in order to heighten the flavour of a particular meat or seafood, it should be cooked by itself, with a few spices and aromatics. The addition of vegetables would only dilute the flavour. So, from a Vietnamese perspective, a meat dish should taste like a meat dish and a vegetable dish should be served separately. Meat is generally expensive, so it's usually generously salted so it can be stretched and eaten with a lot of rice (which is unsalted) and other foods. Since rice is at the heart of these meals I've included a foolproof recipe for steamed rice. When serving steamed rice as part of a meal, allow 1 to 2 cups per person.

Poached Whole Chicken with Ginger-lime Dipping Sauce

ga luoc nuoc mam gung

THIS RECIPE USES an old Chinese technique of submerging a whole chicken in boiling water, turning off the heat, and letting it steep. The technique produces a moist and succulent bird, ready to be served or used in any recipe calling for cooked chicken. Many Chinese chefs cook the chicken so the meat is white but the bones are still red. I like chicken well done, so I've increased the cooking time.

When boiling or poaching foods, Vietnamese cooks typically do not use salt because the dish is often served with a dipping sauce and the last-minute balancing of flavours is done at the table. To serve, cut the chicken through the bones into large chunks and arrange them on a plate. To eat, remove the skin and dip the meat in a sauce. The Chinese vendors in Saigon like to serve this with Sweet Soy Sauce with Chillies and Ginger, but I also love it with Ginger-lime Sauce. Steamed or fried rice and a vegetable dish are the traditional accompaniments.

Serves 6

1 fresh whole chicken, about 1.125 kg (2½ lb), preferably free range, trimmed of excess fat

5 sprigs of coriander

2 recipes of Sweet Soy Sauce with Chillies and Ginger (see page 28) or

1 recipe of Ginger-lime Dipping Sauce (see page 24)

- Place 4 litres (7 pints) water in a large soup pot and bring to a rolling boil. Add the chicken and bring to the boil again. Boil for 10 minutes, then turn off the heat. Cover the pot and let the chicken steep, undisturbed, for about 1 hour until cooked through.

- Remove the chicken and transfer to a deep dish. Loosely wrap a piece of clingfilm around it to prevent the skin from drying out. When cool enough to handle, use a cleaver or heavy knife to cut the chicken into the desired-sized pieces. Arrange on a plate and garnish with the coriander. Serve with the dipping sauce of choice on the side.

Perfect Steamed Rice

com

IT'S IRONIC THAT many times, the most important food at the table — the rice — gets the least amount of attention. To ensure that this critical part of the meal is as good as the rest of the dishes, start with good-quality rice and make sure it's properly cooked each time. I prefer jasmine rice from Thailand and Vietnam but, even then, each batch differs in quality: some are fragrant, some are too mushy, and some are dry and bland. In an effort to avoid bad rice, I buy from the busy Asian stores with high turnover and stick to the brands that I'm familiar with, like Phoenix and Three Ladies.

Good rice is fresh-cooked rice. You can start with the best batch of grains, but if it's been cooked even half an hour in advance, its taste and texture will be less than optimal. Try to time the cooking of the rice so that it's done just minutes before you eat.

The easiest way to make great rice is to boil it in an automatic insulated rice cooker. (Even though cooked rice is often referred to as steamed, it is actually boiled.) With an automatic cooker, the heat is more evenly distributed, and the insert creates more steam, thus resulting in better rice. Besides, if the most important part of the meal can be taken care of by this machine, why not use it and save your energy for other dishes?

Whether you are using an automatic rice cooker or the traditional stove-top method, I strongly suggest rinsing your rice before cooking, as the Vietnamese cooks do. Rinsing removes the excess starch that tends to mask the delicate flavour of rice. Once the rice is rinsed, measure out the water. The amount needed can vary because each batch of rice has a different moisture level. If it's from a new crop, the rice will be high in moisture and will need less water. Jasmine rice often falls in this category. But as a general guideline, use 1 part rice to 1½ parts water. Properly cooked rice is soft and fluffy with the grains still maintaining their shape.

Serves 4 to 6
400 g (14 oz) jasmine rice
750 ml (25 fl oz) water

- If using a rice cooker, place the rice in the insert and rinse with cold water until the water runs clear. Tilt the insert to drain the rice, using your hand to keep the rice from spilling. Drain completely. Add the water and cook the rice. Serve the rice minutes after the timer goes off.

- To cook in a regular pan, place the rice in the pan and wash with several changes of cold water. Drain the rice, then add the water. Bring the pan to the boil and let it continue to boil for about 2 to 3 minutes. Stir gently once, then cover the pan. Reduce the heat to very low and simmer, covered, for about 20 minutes until all the water is absorbed and the rice is done. Turn off the heat and let it sit for 5 minutes before serving.

Vietnamese Fried Rice
com chien

UNLIKE THE MORE traditional recipes for fried rice that call for ham or Chinese sausage, this family favourite has a bit of a Western influence: it's stir-fried in butter, with a little ketchup. This makes a great accompaniment to barbecued meats such as Barbecued Five-spice Chicken (see page 167) and Lemongrass Roasted Chicken (see page 160). It also makes a wonderful lunch dish when embellished with cooked meat and vegetables (or even eggs) and served with Soy-lime Dipping Sauce (see page 27).

Serves 4 to 6
3 tablespoons butter
1 teaspoon chopped garlic

3 tablespoons chopped onion

2 tablespoons ketchup

½ tablespoon fish sauce

Salt to taste

1 teaspoon sugar

740 g (1 lb 10 oz) cold cooked rice, preferably long grain (see Glossary page 263)

2 spring onions, cut into thin rings

5 sprigs of coriander, cut into 5 cm (2 inch) lengths

• Heat the butter in a wok or nonstick frying pan over moderate heat. Add the garlic and onion and stir for about 20 seconds until fragrant. Add the ketchup, fish sauce, salt and sugar and simmer for 2 to 3 minutes until the sauce is slightly reduced. Add the rice and stir-fry for 4 to 5 minutes until it is hot. Add the spring onions and stir for another 2 minutes. (Sprinkle on some water if the pan is dry.) Transfer to a serving dish, garnish with the coriander and serve immediately.

Chicken Curry with Sweet Potatoes
ca ri ga

TRUE TO THE Vietnamese style of curry-making, this recipe is milder and lighter than Indian or Thai curries. You can make this with chicken stock, but the coconut milk adds body and enhances the overall flavour. Depending on my mood and the time of year, I sometimes serve this with a warmed baguette (a French influence) instead of steamed rice. Other times, I just make the curry with more broth and serve it with rice noodles. Like other curries, it's delicious the next day.

Serves 4

3 tablespoons curry powder, Three Golden Bells brand if you can find it

½ teaspoon salt, or to taste

900 g (2 lb) skinless chicken thighs

2 tablespoons vegetable oil

1 tablespoon chopped shallot

2 teaspoons minced garlic

2 teaspoons ground chilli paste (see Glossary page 259) or dried chilli flakes, or to taste

3 tablespoons fish sauce

1 tablespoon sugar

2 lemongrass stalks, cut into 7.5 cm (3 inch) pieces and bruised with the flat side of a knife

2.5 cm (1 inch) piece of ginger, peeled, cut into 3 slices and bruised with the flat side of a knife

375 ml (12 fl oz) fresh Chicken Stock (see page 38) or store-bought reduced-salt chicken stock

3 carrots, peeled, cut on the diagonal into 1.5 cm (⅝ inch) pieces

375 ml (12 fl oz) unsweetened coconut milk or cow's milk

1 onion, cut into thin wedges

1 medium sweet potato, about 450 g (1 lb), peeled and cut into 2.5 cm (1 inch) cubes

For the garnish:
25 g (1 oz) Asian basil leaves, cut in half
8 sprigs of coriander, cut into 5 cm (2 inch) pieces
2 spring onions, chopped

- Combine 2 tablespoons of the curry powder and the salt in a bowl. Add the chicken and turn to coat the meat evenly. Set aside for 30 minutes.

- Heat the oil in a medium pan over moderate heat. Add the shallot, garlic, chilli paste and the remaining 1 tablespoon curry powder and stir for about 10 seconds until fragrant. Add the chicken and cook for 3 to 4 minutes until the edges of the pieces are golden. Add the fish sauce, sugar, lemongrass, ginger and chicken stock. Bring to the boil, then reduce the heat. Add the carrots and cook for 10 minutes. Add the coconut milk, onion and sweet potato and cook for about 15 minutes until the vegetables are tender. Transfer to a serving bowl, garnish with Asian basil, coriander and spring onions and serve.

Making Fresh Coconut Milk

MY GRANDMOTHER, who owns a coconut plantation in the Mekong Delta, grows two main varieties of coconuts. One is harvested for the sweet juice, used as a beverage and cooking liquid, and the other is used to make *nuoc cot dua*, or coconut milk.

To make coconut milk the traditional way, Co Muoi (Tenth Aunt), who now does all the cooking for my grandmother, relies upon a special tool. Using a round serrated blade, she scrapes the inside of the coconut flesh, turning the fruit as she goes. To extract the milk, she steeps the grated coconut in hot water, then squeezes it over a bamboo basket. The first pressing yields a rich creamy liquid commonly used in desserts. The second and third pressings, made by adding additional boiling water, are used to make curry sauce, soups and lighter desserts.

If you want to make fresh coconut milk, you can use the same basic technique. To crack open a coconut, hold it with a towel over the sink and use the back of a cleaver to whack crossways along the middle. It usually takes several whacks (depending on its thickness) before the nut cracks. Using the tip of the cleaver, prise it open just enough to drain the juice. Drink the juice or use as a cooking liquid.

Bake the cracked coconut in a preheated 170°C/325°F/Gas Mark 3 oven for about 30 minutes. Remove and let cool. Once cool, wrap a towel around it and lay it on a hard surface. Using a hammer or mallet, give it a few whacks to break it into several pieces. Remove the flesh with a screwdriver, then use a vegetable peeler to peel the outside brown skin.

Chop the coconut into coarse pieces, then add to a food processor. Grind as fine as you can, gradually adding 250 ml (8 fl oz) hot water. (You may have to do this in batches.) Transfer to a bowl and add 250 ml (8 fl oz) boiling water. When the coconut mixture is cool enough to handle, use your hands to massage and squeeze the pulverized coconut for about 5 minutes. Place a fine-mesh strainer over a bowl and pour the coconut mixture through. Again using your hands, squeeze the solids over the strainer, extracting as much liquid as possible. The creamy coconut milk is now ready for use. To make a less creamy version, add 500 ml (16 fl oz) more boiling water to the solids and repeat the process. Fresh coconut milk is highly perishable and should be used within 2 days.

These directions may sound daunting but it's really hard to beat fresh coconut milk. It's worth doing at least once so you can taste the difference between fresh coconut milk and the canned products. The good news about canned coconut milk is that the number of brands available these days is increasing. Many are quite good and consistent, like Mae Ploy and Chao Koh, both from Thailand.

Lemongrass Roasted Chicken

ga nuong xa

IN VIETNAM, most homes don't have an oven, so chicken is usually cut into chunks for easy grilling or stove-top cooking. However, for this dish, I prefer using a whole chicken. Just imagine pulling out of the oven a freshly roasted chicken, its golden skin covered with a last-minute basting of aromatic lemongrass and coriander. For a satisfying meal, serve this with steamed or fried rice (see pages 153 and 155) and a salad such as Cabbage Salad with Prawns and Pork (see page 96).

Serves 4 to 6
4 tablespoons minced lemongrass
2 tablespoons minced shallot
2 tablespoons minced garlic
2 tablespoons soy sauce
2 tablespoons sugar
2 tablespoons fish sauce
1 tablespoon dried chilli flakes, or to taste
1 teaspoon sea salt, or to taste
1 whole chicken, about 1.35 kg (3 lb), preferably free range, rinsed and patted dry

2 tablespoons minced coriander
3 tablespoons vegetable oil
125 ml (4 fl oz) Soy-lime Dipping Sauce (see page 27)

- Remove 2 tablespoons of the lemongrass and set aside in a small bowl. Combine the remaining lemongrass, shallot, garlic, soy sauce, sugar, fish sauce, chilli flakes and salt in a large bowl. Add the chicken and turn to coat, tucking some marinade underneath the skin. Pour any excess marinade into the bird cavity. Cover the chicken with clingfilm, then marinate in the refrigerator for at least 4 hours, preferably overnight. Bring the chicken to room temperature before roasting.

- Preheat the oven to 180°C/350°F/Gas Mark 4. Put the chicken, breast side down, on a rack in a roasting pan. Roast for 40 minutes. Turn the bird over and roast for about 20 to 30 minutes more until the chicken is cooked and nicely browned. About 10 minutes before the chicken is done, combine the remaining 2 tablespoons lemongrass with the coriander and oil. Brush the mixture on the bird, then continue to roast until it is done and the juices run clear. Let the chicken rest for 10 minutes before carving. Serve with Soy-lime Dipping Sauce and fried or steamed rice. (The pan juices are delicious on the rice.)

Ginger Chicken
ga kho gung

KHO (BRAISED) DISHES are an important part of Vietnamese cuisine, particularly in the south. They're usually prepared in a claypot, with pork, chicken or seafood, without any vegetables. For working families in the villages, a *kho* dish is ideal because if generously salted, it can be stretched to feed lots of people. This simple recipe will surprise you with its robust flavours.

For this recipe, it's best to use a 900 ml (1½ pint) Asian claypot (see page 163), but you can also prepare this in a regular covered pot or casserole. Serve with a vegetable dish and steamed rice.

Serves 4

5 cm (2 inch) piece of ginger

325 g (11 oz) boneless, skinless chicken thighs or breast, cut into bite-sized strips

2 tablespoons vegetable oil

2 teaspoons minced garlic

¼ onion, thinly sliced lengthways

1 teaspoon chopped fresh red chillies or dried chilli flakes

1½ tablespoons fish sauce

2 teaspoons sugar

¼ teaspoon salt

125 ml (4 fl oz) fresh Chicken Stock (see page 38) or store-bought reduced-salt chicken stock

½ tablespoon Caramel Sauce (see page 33) or 1 tablespoon light brown sugar

2 spring onions, cut into 5 cm (2 inch) lengths

6 sprigs of coriander, cut into 2.5 cm (1 inch) pieces

• Peel the ginger and cut on the diagonal into 2 mm (⅛ inch) thick slices. Take a few slices and finely chop enough to measure 1 tablespoon. Combine the minced ginger and the chicken in a bowl. Set aside to marinate for 30 minutes.

- Heat the oil in a large frying pan over moderate heat. Add the garlic, onion and chillies and stir for about 10 seconds until fragrant. Add the chicken, ginger slices, fish sauce, sugar and salt and stir for 2 to 3 minutes. Transfer to a preheated claypot, if using, at this point.

- Add the chicken stock and Caramel Sauce and reduce the heat to a simmer. Cover and cook for about 5 minutes until the chicken is halfway done. Uncover and continue cooking for another 5 minutes until the sauce is thickened. Stir in the spring onions. Remove the pot from the heat. Garnish with the coriander and serve.

Cooking with Claypots

MADE OF SAND and clay, the claypot is an ancient Chinese creation used throughout Asia. It imparts a deep, smoky flavour to foods and is especially good for slow braising recipes, such as stews and casserole-type dishes. The pot comes in two styles: one with a single thick handle, the other with two smaller handles. Some pots have a protective wire brace, a clever feature since they do sometimes crack. Both styles have an unglazed off-white exterior, while the lid and the interior are glazed dark brown.

Claypots are available in many different sizes, but I recommend getting the 900 ml (1½ pint) and 2.65 litre (4½ pint) sizes since most recipes call for one or the other. The smaller size is suitable for dishes with only a few ingredients like Aunt Tam's Pork in Claypot (see page 173), while the larger one is better for rice dishes that need more steam, such as Vegetarian Claypot Rice with Ginger (see page 225). When cooking, you can set the claypot on the gas stove, then bring up the heat gradually. If you have an electric stove, use a heat diffuser to be on the safe side. To prevent sudden cracks, avoid setting a cold pot on a very hot stove and always cook on moderate, not high, heat. Also, refrain from washing a hot claypot in cold water.

Claypots don't need to be seasoned in any special way, although I've found that boiling water in a new pot helps remove the smell of the clay. Over time, if you use claypots often, they will blacken and start to have a few unharmful cracks. It's all part of the beauty of claypot cooking.

Stir-fried Chicken with Lemongrass and Chillies

ga xao xa ot

I WAS RAISED on this dish, eating it almost twice a week. I never grew tired of it, especially the gooey sauce. The secret is lots of onions, lemongrass and chillies: not only do the onions impart a savoury sweetness, but they help bring out the flavours of the spices and herbs. You can also make this dish with pork, seafood or eel, which is quite popular in Vietnam. Make sure the lemongrass is very fresh.

Serves 4
2 teaspoons cornflour
1 tablespoon water
325 g (11 oz) boneless, skinless chicken thighs or chicken breast, cut into thin bite-sized strips

3 tablespoons vegetable oil

2 garlic cloves, chopped

2 teaspoons chopped fresh chillies or dried chilli flakes

2 lemongrass stalks, bottom white part only, finely
    chopped

1 onion, thinly sliced lengthways

125 ml (4 fl oz) fresh Chicken Stock (see page 38) or
    store-bought reduced-salt chicken stock

1 tablespoon fish sauce

1 teaspoon sugar

2 teaspoons Caramel Sauce
    (see page 33) or 1 teaspoon light brown sugar

5 sprigs of coriander, cut into 5 cm (2 inch) lengths

- Combine the cornflour, water and chicken in a bowl. Toss to coat the meat evenly. Set aside to marinate for 15 minutes.

- Heat 1½ tablespoons of the oil in a frying pan over high heat. Add the chicken and stir for about 3 minutes until the edges turn white. Transfer to a plate and keep warm.

- Wipe the pan clean. Add the remaining 1½ tablespoons oil and heat over moderate heat. Add the garlic, chillies and half of the lemongrass and stir for about 10 seconds until fragrant. Add the onion and chicken stock and cook for about 10 minutes until the onion is soft.

- Stir in the chicken, remaining lemongrass, fish sauce, sugar and Caramel Sauce and cook for about 3 to 4 minutes until the chicken is cooked through. Transfer to a plate, garnish with the coriander and serve immediately.

Grandmother's Chicken with Wild Mushrooms

ga xao nam

AT MY GRANDMOTHER'S house, many of the best meals are those made with *nam moi*, a type of wild mushroom that grows profusely on her coconut plantation during the rainy season. Resembling a small but leggy straw mushroom, it has a distinct, earthy flavour. Since it's not available in the West, I've substituted other delicious mushrooms. This dish is typically made with young coconut juice (not milk) as a cooking liquid but since it's difficult to find, I've substituted chicken stock.

Serves 4

2 tablespoons soy sauce
2 teaspoons fish sauce
2 teaspoons sugar
2 teaspoons cornflour
225 g (8 oz) boneless skinless chicken breasts and/or thighs, cut into thin bite-sized strips
3 tablespoons vegetable oil
2 shallots, sliced
8 dried black mushrooms (shiitake), soaked in warm water for 30 minutes, drained, stemmed and halved
90 g (3½ oz) white or brown mushrooms, clean and halved
90 g (3½ oz) oyster mushrooms, cleaned and cut into bite-sized pieces
½ teaspoon salt
2 teaspoons chopped garlic

125 ml (4 fl oz) fresh Chicken Stock (see page 38) or
store-bought reduced-salt chicken stock
5 sprigs of coriander, cut into 5 cm (2 inch) lengths

- Place the soy sauce, fish sauce, sugar and cornflour in a bowl and stir well. Add the chicken and toss to coat the meat evenly.

- Heat 1½ tablespoons of the oil in a large frying pan over moderate heat. Add the shallots and stir for about 20 seconds until fragrant. Add the black mushrooms, white mushrooms, oyster mushrooms and salt. Cook for 3 to 4 minutes until the mushrooms are soft. (Add 2 to 3 tablespoons water if the pan gets too dry.) Transfer the mushrooms and their juices to a bowl and keep warm.

- Wipe the pan clean. Add the remaining 1½ tablespoons oil over moderate heat. Add the garlic and the chicken and stir-fry for about 2 to 3 minutes until the meat turns white. Add the chicken stock and mushrooms and cook for about 3 minutes until all the ingredients are cooked. Transfer to a serving plate, garnish with the coriander and serve.

Barbecued Five-spice Chicken
ga ngu vi huong

THE BEST FIVE-SPICE chicken I have had in Vietnam was made by a street-food vendor in the port town of Hoi An in the central region. The vendor used a spice mix of freshly toasted star anise and turmeric. When she grilled the chicken, the whole neighbourhood was perfumed with the most enticing fragrance. This is my version of that dish. It's great with Vietnamese Fried Rice (see page 155) and Cucumber Salad (see page 86).

Serves 4
1 whole chicken, about 1.125 kg (2½ lb), preferably free
   range, rinsed
3 tablespoons vegetable oil
2 tablespoons soy sauce
3 tablespoons minced ginger
2 tablespoons minced garlic
2 tablespoons sugar
2 teaspoons ground turmeric
1 teaspoon Chinese five-spice powder (see Glossary page
   260)
½ tablespoon sea salt
4 whole star anise, lightly toasted in a dry pan for
   3 minutes, pounded or ground into a fine powder
125 ml (4 fl oz) Soy-lime Dipping Sauce (see page 27)

- Cut the chicken into 6 pieces and make 1 or 2 slashes in each piece for faster cooking. Trim and discard any excess fat. Pat the chicken dry.

- In a bowl, combine the oil, soy sauce, ginger, garlic, sugar, turmeric, five-spice powder and salt. Stir well to blend. Add the chicken pieces and turn several times to coat them evenly. Marinate in the refrigerator for at least 4 hours.

- Start a barbecue or preheat a grill to moderate heat. Thirty minutes before cooking, add the freshly toasted star anise powder to the marinated chicken, turning so the meat is coated evenly.

- Place the chicken, skin side up, on the grill. Cook for 10 minutes, then turn over and grill for another 10 minutes until the chicken is cooked and the juices run clear, depending on the thickness. While grilling, move the chicken pieces around so that they cook evenly. Transfer the chicken to a serving platter and serve with the dipping sauce.

Braised Duck with Pineapple
vit nau thom

AT MY GRANDMOTHER'S house, this dish often appears during *do ong noi* (paternal grandfather's death anniversary). My aunts think it's an adaptation of duck *à l'orange*, one of many dishes left behind from the French colonial days. Since oranges, except for the green-skinned variety, are not grown in Vietnam, pineapples are used.

Serves 6

3 shallots, minced

3 garlic cloves, minced

1 tablespoon fish sauce

2 tablespoons soy sauce

1 teaspoon sea salt, or to taste

½ teaspoon freshly ground black pepper

1 whole duck, excess fat trimmed, cut into 8 pieces

1 ripe pineapple

2 tablespoons vegetable oil

1 onion, cut into thin wedges

2 carrots, peeled and cut on the diagonal into 1.5 cm
   (⅔ inch) slices

2 tablespoons dark rum
5 sprigs of coriander

- Combine the shallots, garlic, fish sauce, soy sauce, salt and pepper in a large bowl. Add the duck and turn to coat the meat evenly. Cover and marinate for at least 4 hours but preferably overnight.

- Peel the pineapple and cut in half lengthways. Save one half for another use. Cut the remaining half in two and remove the core. Cut crossways into 5 mm (¼ inch) thick slices. Set aside half of the pineapple slices. Finely chop the other half. Using your hands, squeeze the finely chopped pineapple over a strainer into a bowl, extracting as much juice as possible. Reserve the juice.

- Heat I tablespoon of the vegetable oil in a frying pan over high heat. Add the reserved pineapple slices and sear for 2 to 3 minutes on each side until the edges are slightly browned. Remove from the heat and drain on paper towels.

- Wipe the pan clean. Heat the remaining I tablespoon oil in the pan over moderate heat. Add the duck, skin side down (do not crowd the pan), and cook for about 3 to 4 minutes until slightly browned. If necessary, cook in batches.

- Transfer the duck and any marinating liquids to a pot and add the reserved pineapple juice. Add enough water to cover the duck. Bring the liquid to a boil, then reduce the heat. Simmer for 20 minutes. While the duck cooks, skim the surface of any foam or fat.

- Add the onion, carrots and dark rum. Continue cooking for about 15 minutes until the duck and carrots are tender. Stir in the reserved pineapple slices and cook for 2 to 3 minutes until thoroughly hot. Transfer the mixture to a serving dish, garnish with the coriander and serve with steamed rice.

Broken Rice with Shredded Garlic Pork

com tam bi

THE PORK IS very tasty in Vietnam, especially when it's cooked as it is in this dish, which is served at market kitchens and street cafés all over the country. It calls for broken rice – the grains that break when the rice is milled. It's often served with a combination of pork toppings, from the basic *bi*, or shredded pork, to grilled pork chops, pork sausages and pork meatloaf. In this version, the pork skin, which is cooked and available at Asian stores, adds texture. However, the dish is also delicious without it. What makes this particularly enticing is the wonderful oil, dipping sauce and salad accompaniments. If you don't have broken rice, use regular rice. The texture is different but the flavours are just as delicious. Toasted rice powder is available at Asian stores.

Serves 2

400 g (14 oz) broken rice or regular long-grain rice

3 tablespoons vegetable oil

325 g (11 oz) pork shoulder, excess fat trimmed, cut into
    two 2.5 cm (1 inch) thick pieces

10 whole garlic cloves, peeled

2 handfuls of shredded cooked and frozen pork skin,
    rinsed in hot water and very well drained

1 tablespoon sugar

½ teaspoon sea salt

1½ tablespoons toasted rice powder (see Glossary
    page 267)

For the garnish:
125 ml (4 fl oz) Spring Onion Oil (see page 31)
125 ml (4 fl oz) Chilli lime Dipping Sauce (see page 29)
Cucumber Salad (see page 86)

- Rinse the broken rice. Place in a pan with 500 ml (16 fl oz) water. Bring to the boil, stir a few times, then reduce the heat to the lowest possible temperature. Cover and cook for 20 minutes. (If you use regular rice, use 560 ml/18 fl oz water and cook in a similar fashion.)

- Heat the oil in a frying pan over moderately low heat. Add the pork pieces. Cover and cook for about 5 minutes until the edges are golden. Turn the meat and add the garlic. Cook for another 5 to 7 minutes until the pork is just done. When the garlic starts to brown, remove and drain on paper towels. Remove the meat and drain on paper towels.

- Cut the shredded pork skin into 5 cm (2 inch) lengths and set aside.

- When the pork is cool enough to handle, cut into thin narrow strips about the length and width of a short matchstick. Place the shredded pork in a bowl. Finely chop the garlic and add it to the bowl. Add the pork skin, sugar, salt and toasted rice powder and stir to combine.

- To serve, place the hot broken rice in the centre of a plate. Top with the shredded pork and Spring Onion Oil (spring onions and a little oil). Drizzle with the dipping sauce and serve with the Cucumber Salad on the side.

Aunt Tam's Pork in Claypot
thit kho tieu

IF THERE'S SUCH a thing as Vietnamese comfort food, this would be it. Every cook has his or her own recipe for this delicious pork, but Aunt Tam's is my favourite. Cooked in a rustic claypot or sandpot, the meat is simmered with fish sauce and caramel sauce, which adds a distinctive sweetness and smokiness to the dish. Then a generous amount of black pepper is added at the end. For a thoroughly authentic menu, cook this in a claypot and serve it with Sweet-and-sour Prawn Soup with Fresh Herbs (see page 76) and a vegetable dish.

Serves 4
2 tablespoons fish sauce
1½ teaspoons Caramel Sauce (see page 33)
1 tablespoon sugar
225 g (8 oz) boneless pork shoulder, sliced into thin bite-sized strips
3 tablespoons water
1 teaspoon freshly ground black pepper
4 sprigs of coriander, cut into 2.5 cm (1 inch) pieces

- Combine the fish sauce, Caramel Sauce and sugar in a bowl and stir well to blend. Add the pork and marinate for 30 minutes.

- Place the pork and any of the marinating juices in a 900 ml (1½ pint) claypot. Bring to the boil, then reduce the heat to a simmer. Add the water and cook for about 7 to 10 minutes, uncovered, until the sauce is slightly thick. Stir in the black pepper. Remove the pot from the heat. Garnish with the coriander and serve in the claypot.

Vietnamese Rice Cake in Banana Leaves

banh chung

ALMOST SYNONYMOUS with Tet, the lunar new year, *banh chung* is a highly regarded food in Vietnam. It's said to have originated centuries ago when King Hung Vuong VI challenged his many sons that whoever came up with the best recipe for Tet would inherit his throne.

The eldest one, eager to impress his father, travelled far and wide to procure the most exotic recipes. But the youngest son, the shy and quiet one, stayed closed to home and cooked a dish based on a dream. A genie had told him to take sticky rice (which symbolized the earth), wrap it around a ball of mung bean paste (which represented the sun), then boil it for one day and one night. Upon tasting the dish and hearing the story, the king was so impressed he proclaimed his youngest son the heir to his throne and ordered the recipe to be shared with all commoners.

Since that day, *banh chung* has enjoyed a central place in Vietnamese culture – at the family table and on the ancestor worship altar. Since it's considered taboo to work or cook during the first three days of Tet, these cakes are usually made before the festivities begin. Serve this dish at room temperature with salt and pepper or reheat slightly in the microwave and serve as part of a meal.

Makes 1 cake or 4 servings
350 g (12 oz) sticky (glutinous) rice, preferably long-grain
1 drop of green food colouring (optional)
60 g (2 oz) dried split mung beans
¼ teaspoon salt

2 tablespoons chopped shallots
1½ tablespoons fish sauce
1 teaspoon ground black pepper
150 g (5 oz) pork shoulder, cut into 5 mm (¼ inch) thick
   chunks
1½ tablespoons vegetable oil
2 x 35 x 40 cm (14 x 16 inch) sheets of clingfilm plus extra
35 x 40 cm (14 x 16 inch) sheet of aluminium foil
2 x 35 x 35 cm (14 x 14 inch) pieces of banana leaf

- Place the sticky rice in a large bowl and cover with 7.5 cm (3 inches) of water. Stir in the food colouring, if using, and let the rice soak overnight. (Once soaked, the rice will double.) In a separate bowl, soak the mung beans for at least 4 hours. Drain both just before using and set aside in separate bowls. Add the salt to the rice and stir to blend.

- Combine the shallots, fish sauce, black pepper and pork pieces and let marinate for 30 minutes.

- Heat the oil in a frying pan over moderate heat. Add the pork pieces and all the marinade and stir for about 3 to 4 minutes, just until the meat is brown around the edges. Remove the pan from the heat and set aside.

- Using a steamer basket, steam the mung beans for about 10 minutes until they're soft. Remove from the heat and set aside.

- To make the packet, neatly lay down the wrappers in this order: 1 sheet of clingfilm (leave the other for use later), the aluminium foil, 2 sheets of banana leaves (one perpendicular to the other). Place one-quarter of the rice in the centre of the banana leaf, spreading it to cover a 13 cm (5 inch) square. Place half of the mung beans on top, then add the pork pieces. Cover with the remaining mung beans and place another quarter of the rice on top. Bring the narrow sides of the wrappers together. Fold the gathered edges over twice, then flatten against the packet. (You now have two open ends.) Fold one end over and hold the packet upright. Add half of the remaining rice, tapping it and pushing it down so that the packet will be an even square. Fold the end over and repeat on the other side.

- Place the packet with the folded sides down in the centre of the remaining clingfilm. Wrap tightly so that water will not seep into the packet during cooking.

- Tightly tie the packet with two parallel strings in both directions (as in a noughts and crosses pattern).

- Fill a large stockpot with water. Add the packet and bring to the boil. Reduce the heat to a simmer. Place a colander or something heavy on top of the packet to keep it submerged in the water. Cook uncovered for about 6 hours until done, adding more water as necessary. Remove from the heat and set aside to cool for 1 hour.

- To serve, cut the packet (without unwrapping) into 1 cm (½ inch) slices. Remove the wrapping and arrange the slices on a serving plate. Serve warm or at room temperature. If wrapped in clingfilm and refrigerated, the cake will keep for 1 week.

Shaking Beef
bo luc lac

FOR MOST FAMILIES in Vietnam, the dish that comes closest to a steak is *bo luc lac*, which is made by shaking the beef in a pan over high heat. Inspired by the French, who introduced and popularized beef, it can be served either as a snack or as part of a meal. I remember my sister Denise and I often ate this at a French country club where we used to go swimming after school. The salad, which was served with warm baguette, was always the highlight of our outing. We'd eat everything on the plate, finishing by taking bread and soaking up every single drop of the dressing.

To me, this dish makes an easy and delicious light supper in the summer. I like it with either bread or steamed rice.

Serves 4

1½ tablespoons fresh lime juice

1 tablespoon fish sauce

1 tablespoon sugar

2 Thai bird's eye chillies or ½ serrano chilli, chopped

1 tablespoon oyster sauce

2 teaspoons soy sauce

325 g (11 oz) beef sirloin or flank steak, cut into 1 cm
(½ inch) cubes

2 to 3 tablespoons vegetable oil

2 garlic cloves, sliced

¼ ripe pineapple, cut into bite-sized slices about 5 mm
(¼ inch) thick (optional)

25 g (1 oz) Asian basil leaves, cut in half

¼ red onion, thinly sliced lengthways

90 g (3½ oz) watercress, washed, picked over and torn into
bite-sized sprigs

1 ripe tomato, cut into
thin wedges

- Combine the lime juice, fish sauce, sugar and chillies in a large bowl. Set aside.

- Place the oyster sauce, soy sauce and beef in a medium bowl and toss to coat the meat evenly.

- Heat the oil in a large frying pan over high heat. Add the garlic and stir for about 5 seconds until fragrant. Add the beef and quickly stir-fry it for about 2 to 3 minutes until just charred on the edges. Add to the bowl with the lime sauce.

- Add the pineapple slices, if using, Asian basil and red onion to the beef mixture. Spread the watercress and tomato in an attractive manner on a serving platter. Arrange the beef mixture and all its juices on the watercress and serve immediately.

NOTE: Another way of presenting *bo luc lac* is to omit the lime dressing completely and serve the beef with a dipping salt mixture made with 1½ tablespoons sea salt, 1 teaspoon freshly ground black pepper and 1 tablespoon fresh lime juice.

Beef Stew with Star Anise and Basil
thit bo kho

IN VIETNAM, there are people who would travel great distances each morning just to get a perfect bowl of *thit bo kho*, an aromatic beef stew simmered with chillies and lemongrass and made with annatto oil, which gives it a reddish-orange colour. Although hearty, this dish gets its refreshing twist from the last-minute addition of fresh basil and onion. At breakfast, *thit bo kho* is served with a French baguette, but at other meals it's usually accompanied by noodles or steamed rice.

Serves 6

3 tablespoons vegetable oil

2 tablespoons annatto seeds (see Glossary page 257)

2 tablespoons chopped shallots

½ tablespoon chopped garlic

450 g (I lb) beef chuck, cut into 4 cm (I½ inch) cubes

750 ml (25 fl oz) fresh water, Chicken Stock (see page 38) or store-bought reduced-salt chicken stock, boiling

2 lemongrass stalks, lightly crushed with the flat side of a knife and cut into 7.5 cm (3 inch) pieces

2 tablespoons fish sauce

I tablespoon soy sauce

I tablespoon sugar

3 whole star anise

I tablespoon curry powder, Vietnamese Three Golden Bells brand if you can find it

2 teaspoons chopped fresh red chillies or dried chillies, or to taste

3 carrots, peeled and cut on the diagonal into I cm (½ inch) rounds, blanched in boiling water for 3 minutes and drained

25 g (I oz) Asian basil leaves

¼ small onion, sliced paper-thin

5 sprigs of coriander, cut into 5 cm (2 inch) lengths

- Heat the oil in a small saucepan over low heat. Add the annatto seeds, stir a few times and remove immediately from the heat. (The seeds should foam upon contact but not burn.) Let stand for 10 minutes, then strain the oil and discard the seeds.

- Heat half the annatto oil in a medium pan over moderate heat. Add half the shallots and half the garlic and stir for about 10 seconds until fragrant. Add the beef and stir for about 3 to 4 minutes until lightly seared. Add the boiling chicken stock, lemongrass, fish sauce, soy sauce and sugar and bring to the boil. Reduce the heat to a simmer. Cook for about 40 minutes until the beef is tender, skimming the top occasionally.

- While the beef is cooking, lightly toast the star anise in a dry pan over low heat for about 3 to 4 minutes until fragrant. Transfer to a mortar and pound to a fine powder. (You can also use a spice mill.)

- Heat the remaining annatto oil in a small saucepan over moderate heat. Add the remaining shallots and garlic, star anise powder, curry powder and chillies and stir for about 20 seconds until fragrant. Set aside.

- Fifteen minutes before the beef is done, add the carrots and cook until they are tender. Add the spice mixture and stir a few times. Stir in half the basil and transfer the stew to a serving bowl. Garnish with the remaining basil, onion and coriander and serve immediately.

Seafood

THE CANVAS TOPSAIL of our junk flaps gently in the wind and the bamboo rods clang against one another. Underneath the deck, the waves ripple and splash.

Never before have I been so enchanted by nature. We have been sailing since dawn, drifting and floating on the calm Ha Long Bay. Just an hour ago this magical body of water, located just off the coast of northern Vietnam, was blanketed with fog. Then, as the blurry red sun rose above the silvery surface of the water, the fog slowly disappeared.

As we drift along, hundreds if not thousands of limestone formations fade in and out of view – some clear, some in graduating shades of blue. No wonder this bay is named the Descent of the Dragon, where, according to one tale I often heard when I was a child, Vietnamese civilization was said to have originated.

In the beginning of time, so goes the tale, one hundred eggs were born to a dragon and a fairy. Fifty children went with the fairy mother and settled in the mountains and valleys where they cultivated rice. The rest followed the dragon father and conquered the sea. Growing up with such a tale, it's no wonder we're in awe of this panorama, especially when told we are *con rong chau tien* (children of the dragon and fairy).

As I look closely, I realize the formations do indeed look like the animals and objects after which they've been named – Fighting Cocks, Turtle, Rice Ball and Elephant. I can see now why Ha Long Bay is considered to be the Eighth Wonder. The mountains seem to jut right out of the sea and touch the sky. Grottoes are filled with amazing stalactites and stalagmites, creating stunning temples of nature.

We manage to reach one such temple by squeezing through a passage underneath a rock that leads to a lagoon. Once inside, I'm captivated by the stillness of the warm water, the continuous cliffs that surround it, and the silence that breaks only when birds move from one treetop to another. Suddenly a voice startles me.

'How about some delicious crabs?' shouts a woman from a small fishing vessel, her hands grabbing the edge of our boat. She must have choked off the motor before getting close. Many fishing families around Ha Long Bay spend their entire life at sea, making a living by selling their catch to tourists like us.

The woman's husband waves a huge crab at me. His two toddlers, bundled in warm clothes and faces darkened by the sun, stare at me intently.

'Please, help our family and buy this fresh fish and prawns. We just caught them this morning,' the woman pleads. The crew already brought plenty to cook a big lunch with, including mackerel, squid and clams, but I can't resist her offer. With these prawns, I can make a pot of exquisite Vietnamese seafood stew, flavoured with beer, lemongrass and dill. 'Okay,' I answer, 'we'll take them both.'

I can hardly contain my excitement as I pay for my purchases. I know that cooking and savouring this fresh seafood in this most breathtaking setting will truly be an experience of a lifetime.

Looking down at the fishing vessel, I can see the family watching us in such a poignant way. The couple stand motionless, their eyes fixed on us, their kids wrapped around their legs. Never mind the blue skies, the limestone peaks, the temples of nature. The family seems infinitely more interested in us than in anything else around them.

Seafood plays a critical role in the Vietnamese diet, thanks to the more than 3,000-kilometre-long coastline, stretching from the Gulf of Tonkin to the Gulf of Thailand, and all the rivers and tributaries that flow throughout the countryside. At any number of bustling fish markets, one can find all kinds of fish and shellfish – from the ordinary tuna and mackerel to the more exotic species such as angelfish, razor clams and seaworms.

While many types of seafood are prized, fish, eel, crab and prawns are the most commonly prepared. Fish – both saltwater and freshwater – are usually served whole, fried or steamed, and accompanied by a dipping sauce. When they are cut into smaller pieces, the bones and skin are left on to preserve flavour and moisture. At the Vietnamese table, it's acceptable to chew on a piece of fish and remove a bone or two, leaving them on the table. Shellfish and prawns are cooked with their shells on for the same reason. The Vietnamese believe simplicity is the best approach to freshly caught fish and shellfish, so most of the recipes in this chapter are very uncomplicated.

Seafood Stew with Lemongrass and Dill
lau bien

WHEN I FIRST had this delicious dish in Ha Long Bay, I was a little shocked. It came in a pot set on a table-top stove and it was filled with all kinds of seafood, including live prawns. When the broth boiled, the prawns started jumping. Our server said this was the only sure sign of freshness. Like the Chinese, the Vietnamese prize live fish and shellfish.

This version of *lau*, which is a fairly new creation based on the Chinese hotpot, has become quite popular in recent years. It's considered status food because it contains seafood that is cooked with beer or other alcohol. Try to get the freshest seafood you can and use very ripe tomatoes. You can serve this dish with rice or bread, which is great for soaking up the wonderful broth.

Serves 6
2 tablespoons vegetable oil
2 shallots, thinly sliced
2 garlic cloves, thinly sliced
½ teaspoon dried chilli flakes, or to taste
2 tomatoes, preferably vine-ripe, cut into large chunks
2 tablespoons fish sauce
I lemongrass stalk, cut into 7.5 cm (3 inch) pieces and lightly bruised with the flat side of a knife
500 ml (16 fl oz) Chicken Stock (see page 38)
125 ml (4 fl oz) water
125 ml (4 fl oz) light beer
4 Asian celery stalks or 2 regular celery stalks (leafy parts included), cut on the diagonal into 5 mm (¼ inch) thick slices
I bunch of fresh dill, leaves only, cut into 2.5 cm (I inch) pieces
110 g (4 oz) raw medium prawns, peeled and deveined
150 g (5 oz) skinless red snapper fillets, or any firm fish, cut into large chunks
225 g (8 oz) black mussels, scrubbed clean and debearded, or Manila clams

- Heat the oil in a medium pan over high heat. Add the shallots and garlic and stir for about 20 seconds until fragrant. Add the dried chilli flakes, half of the tomatoes, the fish sauce and lemongrass and stir for about 2 minutes until fragrant. Add the stock, water, beer, celery and half of the dill. Bring to the boil, then reduce the heat to low. Cover and simmer for 15 minutes.

- Add the prawns, red snapper, mussels and the remaining tomatoes and dill and cook for about 3 minutes until the fish turns white and the mussels have opened. Transfer to a large preheated bowl and serve immediately.

Tamarind

TAMARIND IS USED extensively in Vietnamese cuisine as a souring agent. It's sold in three basic forms – dried pulp (sometimes labelled 'candy') packaged in a 225 g (8 oz) or 450 g (1 lb) plastic-wrapped block; liquid concentrate; and fresh pods. The dried pulp is readily available at Asian stores and is quite convenient to use. To make tamarind juice, soften the pulp in warm water for about 30 minutes. Use 1 part tamarind to 3 parts water. If this is too sour, add more water. Put the mixture through a strainer, scraping the pulp to extract as much juice as you can. When buying this product, look for the 'sweet' tamarind, which is not as sour as regular tamarind. That way, you can use a larger amount to get more tamarind flavour without making the dish too sour.

There's not much sense in using the liquid concentrate when the dried pulp is available. If you are able to find fresh ripe pods, handle them as you do the pulp: scrape the flesh from the pods, soften it in hot water, then press through a sieve to extract the juice.

Tamarind Crab

cua rang me

MY AUNT Co Tam serves me this dish every time I'm in Saigon. It's a little messy to eat because you have to pick up the crab with your fingers and suck on the gooey sauce before cracking the shells, but it's well worth the effort. In fact, this hands-on approach is the proper etiquette for crab-feasting. In Vietnam, this dish is made with the sweet and meaty mud crab, but you can use whatever's available.

Serves 4
3 tablespoons vegetable oil
2 shallots, minced
I tablespoon chopped garlic
900 g (2 lb) fresh crab, cleaned, cut into 4 or 6 pieces
    and the liver reserved (see How to Clean a Crab on
    page 187)
2 to 3 tablespoons tamarind pulp, juiced (see page 185)
I½ tablespoons fish sauce
I tablespoon sugar
125 ml (4 fl oz) fresh Chicken Stock (page 38), store-
    bought reduced-salt chicken stock or water
2 spring onions, cut into 5 cm (2 inch) lengths
5 sprigs of coriander, cut into 5 cm (2 inch) lengths

- Place the oil in a frying pan large enough to hold all the crab pieces and heat over high heat until the oil is very hot. Add the shallots and garlic and stir for about 10 seconds until fragrant. Add the crab liver, reduce the heat slightly, and stir for 2 minutes. Add the crab, tamarind juice, fish sauce and sugar. Stir so that the crab is well coated with the sauce. Add the chicken stock and cover. Simmer for about 10 minutes until the meat of the crab turns white. (Add a little water if the pan gets too dry.) Stir in the spring onions. Transfer to a serving plate and garnish with the coriander.

How to Clean a Crab

IF YOU'RE A crab lover like me, it's helpful to know how to select a good live crab and clean it. While cooked crabs also work in the recipes in this book, live ones are better because the meat is fresh, firm and sweet. In Vietnam, crabs are only sold live.

Nho and Suong Pham, the husband-and-wife team who have been supplying fresh seafood to our Lemon Grass Restaurant since day one, personally handpick every crab that we serve. They look for those with very firm legs, a sign that they're meaty and juicy. Holding a crab with tongs, they press against the upper part of a leg. If it's very hard and doesn't give, it's a good crab.

To kill a crab, bring a pan of water to a rolling boil. Drop the crab in and cook for 2 to 3 minutes. When it stops moving, remove it from the water. (If you want to parboil the crab, let it cook longer, for about 10 minutes.) Set aside to cool.

To clean, turn the crab belly side up and remove and discard the 'apron' – the V-shaped flap on the bottom. Holding the crab firmly, pull the top shell away from the body. Remove the soft, yellowish liver located on the inside of the shell, behind the eyes. Called *gach*, it's a prized part of the crab that Vietnamese cooks use to enrich the flavour of a dish. Discard the sets of feathery gills in the body of the crab, then rinse with cool water. Snap off the legs and claws. Using a heavy knife, cut the body into 2 or 4 pieces, depending on the size. You can crack the claws and legs lightly, although I prefer to leave them uncracked because the meat remains more moist when cooked that way.

Salt-and-pepper Crab with Ginger
cua rang muoi

OFTEN CALLED salt-baked crab in restaurants, this dish of Chinese origin is traditionally made by first deep-frying the crab, then stir-frying it with garlic and ginger. In order to make it a bit lighter, I've eliminated the deep-frying step. Instead I simply parboil the crab, then add it to the stir-fry. For the best flavour, purchase crab – preferably live – at a reputable seafood market. When it comes to eating, don't be bashful. Use your hands, nibble on the garlic and ginger, and retrieve every morsel of meat from the crab that you possibly can. I can eat this at least once a week come crab season. Try serving this with a side dish of Spring Onion Noodles (see page 127) or just steamed rice and Cucumber Salad (see page 86).

Serves 2 as a main dish

2 tablespoons vegetable oil

2 garlic cloves, minced

I shallot, minced

2.5 cm (I inch) piece of ginger, peeled and cut into matchstick strips

1.125 kg (2½ lb) live crab, parboiled for 10 minutes, cleaned and cut into smaller segments, the liver reserved (see How to Clean a Crab on page 187)

2 teaspoons coarse sea salt

I teaspoon sugar

½ teaspoon freshly ground black pepper

I teaspoon soy sauce

2 spring onions, cut into 5 cm (2 inch) lengths

5 sprigs of coriander, cut into 5 cm (2 inch) lengths

- Heat the oil in a large wok or frying pan over moderate heat. Add the garlic, shallot and ginger and stir for about 15 seconds until fragrant. Add the reserved liver, stirring to break it up. Cook for 1 minute, sprinkling with 2 to 3 tablespoons of water if the pan is too dry.

- Add the salt, sugar, pepper, soy sauce and crab, and stir so that the crab pieces are evenly coated with the seasonings. Add the spring onions and cook for about 5 minutes until the crab is thoroughly hot. Transfer the crab and all the bits and pieces of the seasonings to a serving plate. Garnish with the coriander and serve with lots of napkins.

Southern-style Catfish in Claypot

ca kho to

TO ME, if there's one dish that best represents Vietnamese home cooking, it has to be this classic *ca kho to*. Made with catfish and fish sauce simmered in a claypot, it's a favourite at every family table. Originally a southern creation, it is now eaten throughout the country.

Every time our mother made this, my siblings and I would fight over the gooey, smoky sauce in the bottom of the claypot. Interestingly, many customers at our Lemon Grass Restaurant do the same thing. A claypot will enhance the flavour of this dish, but it's also delicious cooked in a regular pot. Serve it with steamed rice, a soup and a vegetable dish and you'll have yourself an authentic Vietnamese meal.

Serves 4

2 tablespoons sugar
1 tablespoon vegetable oil
1 garlic clove, minced
125 ml (4 fl oz) boiling water
3 tablespoons fish sauce
325 g (11 oz) fresh catfish or other firm-fleshed fish fillets, cut in halves or thirds
1 spring onion, cut into 2.5 cm (1 inch) lengths
4 sprigs of coriander, cut into 2.5 cm (1 inch) lengths
½ teaspoon freshly ground black pepper

- Place the sugar in a 900 ml (1½ pint) claypot and add just enough water to barely wet it. Heat for about 3 to 5 minutes over moderate heat until the sugar starts to turn brown. Stir once, then add the oil and garlic. Stir for 1 minute, then add the boiling water, fish sauce and catfish pieces. Turn the pieces so that they're evenly coated with the sauce. Reduce the heat to a simmer. Cook, covered, for about 5 minutes until the catfish is firm and almost done. Uncover, and continue to simmer for another 2 to 3 minutes so that the sauce is slightly thickened.

- Remove the claypot from the heat and garnish with the spring onion, coriander and black pepper. Serve immediately in the claypot.

Sea Bass with Lily Buds, Mushrooms and Cellophane Noodles

ca chung tuong

THIS DISH IS as delicious as it sounds. The soy-infused broth, seasoned with ginger, brings out the delicate flavours of the fish. In Chinese cookery, dried ingredients are prized for certain flavours and textures, as well as for the medicinal qualities that fresh foods don't have. In this dish, the *kim cham* (lily buds) add delightful chewiness and are said to be a mild pain reliever. The traditional way of preparing this dish is in a steamer (see page 198), but you can also cook it in a pan. Just prepare the aromatics and noodles, then add the fish towards the end so it doesn't overcook.

Serves 4

35 dried lily buds (see Glossary page 262), each tied into
  a knot

6 small dried black mushrooms (shiitake)

25 g (1 oz) dried wood-ear mushrooms, preferably the
  small black variety (optional)

25 g (1 oz) dried cellophane noodles (see page 124)

2 tablespoons vegetable oil

1 shallot, sliced

1 garlic clove, minced

½ teaspoon dried chilli flakes

½ teaspoon sugar

2 tablespoons soy sauce

170 ml (5½ fl oz) fresh Chicken Stock (see page 38) or
  store-bought reduced-salt chicken stock

2 x 175 g (6 oz) skinless sea bass fillets

5 cm (2inch) piece of ginger, peeled and cut into slivers

1 spring onion, cut into 5 cm (2 inch) slivers

5 sprigs of coriander, cut into 5 cm (2 inch) pieces

Freshly ground black pepper

- Soak the lily buds, black mushrooms, wood-ear mushrooms, if using, and noodles in hot water for 30 minutes. Drain and squeeze dry. Remove the tough knobs and stems from the mushrooms and slice into bite-sized pieces. Cut the noodles into 25.5 cm (10 inch) lengths. Set aside.

- Heat the oil in a pan over moderate heat. Add the shallot, garlic and chilli flakes and stir for about 10 seconds until fragrant. Add the sugar, soy sauce and black mushrooms. Stir a few times, then add the stock, wood-ear mushrooms and noodles. Quickly transfer the mixture to a deep casserole that will fit inside your steamer. Place the fish fillets on top, then sprinkle half of the ginger on the fish.

- Place the casserole on a steamer rack. Fill a wok or steamer pan with 7.5 cm (3 inches) water. Cover and steam over high heat for about 15 minutes until the fish is just done. Remove from the heat and garnish with the remaining ginger, the spring onion, coriander and black pepper. Serve immediately.

Fish with Fresh Tomato Sauce
ca chien sot chua ngot

HOT, CRISPY FISH topped with fresh, tangy tomato sauce. In Hanoi, these simple ingredients come together in such a delightful manner. What makes this dish so special are the vine-ripe tomatoes and the freshly harvested young spring onions from nearby villages. Prior to my trips, I had thought baby vegetables and greens were a uniquely Western phenomenon, but in Vietnam it's the only way many vegetables, especially the spring onions and aromatic herbs, are sold.

Cu kieu (pickled spring onion bulbs), a popular Vietnamese condiment, adds complexity to the sauce. It's available at Asian stores, but the dish will still be wonderful without it.

Serves 4
Vegetable oil
2 shallots, minced
1 garlic clove, chopped
1 teaspoon dried chilli flakes, or to taste
2 tablespoons pickled spring onions with juice, sliced

1 tablespoon fish sauce

½ tablespoon sugar

2 ripe tomatoes, cut into 7.5 mm (⅓ inch) cubes

2 teaspoons cornflour

150 g (5 oz) Chicken Stock (see page 38) or store-bought reduced-salt chicken stock

1 whole red snapper, about 900 g (2 lb), cleaned, with or without head and tail, scored with 3 slashes on each side, or 450 g (1 lb) sea bass fillets

1 spring onion, cut into 2.5 cm (1 inch) pieces

5 sprigs of coriander, cut into 5 cm (2 inch) pieces

Heat 2 tablespoons vegetable oil in a small saucepan over moderate heat. Add the shallots, garlic and chilli flakes and stir for about 1 minute until fragrant. Add the pickled spring onions and juice, if using, fish sauce, sugar and two-thirds of the tomatoes. Reduce the heat and simmer for 3 to 4 minutes.

- Combine the cornflour and stock. While stirring, drizzle the cornflour mixture into the sauce and cook until the sauce is thick enough to just coat the spoon. Remove the pan from the heat and set aside until ready to use.

- Into a frying pan large enough to hold the whole fish, pour 1 cm (½ inch) oil and heat it over moderate heat until it reaches about 180°C (350°F). Carefully add the fish and cook for about 5 minutes on each side until the meat turns white. (If using fillets, reduce the cooking time.) Remove and drain on paper towels. Transfer the fish to a serving plate.

- Add the remaining chopped tomatoes to the sauce and reheat. Spoon the sauce over the fish. Garnish with the spring onion and coriander and serve immediately.

Grilled Lemongrass Prawns
tom nuong xa

WHAT CAN BE more enticing than the aroma of sweet, plump prawns with lemongrass on the grill? It's a fragrance I often encounter at the market stalls in Vietnam, and it's always hard to walk by without surrendering to a plateful. Fortunately, this delicious dish is easily prepared at home and gets rave reviews from everyone, including children. Just make sure that the prawns are of high quality and the lemongrass is really fresh. Serve this as an appetizer or as a main dish with the prawns as the topping for Rice Noodles with Fresh Herbs (page 133).

Serves 4 as an appetizer

4 tablespoons minced lemongrass (see page 42)
1 teaspoon minced garlic
1 teaspoon soy sauce
1 teaspoon fish sauce
½ teaspoon ground chilli paste (see Glossary page 259)
Pinch of salt
1 teaspoon sugar
2 tablespoons vegetable oil
450 g (1 lb) medium raw prawns, peeled and deveined
4 x 25 cm (10-inch) bamboo skewers, soaked in hot water
    for 30 minutes and drained

• Combine the lemongrass, garlic, soy sauce, fish sauce, chilli paste, salt, sugar and oil in a bowl. Add the prawns and marinate for 15 minutes. Thread the prawns on the skewers and set them aside.

- Start a charcoal barbecue or preheat a gas grill to moderate heat. Just before serving, grill the prawns, turning the skewers, for about 2 to 3 minutes total, depending on the size, until just done. If you don't have a grill, trim the skewers and cook in a pan with a little oil on the stovetop.

Steamed Sea Bass with Soy Sauce, Ginger and Spring Onions

ca hap gung

WHENEVER I'M IN the mood for this dish, I head out to a fish market, pick out a live bass and have it killed and cleaned right on the spot. When a fish is that fresh, you want to serve it simply, as in this recipe. Any white-fleshed fish including red snapper or cod will work.

Look for the very young spring onions and use young ginger, with the smooth pinkish skin. The best way to cook this dish is in a Chinese aluminium steamer (page 198). If you don't have one, improvise: place a wire rack in a large pan (with water below the rack) and set your platter on top. Be sure the pan has a tight-fitting lid.

Serves 6
1 whole sea bass, about 900 g (2 lb), cleaned and patted dry
2 tablespoons sea salt

2 tablespoons vegetable oil
1 shallot, thinly sliced
2 tablespoons thin soy sauce, or to taste
1 tablespoon rice wine or
   dry sherry
60 ml (2 fl oz) fresh Chicken Stock (see page 38) or water
4 cm (1½ inch) piece of young ginger, peeled and cut into
   thin slivers
2 thin spring onions, cut on the diagonal into very thin
   slivers
3 sprigs of coriander, cut into 5 cm (2 inch) lengths
½ teaspoon chopped red chilli, or to taste (optional)

- Rinse the fish. Rub it with the sea salt inside and out, rinse again and pat dry. If you like, or if your steamer is small, remove the head and tail and use only the middle section of the fish. Place the fish in a heatproof dish and place on a steamer rack. Fill the steamer pan one-third full with water and place the rack in the pan. Cover and steam over high heat for about 12 to 15 minutes, depending on the thickness, until the fish flakes easily.

- While the fish is steaming, prepare the sauce: heat the oil in a pan over moderate heat. Add the shallot and stir for about 10 seconds until fragrant. Add the soy sauce, rice wine, chicken stock and half the ginger. Reduce the heat and simmer for 2 minutes. Remove from the heat and set aside.

- When the fish is done, turn off the heat and carefully remove the platter. Drain most of the liquid from the platter. Pour the sauce on top. Garnish with the remaining ginger, spring onions, coriander and chillies, if using, and serve immediately.

Chinese Steamers

THE STEAMER IS one of the best tools created for the Asian kitchen. It's ideal for steaming all different kinds of foods – fish, crab, vegetables or rice. There are two main types of steamers to consider: the modern two-tier aluminium steamer set and the bamboo steamer that requires a wok or a large pan to hold the water. I prefer the aluminium one (although I own both). The aluminium version, which is quite inexpensive and very practical, comes with a water pan, two steamer racks and a big dome lid. The perforated racks have sturdy handles and can be used as colanders, and the water pan can double as a pot. It's especially good for steaming whole fish or chicken, as well as for making desserts, such as sticky rice. It's important to purchase one that is big enough to hold a whole fish, 40 cm (16 inches) or larger.

The bamboo version is more traditional and attractive, but a large one can be difficult to find. The small sizes are most available and are more appropriate for steaming foods such as dumplings and other *dim sum* items.

Coriander Prawns in Claypot
tom kho to

Although this recipe is not Vietnamese, it's one of our family favourites. In the late sixties when our family lived in Thailand, our Thai nanny often spoiled us with this dish. It calls for simmering whole prawns with a generous amount of coriander, black peppercorns and ginger in a claypot. Just remembering the fragrance of this dish makes me hungry.

The shells add tremendous flavour and colour, so before you're tempted to peel the prawns, try them unpeeled first. At the Vietnamese table, it's perfectly acceptable to suck on the whole prawns, peeling and discarding the shells as you go.

Serves 4

1 teaspoon black peppercorns, lightly toasted, or
½ teaspoon freshly ground black pepper
3 garlic cloves, chopped
2 teaspoons chopped ginger
4 tablespoons chopped coriander
3 tablespoons vegetable oil
½ small onion, cut into thin wedges
225 g (8 oz) raw unpeeled prawns, slit through the back
and deveined
375 ml (12 fl oz) fresh Chicken Stock (see page 38) or
store-bought reduced-salt chicken stock
1½ tablespoons soy sauce
2 teaspoons sugar
1 tablespoon rice wine or dry sherry
2 teaspoons fish sauce, or to taste
2 teaspoons sesame oil
50 g (2 oz) bean thread noodles (see page 125), soaked in
hot water for 30 minutes, drained and cut into 30 cm
(12 inch) lengths
2 celery stalks, leaves included, sliced on the diagonal into
5 mm (¼ inch) thick pieces
3 spring onions, cut into 2.5 cm (1 inch) pieces

- Place the peppercorns, garlic, ginger and half the coriander in a mortar and pound into a coarse paste. (You can also grind the peppercorns in a spice mill, then chop the remaining ingredients by hand.)

- Heat the oil in a 1.75 litre (3 pint) claypot over moderate heat. Add the herb paste and stir for about 20 seconds until fragrant. Add half the onion and all the prawns and stir-fry for about 2 minutes until the prawns just turn pink. Transfer to a plate and keep warm.

- Return the claypot to the stove. Add 250 ml (8 fl oz) of the stock, the soy sauce, sugar, rice wine, fish sauce and sesame oil. Bring to the boil, then add the bean threads. Stir so the noodles are well coated with the sauce. Add the celery and remaining onion. Reduce the heat slightly and cook, uncovered, for 3 minutes. Stir in the cooked prawns, spring onions and the remaining stock and simmer for another minute or so until thoroughly hot. (The claypot retains heat for a long time so it's best to undercook slightly.) Garnish with the remaining coriander and serve immediately in the claypot.

Caramelized Garlic Prawns
tom rim man

WHILE GROWING UP in Vietnam, my aunts often made this dish using live freshwater prawns caught from one of the tributaries on the Mekong River near my grandmother's house. They actually went shopping at the riverbanks, waiting as the fishermen came to shore with buckets of live prawns. In this southern dish, the prawns are first stir-fried in oil and sugar and then seasoned with garlic and fish sauce. What makes it is especially delectable is the intense caramelized flavour and the savouriness of the shell-on cooked prawns. To enjoy this dish, just suck on the shells, peeling and eating as you go.

For a simple but satisfying country-style meal, serve this with steamed rice, a clear broth soup and a vegetable dish such as Chopstick Beans in Garlic (see page 234).

Serves 4
325 g (11 oz) raw medium prawns, unpeeled
2 tablespoons vegetable oil
1½ tablespoons sugar
1 garlic clove, chopped
1 shallot, chopped
4 tablespoons water
1 tablespoon fish sauce
¼ teaspoon salt
5 sprigs of coriander, cut into 5 cm (2 inch) lengths

- Lay the prawns on a chopping board. Holding a prawn down securely, use a sharp paring knife and carefully make a shallow cut through the shell in the back. Remove the black vein (but not the shell), and rinse. Clean all the prawns in this way. Pat the prawns dry with paper towels.

- Heat the oil in a frying pan over moderate heat. Add the prawns and sugar and stir for 1 minute. Add the garlic and shallot, stir for 1 minute, then add the water, fish sauce and salt. Reduce the heat and cook for about 1 minute or so until the prawns are done and the pan is almost dry. Transfer to a plate, garnish with the coriander and serve immediately.

Seared Sea Bass
with Ginger-lime Sauce
ca chien nuoc mam gung

TAKE ONE BITE of this dish and you'll be amazed at how the ginger and fish sauce can enliven the flavour of fried fish. At the market food stalls that serve *com binh dan* (inexpensive home-cooked foods), this classic dish is prepared with just about any small whole fish, including yellow-fleshed catfish, perch, mackerel and snapper.

What I love about this recipe is the cucumber garnish. It's a traditional Vietnamese touch, made by cutting the cucumber into long thin strands and soaking them in the sauce. It's actually quite a clever concept because without the cucumber garnish, the sauce would just sit on the plate rather than on the fish.

Serves 4
½ cucumber, unpeeled
250 ml (8 fl oz) Ginger-lime Dipping Sauce (see page 24)
60 ml (2 fl oz) vegetable oil
450 g (1 lb) skinless sea bass fillets, cut into 2 or 3 pieces
6 small whole garlic cloves

- Seed the cucumber and use a Japanese mandoline to cut it into long, thin strips about the thickness of angel hair (capellini) pasta. Add the cucumber to the dipping sauce and set aside.

- Heat the oil in a large nonstick frying pan over moderate heat. Add the fillets and carefully sear them for 3 to 4 minutes on each side, depending on the thickness, until golden and just done. Halfway into the cooking, add the whole garlic cloves and cook until soft. (If the fillets are thick, cover and cook for a few minutes more.) Remove the fish and garlic and place on paper towels to drain.

- Arrange the fillets on a serving dish. Scatter the garlic cloves on top. Remove the cucumber strips from the sauce and place neatly on the fish. Pour half of the sauce on top and serve the remaining sauce on the side.

Chilli Clams with Fermented Black Beans and Basil
ngheu xao tau xi

THE DISTINCTIVE FLAVOURS of ginger and fermented black beans in this dish can be traced back to its Chinese roots. The addition of the Asian basil, however, gives it a refreshing Vietnamese touch. Be sure to soak and scrub the clams clean before using them. For variations, try mussels and prawns. You can serve this as an appetizer or as part of a meal.

Serves 4
2 tablespoons vegetable oil
2 teaspoons chopped garlic
2 teaspoons minced ginger
1½ teaspoons fermented black beans, rinsed (see page 204)
6 Thai bird's eye chillies or 1 serrano chilli, cut into slivers, or to taste
50 g (2 oz) Asian basil leaves

I tablespoon oyster sauce
900 g (2 lb) clams, scrubbed
I teaspoon cornflour
60 ml (2 fl oz) Chicken Stock (see page 38) or water

- Heat the oil in a wok or large frying pan over high heat. Add the garlic, ginger, black beans, chillies and half the Asian basil leaves. Stir for about 10 seconds until fragrant. Add the oyster sauce and clams and stir several times.

- In a cup combine the cornflour and stock and stir into the pan. Cook for about 3 to 4 minutes until the clams are all opened. Stir in the remaining basil. Transfer to a serving plate and serve immediately.

Fermented Black Beans

CALLED *TAU XI*, this ancient Chinese seasoning is used to add pungent, savoury flavour to food. Fermented black beans (also called salted black beans or preserved beans) are sold in 450 g (1 lb) plastic bags, in cartons or in earthenware jars. Rinse them briefly to remove any gritty substances but don't soak them because that will diminish their flavour. Asian stores carry a variety of brands but I find that the Yang Jiang Preserved Beans with Ginger (by Pearl River Bridge) are the most aromatic and assertive in flavour if you can find them.

Fermented black beans will keep indefinitely if transferred to a clean, covered jar and stored in the refrigerator.

Steamed Mussels with Lemongrass
so hap xa

IN VIETNAM, one of the most popular ways of preparing mussels, clams and snails is to steam them with lemongrass or other aromatic leaves like ginger or guava, then serve them with a zesty and spicy dipping sauce. The traditional version calls for using a steamer, with the herbs added to the liquid. This modified version is a little simpler and yields a more intense flavour because the lemongrass is actually cooked in the stock before the mussels are added.

Serves 4 to 6
500 ml (16 fl oz) Chicken Stock (see page 38) or water
¼ teaspoon sea salt
3 lemongrass stalks, cut into 5 cm (2 inch) pieces and lightly bruised with the flat side of a knife
2 shallots, sliced
I red serrano chilli or other fresh chilli, seeded and cut into matchstick strips
900 g (2 lb) black mussels, scrubbed cleaned and debearded
125 ml (4 fl oz) Chilli-lime Dipping Sauce (see page 29)

- Place the stock, salt, lemongrass and shallots in a medium pan and bring to the boil over moderate heat. Reduce the heat, cover and simmer for 10 minutes.

- Add the chilli and mussels. Cover and cook for about 2 minutes until the mussels open. Transfer to a preheated large bowl and serve steaming hot, with the dipping sauce on the side.

Vegetarian Dishes

WHENEVER I COOK a vegetarian meal, I'm reminded of my grandmother – who is 102 years old at this writing – and of that special reunion at her home in the Mekong Delta.

It was only my second trip back to Quoi Son, my ancestral village, since the war had ended in 1975. We had barely finished unloading a special gift from the van – a sparkling lightweight wheelchair that I had wanted to give my grandmother for years – when a crowd of relatives came running out. The well-wishers surrounded us, hugging us and hanging on to our clothes as we stumbled towards the house. I looked up and saw my grandmother standing in the doorway, calling and beckoning us to come inside. She waved, her face beaming and her eyes – though drowned in tears – still shining bright.

We embraced and chatted. Except for a cut on her forehead from a recent fall, she was in good health. Had the whole village not prayed by her bedside, she confided, she might not have pulled through. As we talked, the well-wishers quietened down. Their mouths dropped as they admired what must have been the first wheelchair to roll into the village. 'Fancy!' 'Must be expensive,' said the onlookers as they touched and caressed the shiny chrome.

The commotion made my grandmother excited to try her new wheelchair. When her ninety-pound frame fell into the nylon seat, her eyes widened. She seemed a bit puzzled but quickly laughed, marvelling at how comfortable it felt. I placed her feet on the rest and started to push her towards the street. She giggled, but became nervous and fearful about falling into the potholes. 'I'll be careful,' I reassured her. I pushed her out to the front, then up and down the road where she's lived all her life. We rolled past the coconut plantations where she once worked, past the longan orchards that she helped plant, the ones that would later produce unusually big, juicy fruits.

She seemed overjoyed, her words barely understandable. Her bony arms flew, one moment pointing this way and another that. This village had been her home all these years, but only now was she able to see it again up close. The last time she had walked this land was more than two decades ago, before arthritis struck and left her practically immobile.

In the bright sunlight, my grandmother's face was pinkish-white. Her eyes squinted and her silvery hair glistened. Whenever the breeze blew her hair into her face, she seemed pleased as she pushed it behind her ears. She liked being out here. She loved the sun, the air, the feeling of movement. I tried to extend the moment, pushing the wheelchair slowly, step by step, basking in the happiness as it unfolded. I felt ecstatic, not only because I'd brought a meaningful gift but also because I was reunited with someone I've admired all my life.

When my grandfather died years ago at an early age, my grandmother was forced to raise seven kids by herself while running the family plantation. That twist of fate turned her into a vegetarian, in part because vegetarianism is a form of merit-making. In Asian culture, it's not uncommon for one to abstain from eating meat as a way to *duoc phuoc* (gain merit). In doing so, one's wishes would be granted. In my grandmother's case, she prayed for the well-being of her children, now made more challenging with the passing of her husband. To support all the kids, she had to work very hard. Even in her sixties she still went to the fields every day to harvest coconuts and other fruits. Despite her hard life and difficult circumstances, she remained compassionate, caring and generous.

Every time she visited our family in Saigon, she brought baskets of live chickens and ducks, fresh bamboo shoots, wild mushrooms and other vegetables from her garden. They were her gifts of love. Although she didn't eat meat, she spent endless hours in the kitchen, cooking up sumptuous meals. Then at night, she spoilt us even more, sharing fascinating and endearing stories about life on the coconut plantation.

She taught me that family is sacred, that food is love and love is food. Though I had a lot to say and thank her for, I felt awkward. I just kept my eyes on the wheelchair. My grandmother, too, didn't say much after that.

By the time I wheeled her back to the house, my aunts had finished cooking all my grandmother's favourites – salad rolls with jícama (see Glossary, page 261) and peanuts and basil, spicy lemongrass tofu and black mushrooms and bean threads in a claypot. While savouring the food, we chatted, joked and laughed with one another. But when my grandmother started to talk, the noise quickly subsided.

'That's a great wheelchair,' she said, almost whispering, as she pointed to the prized gift parked beneath the side porch. 'When I go, you all can take turns using it. It stays in the family.' Since that reunion, I've been back to Quoi Son several times, but I still yearn to share many more meals with my grandmother. I want to go for that walk again, she in that wheelchair and me by her side, strolling up and down her favourite road.

The Vietnamese have a high regard for vegetables, in large part because meat is too expensive to be consumed on a regular basis. But beyond that, we were raised with the notion that vegetables are just as important as meat proteins and starches. As kids we often heard our mother say, '*An rau cho mat va bo*' or 'Eat vegetables so you will be strong.'

We learnt to appreciate vegetables in every form imaginable – raw, cooked, pickled, salted and dried – and even as kids we were able to distinguish the different ways a vegetable could taste depending on how it was cut or prepared. For example, if the cucumbers were served with tender meat, they'd be cut thick for contrast. If they were used as a garnish with fried fish, they'd be cut into long thin strands so they could easily soak up the sauce and flavour the fish. In other words, we learnt to treat and prepare vegetables with the same level of attention and care as one would treat meat.

This attitude also stems from the fact that many Vietnamese are Buddhists who practise vegetarianism on one level or another. At many temples and restaurants, cooks go to great lengths to make vegetarian meals look and taste as if they contain meat. Tofu is pressed, moulded and flavoured to resemble a whole fish or pork chops. Spring rolls are stuffed with shredded coconut, taro root, and tofu instead of the usual crabmeat and pork. One time, just when I thought I was digging into catfish in a claypot, it turned out to be pressed tofu that had been simmered in soy sauce! With the shortage of animal protein and the pervasiveness of the Buddhist influence in the culture, it is not uncommon to find many Vietnamese dishes eaten in two ways – *man* (with meat) and *lat* (without meat). Indeed, almost every meat dish in this book can be made vegetarian.

This chapter includes many of my favourite meatless recipes. Some are hearty noodle soups and noodle main courses that can be served by themselves; others are smaller side dishes that are meant to accompany other foods. When making vegetable dishes, try the many varieties of vegetables that are becoming increasingly available at Asian stores, farmers' markets and even supermarkets around the country. For example, the recipes for loofah squash and long beans are delicious, but they also can be made with just about any vegetables you like.

As you're cooking from the recipes, notice how the concept of building flavours that I talked about in chapter 1 – the layering techniques, the contrasting of textures and temperatures and the use of dipping sauces and garnishes – still all apply to vegetable cooking. In fact, when you don't have that savoury meat to work with, these techniques become even more important.

Salad Rolls with Jícama, Peanuts and Basil
bo bia chay

ONE OF THE biggest attractions in Saigon at night is the area around the main post office where the *bo bia* (salad roll) carts assemble. When the weather is warm, nothing is better than to sit on a low stool and watch the world go by while snacking on these delicious rolls. Unlike the more common *goi cuon*, which are stuffed with room-temperature prawns and pork, these rolls are typically made to order, so that the filling is slightly warm.

The original recipe calls for Chinese sausage, which I've replaced here with tofu and eggs. If you want to make the dish vegan, omit the eggs. This is a great do-it-yourself finger food and is wonderful for outdoor events. Simply place the ingredients on a table and invite guests to make their own rolls. Note that this dish is not served with any sauce because the hoisin sauce is added to the rolls during assembly. Serve this as a snack or appetizer.

Makes about 24 rolls
4 tablespoons vegetable oil
2 eggs
I teaspoon sea salt
2 tablespoons chopped shallot
I tablespoon soy sauce
I jícama, peeled and cut into matchstick strips
I carrot, peeled and cut into matchstick strips
125 ml (4 fl oz) water
60 ml (2 fl oz) hoisin sauce (see Glossary page 261)
I tablespoon ground chilli paste (see Glossary page 259),
　　or to taste
24 x 15 or 20 cm (6 or 8 inch) dried rice paper rounds plus
　　extras, see page 108
I head green-leaf lettuce,
　　washed, drained and cut into 2.5 x 7.5 cm (1 x 3 inch)
　　pieces
175 g (6 oz) piece of tofu, seared and cut into thin strips
　　(see page 215)
30 g (1 oz) Asian basil leaves
50 g (2 oz) chopped Roasted Peanuts (see page 34)

• Heat I tablespoon of the oil in a large nonstick pan over moderate
heat. In a bowl, combine the eggs and a pinch of salt and beat well.
When the pan is hot, pour in half the beaten eggs and quickly swirl to
cover the bottom of the pan. Cook for about I minute until firm. Flip
the egg crêpe and cook for another minute. Transfer the crêpe to a
plate. Repeat with the remaining egg batter. When the crêpes are cool
enough to handle, cut into thin strips and set aside.

- Heat the remaining 3 tablespoons oil in a large pan over high heat. Add the shallot and stir for about 1 minute until fragrant. Add the soy sauce, jícama, carrot, water and the remaining salt. Cook, uncovered, for about 15 to 20 minutes until the vegetables are soft. Transfer the vegetables to a dish.

- Combine the hoisin sauce and chilli paste in a small bowl and set aside. Set up a work station by placing the ingredients in the order in which they will be needed: rice papers, egg strips, lettuce, jícama mixture, tofu, hoisin mixture, basil, peanuts.

- Fill a large bowl with hot water. Cover a chopping board with a damp towel and place it next to the bowl. Working with 2 rice paper rounds at a time, dip one, edge first, into the hot water and turn for about 10 seconds to wet it completely. Lay the round down on the towel. Repeat with the other round and place it next to the first. (This allows you to work with one while the second sets.)

- Neatly place on the bottom third of the first round a few strips of egg crêpe, 1 piece of lettuce, 2 tablespoons jícama mixture (no juice), 2 pieces of tofu, ½ teaspoon hoisin sauce mix, 2 or 3 basil leaves and a sprinkling of peanuts. Make sure the filling is neatly stacked. Fold the bottom edge over the filling, tuck in the sides and roll into a cylinder. A perfect *bo bia* is about 2.5 cm (1 inch) wide and 10 cm (4 inches) long. Repeat with the remaining ingredients. Serve the rolls whole or cut in half.

Salad Rolls with Tofu and Mushrooms
goi cuon chay

GOI CUON CHAY relies a great deal on how the mushrooms are prepared. To make this a stand-out dish, be sure the pan is extremely hot before adding the onions and mushrooms. If the soy sauce sizzles and caramelizes upon contact, you did it right.

You can prepare these rolls a couple of hours in advance and cover them with a damp towel or wrap them in clingfilm until ready to serve. Do not refrigerate them, as the wrappers will get dry and hard.

Serves 6 to 8 as an appetizer

2 tablespoons vegetable oil

2 shallots, sliced

¼ onion, thinly sliced lengthways

6 dried Chinese black mushrooms (shiitake), soaked in warm water for 30 minutes, drained and thinly sliced

1 tablespoon soy sauce, or to taste

1 teaspoon sugar

8 x 30 cm (12 inch) dried rice paper rounds plus some extra

1 small head red-leaf lettuce, leaves separated and washed

110 g (4 oz) *bun* (rice vermicelli) boiled for 4 to 5 minutes, rinsed and drained (see page 124)

1 carrot, peeled, cut into matchstick strips and blanched

110 g (4 oz) tofu, seared (see page 215) and cut into strips about 5 mm (¼ inch) thick

90 g (3½ oz) bean sprouts
250 ml (8 fl oz) Vietnamese Bean Dipping Sauce (see page 28) or Soy-lime Dipping Sauce (see page 27)
50 g (2 oz) Asian basil or mint leaves (tops reserved for garnish, optional)

- Heat the oil in a pan over high heat. When the pan is very hot, add the shallots and onion and stir for about 20 seconds until fragrant. Add the mushrooms and stir vigorously. Create a well in the centre of the mixture. Add the soy sauce and sugar and stir for about 30 seconds until fragrant. Transfer to a bowl and set aside.

- Set up a work station by placing all the ingredients in the order in which they will be needed: rice papers, lettuce, rice vermicelli, carrots, mushroom mixture, tofu, bean sprouts and basil leaves.

- Fill a large bowl with hot water. (Also keep some nearby to add to the bowl when the water cools.) Cover a chopping board with a damp towel. Working with 2 rice paper rounds at a time, dip one, edge first, into the hot water and turn for about 10 seconds to wet it completely, taking care not to burn yourself. Lay the round down on the towel and pull to remove any wrinkles. Repeat with the other round and place it next to the first. (This allows you to work with one while the second round sets.)

- Tear a lettuce leaf in half lengthways and place it on the bottom third of the rice round. Place 2 tablespoons rice vermicelli, 4 carrot strips, 1 tablespoon mushroom mixture, 2 tofu strips, 2 tablespoons bean sprouts and 4 or 5 basil leaves on the lettuce. Make sure the ingredients are evenly spread out.

- Fold the bottom edge over the filling, fold in the sides and roll into a tight cylinder. The rolls should be about 2.5 cm (1 inch) wide and 10 to

13 cm (4 to 5 inches) long. Repeat with the remaining rice papers and filling ingredients. To serve, cut the rolls into 2 or 4 equal pieces and place them cut side up on a plate. Serve with the dipping sauce of choice on the side. If you like, garnish with the basil or mint sprig tops.

Tofu

SINCE ANCIENT TIMES, tofu and other forms of soy have been regarded as essential foods. They provide not only the necessary amino acids, vitamins and minerals, but also other hormone-like chemicals that researchers now say can help combat cancer and illnesses related to high cholesterol and menopause.

Although tofu by itself is neutral-tasting, it is highly versatile and easily adaptable to sautéing, stir-frying, steaming, simmering or grilling. It can also be puréed for use in sauces and dips. The most common form is fresh tofu that is sold packed in water. Pressed tofu, fermented tofu and tofu skins are other forms of this soy product.

In the West, fresh tofu is available in three textures – soft, medium and firm. Soft tofu is used in soups and steamed dishes, while medium and firm tofu are best in stir-fries and braised dishes and for stuffing. A fourth but not as popular kind is silken tofu, which is served as a dessert, often with a light ginger-flavoured syrup. Unless otherwise specified, use medium-texture tofu for the recipes in this book.

At Asian stores, you can often find deep-fried tofu, which is how a lot of tofu is typically sold and eaten. Many stir-fry and simmering recipes call for precooked tofu because it holds up better and adds flavour to the dish. One way to precook tofu at home is to sear it, which I actually prefer because it's less oily. *To sear tofu*: Cut the tofu slab into 2 or 3 manageable pieces and pat dry. Heat about 2 to 3 tablespoons vegetable oil in a nonstick pan over moderate heat. Add the tofu in one layer and cook for about 5 minutes, turning once, until golden. Drain on paper towels, then cut into the desired size and shape as directed in the recipe.

Another delicious product made from soybeans is *tau hu ky*, or dried bean curd skin (also called dried bean curd sticks). It's made by simmering soy milk until a very thin film forms on top. At one tofu factory in Vinh Long that I visited, the tofu maker used a long, thin bamboo stick to lift the skins on to a clothesline. After several hours, the skins became dried and stiff, taking on the shape of a pair of tongs (hence the name 'sticks').

Available at Asian stores in the dried-food section, *tau hu ky* is cream coloured, about 30 cm (12 inches) long and sold in plastic packages. To use, first soak them in warm water for about 30 minutes, depending on the brand and thickness, and then cut into smaller pieces and add to stews or soups. Like tofu, dried bean curd is delicate-tasting but has a remarkable ability to soak up flavour and impart a unique savouriness to food. It's also available as sheets, which make wonderful wrappers and fillings for dishes such as vegetarian sausages.

Cucumber and Tofu Salad
goi chay

THIS IS THE vegetarian version of a popular salad made with dried jellyfish. While it may sound unusual, it's really a very delicious salad,

with the jellyfish adding a subtly flavoured crunch. This recipe calls for
tau hu ky (dried bean curd skin) and seared tofu instead. Use small
pickling cucumbers, as they're very crisp and take well to blanching.

Serves 4
1 medium carrot, peeled
450 g (1 lb) pickling cucumbers or gherkins, unpeeled
4 tablespoons rice vinegar
3 tablespoons sugar
2 Thai bird's eye chillies, cut into thin rings
½ teaspoon sea salt
2 tablespoons vegetable oil
¼ onion, thinly sliced
2 pieces of dried bean curd skin, soaked in cold water for
**   15 minutes, drained and cut into 1 cm (½-inch) pieces**
2 teaspoons soy sauce
175 g (6 oz) piece of tofu,
**   seared (see page 215) and sliced**
30 g (1 oz) Asian basil leaves plus a few sprigs
3 tablespoons white sesame seeds, lightly toasted
3 tablespoons whole Roasted Peanuts (see page 34)
2 tablespoons Fried Shallots (see page 32)

• Bring a pan of water to a rolling boil. Cut the carrot into bean sprout-
  sized strips. Cut the cucumbers into slightly thicker strips. Place the
  vegetable strips in a sieve with a handle and lower them into the boiling
  water. Blanch for just 5 seconds, remove, rinse under cold water, and
  squeeze gently to remove the excess water.

• Combine the vinegar, sugar, chillies and salt in a large bowl and mix
  well. Add the carrot and cucumber strips to the bowl and marinate for
  10 minutes.

- Heat the oil in a frying pan over moderate heat. Add the onion and stir for about 20 seconds until fragrant. Add the dried bean curd skin and soy sauce and stir for 30 seconds. Remove from the heat and set aside to cool.

- Add the bean curd skin, tofu, basil leaves, sesame seeds, peanuts and shallots to the bowl and toss well. Transfer to a serving dish and garnish with the basil sprigs.

Vegetarian Pho Noodle Soup
pho chay

WHEN I FIRST started writing about *pho*, I received a lot of mail and calls from readers asking about a vegetarian version. At first I was quite apprehensive, wondering how I could come up with such a recipe when the dish is so quintessentially beef oriented. But after much thought, I decided to use the approach that the nuns in Vietnam often resort to – when in doubt, use black mushrooms and tofu as meat substitutes. As with beef *pho*, the success of this soup depends on the garnishings: the paper-thin onions, the spring onions, the coriander, the Asian basil and the chillies.

Serves 4 as a main dish

For the broth:
3 celery stalks, cleaned and cut into 10 cm (4 inch) pieces
4 carrots, peeled and cut in half

6 medium dried Chinese black mushrooms (shiitake),
　soaked in warm water for 30 minutes and drained
5 cm (2 inch) piece of ginger, cut in half lengthways, lightly
　bruised with the flat side of a knife and charred (see
　page 53)
2 onions, charred (see page 53)
60 ml (2 fl oz) light soy sauce (see page 36)
½ tablespoon salt, or to taste
4 whole star anise, lightly toasted in a dry frying pan
4 whole cloves, lightly toasted in a dry frying pan

For the noodle assembly:
450 g (1 lb) dried 1 mm (⅟₁₆ inch) wide rice sticks, cooked,
　drained and rinsed (see page 125)
225 g (8 oz) tofu, seared (see page 215) and cut into 5 mm
　(¼ inch) thick slices
3 spring onions, cut into thin rings
½ bunch of coriander, chopped
450 g (1 lb) bean sprouts
12 sprigs of Asian basil
3 Thai bird's eye chillies or 2 serrano chillies, cut into thin
　rings
6 lime wedges

Make the broth: Bring 3.5 litres (6 pints) of water to the boil in a stockpot. Add the celery, carrots, mushrooms and charred ginger and onions and simmer for 2 hours.

• Thirty minutes before the broth is done, add the soy sauce and salt. Place the star anise and cloves in a spice bag and add to the broth. Simmer for 30 minutes, then remove and discard. (Simmering the spices any longer will make the broth too pungent.) Using a slotted spoon, remove the black mushrooms. Remove the chewy stems and slice the caps into strips.

- To serve, place the cooked noodles in 4 preheated bowls. (If the noodles are not hot, reheat in a microwave or dip briefly in boiling water.) Divide the tofu and mushrooms evenly among the bowls. Pour a generous amount of hot broth over the noodles and garnish with spring onions and coriander. Invite guests to garnish their bowls with bean sprouts, basil, chillies and squeezes of lime before eating.

Vegetable Curry
ca ri chay

SOME OF THE best vegetarian curries in Vietnam are those made at the temples. I think this has to do with two factors – the ingredients are often grown in the temple grounds and the nuns who prepare the curries are very serious cooks. Just imagine how a curry would taste if you could grate a freshly picked coconut to make coconut milk, grow your own sweet potatoes and toast your own curry spices!

For this recipe, use the Vietnamese curry powder called Golden Bells if you can find it. It's milder (having less cumin and fewer fennel seeds) and won't overwhelm the lemongrass and ginger. The bean curd skin enhances the savouriness of the dish and is a real find for vegetarian cooks. For interesting variations, try different vegetable combinations here, such as taro, cauliflower and yard long beans.

Serves 4

2 tablespoons vegetable oil

2 shallots, chopped

2 garlic cloves, chopped

2 to 3 tablespoons Vietnamese curry powder

2 teaspoons ground chilli paste or to taste (see Glossary
   page 259)

2 tablespoons soy sauce

½ teaspoon sea salt

2 teaspoons sugar

500 ml (16 fl oz) unsweetened coconut milk

½ teaspoon ground turmeric

250 ml (8 fl oz) water

2 pieces of dried bean curd skin, soaked in cold water for
   30 minutes, drained and cut into 2.5 cm (1 inch) pieces

1 lemongrass stalk, cut into 7.5 cm (3 inch) lengths and
   lightly bruised with the flat side of a knife

2.5 cm (1 inch) piece of ginger, peeled and cut into 3 slices

1 carrot, peeled and cut into 1 cm (½ inch) rounds

½ onion, cut into wedges

1 sweet potato, cut into 2.5 cm (1 inch) cubes

½ head cauliflower, cut into bite-sized florets

1 tomato, cut into thin wedges

5 sprigs of coriander, cut into 5 cm (2 inch) lengths

- Heat the oil in a large pan over moderate heat. Add the shallots, garlic
  and curry powder and stir for about 20 seconds until fragrant. Add the
  chilli paste, soy sauce, salt, sugar, coconut milk, turmeric, water, bean
  curd skins, lemongrass and ginger. Let the mixture come to the boil,
  then reduce the heat to low. Add the carrot and onion, then cover and
  simmer for 5 minutes.

- Add the sweet potato, cauliflower and tomato and cook for another 15 minutes until the vegetables are tender. Transfer to a serving bowl and garnish with the coriander. Serve immediately with steamed rice.

Spicy Lemongrass Tofu
dau hu xa ot

WHILE TRAVELLING on a train one time to the coastal town of Nha Trang, I sat next to an elderly nun. Over the course of our bumpy eight-hour ride, she shared stories of life at the temple and the difficult years after the end of the war when the Communist government cracked down on religious factions. Towards the end of our chat, she pulled out a bag of food she'd prepared for the trip. It was tofu that had been cooked in chillies, lemongrass and *la lot*, an aromatic leaf also known as pepper leaf. When she gave me a taste, I knew immediately that I had to learn how to make it. This is my rendition of that fabulous dish. Make sure to pat the tofu dry before marinating it and use very fresh lemongrass. I always love serving this to friends who think tofu dishes are bland.

Serves 4
2 lemongrass stalks, outer layers peeled, bottom white part thinly sliced and finely chopped
1½ tablespoons soy sauce
2 teaspoons chopped Thai bird's eye chillies or another fresh chilli
½ teaspoon dried chilli flakes

1 teaspoon ground turmeric

2 teaspoons sugar

½ teaspoon salt

350 g (12 oz) tofu, drained, patted dry and cut into 2 cm
  (¾ inch) cubes

4 tablespoons vegetable oil

½ onion, cut into 2 mm (⅛ inch) slices

2 shallots, thinly sliced

1 teaspoon minced garlic

4 tablespoons chopped Roasted Peanuts (see page 34)

10 *la lot*, or pepper leaves (see page 43), shredded, or 20 g
  (¾ oz) Asian basil leaves

- Combine the lemongrass, soy sauce, chillies, chilli flakes, turmeric, sugar
  and salt in a bowl. Add the tofu cubes and turn to coat them evenly.
  Marinate for 30 minutes.

- Heat half of the oil in a 30 cm (12 inch) nonstick frying pan over
  moderately high heat. Add the onion, shallot and garlic and stir for
  about 1 minute until fragrant. Reduce the heat to low and cook for about
  3 minutes until the onions are soft. Transfer to a plate and keep warm.

- Wipe the pan clean and heat the remaining oil over moderate heat.
  Add the tofu mixture and, using chopsticks or wooden spoons, turn for
  about 4 to 5 minutes so it cooks evenly. Add the onion mixture and
  cook, uncovered, for another 2 to 3 minutes. Add half the peanuts and
  all the pepper leaves.

- Remove from the heat and transfer to a serving plate. Garnish with the
  remaining peanuts and serve immediately with steamed rice.

Rice Noodles with Stir-fried Vegetables
bun chay

IT WAS OUR grandmother who first got our family interested in vegetarian food. Since she is a strict vegetarian, my mother would cook a special meal for her every time she came to stay with us in Saigon. After years of sharing many meals with her, my siblings and I grew fond of her vegetarian meals.

This popular dish is often served at my grandfather's death anniversaries and on other special occasions. *Bun chay* is great for entertaining because you can make the Rice Noodles with Fresh Herbs ahead of time, then stir-fry the topping just before serving.

Serves 4 as a main dish

1 recipe Rice Noodles with Fresh Herbs (see page 133)
2 tablespoons vegetable oil
½ onion, thinly sliced lengthways
½ teaspoon minced garlic
8 dried Chinese black mushrooms (shiitake), soaked in warm water for 30 minutes, drained, stemmed and sliced
2 tablespoons soy sauce
2 teaspoons sugar
3 tablespoons unsweetened coconut milk
1 small jícama, peeled and cut into matchstick strips
175 g (6 oz) tofu, seared (see page 215) and cut into 5 mm (¼ inch) strips
1 carrot, peeled, cut into matchstick strips, blanched for 1 minute and rinsed

80 g (3 oz) chopped Roasted Peanuts (see page 34)
250 ml (8 fl oz) Soy-lime Dipping Sauce (see page 27)

- Prepare the rice noodles according to the recipe on page 133. Divide them among 4 bowls for serving.

- Heat the oil in a large pan over high heat. Add the onion and garlic and stir for 30 seconds. Add the mushrooms, soy sauce, sugar, coconut milk and jícama. Stir, then reduce the heat slightly and cook for 3 to 4 minutes until the jícama softens. Add the tofu and carrot and cook for 2 to 3 minutes until all the ingredients are hot. Add a little water if the pan gets too dry.

- Divide the vegetable topping among the 4 bowls of noodles. Garnish each with 2 tablespoons peanuts. Invite each guest to drizzle 3 to 4 tablespoons sauce over the noodles and gently toss a few times before eating.

Vegetarian Claypot Rice with Ginger
com tay cam chay

IN THE COOLER months, one of my favourite things to eat is *com tay cam chay*, which translates as 'vegetarian hand-held rice'. It's sort of a Vietnamese pilaf, only cooked in a claypot. For this you can use any mushrooms available. To keep the rice moist, use fleshy vegetables like squashes. It's best to cook this in a large 2.65 litre (4½ pint) claypot (the rice steams better in a larger pot), but if you don't have one, a regular pot will do. For a complete meal, serve with another vegetable side dish and a simple soup.

Serves 4 with other dishes

250 g (9 oz) Thai jasmine or any long-grain rice, washed

3 tablespoons vegetable oil

½ small onion, thinly sliced

2 tablespoons minced ginger

1½ teaspoons Chinese five-spice powder (see Glossary page 260), lightly toasted in a dry pan

1 teaspoon minced garlic

½ teaspoon dried chilli flakes, or to taste

2 tablespoons soy sauce

¼ teaspoon salt or to taste

2 teaspoons sugar

6 small dried Chinese black mushrooms (shiitake), soaked in hot water for 30 minutes, drained, stemmed and halved

125 g (4½ oz) canned bamboo shoot slices, rinsed and drained

500 ml (16 fl oz) boiling water

1 courgette, cut into 5 mm (¼ inch) bite-sized slices, blanched for 2 minutes and drained

175 g (6 oz) tofu, seared (see page 215) and cut into 1.5 cm (⅔ inch) cubes

6 sprigs of coriander, cut into 2.5 cm (1 inch) pieces

125 ml (4 fl oz) Soy-lime Dipping Sauce (see page 27)

- Place the rice in a medium frying pan over low heat. Gently stir for about 4 to 5 minutes until it turns opaque. Set aside.

- Heat the oil in a **2.65 litre (4½ pint)** claypot over moderate heat. Add the onion, ginger, five-spice powder, garlic and chilli flakes and stir for about 10 seconds until fragrant. Add the soy sauce, salt, sugar, black mushrooms and bamboo shoots. Add the boiling water and the rice and stir a few times. Let the mixture come back to the boil, then reduce the heat to a low simmer. Cover and cook for about 20 minutes until the rice is done.

- Ten minutes before the rice is done, stir in the courgette and tofu and simmer until all the ingredients are cooked and thoroughly hot. Remove from the heat and garnish with the coriander. Serve from the claypot with the sauce on the side.

Black Mushrooms with Bean Threads in Claypot
nam kho

IF THERE'S A noodle that loves sauce, it's bean threads, also called cellophane noodles. I suggest pre-soaking these dried, clear strands so they don't absorb all of the cooking liquid. For an interesting twist, add ginger and other vegetables like lotus root, bamboo shoots or yard long beans.

This dish is best when prepared in a 1.75 litre (3 pint) or larger claypot but it's also delicious in a regular pot. For a complete meal, serve this dish with a salad or appetizer and a soup.

Serves 4 with other dishes

3 tablespoons vegetable oil

2½ tablespoons fermented soya beans (see Glossary
   page 260)

1 shallot, minced

½ small onion, cut into thin wedges

30 dried lily buds (see Glossary page 262), each tied into a
   knot, soaked for 10 minutes, drained

4 dried black mushrooms (shiitake), soaked in hot water
   for 30 minutes, stemmed and halved

3–4 wood-ear mushrooms, soaked in hot water for
   30 minutes, chewy centres removed, cut into pieces

½ teaspoon dried chilli flakes

2 teaspoons soy sauce, or to taste

2 teaspoons sugar

50 g (2 oz) bean threads, soaked in water for 30 minutes,
   drained and cut into 25 cm (10 inch) lengths

625 ml (20 fl oz) water

175 g (6 oz) tofu, cut into 2.5 cm (1 inch) cubes

125 g (4½ oz) bamboo shoot strips, blanched in hot water,
   drained

2 tablespoons chopped coriander

- Heat the oil in a 1.75 litre (3 pint) claypot over moderate heat. Add the fermented soya beans and shallot and stir for about 2 minutes until fragrant. Add the onion, lily buds, black mushrooms, wood-ear mushrooms, chilli flakes, soy sauce and sugar. Stir for 2 minutes. Add the bean threads, water, tofu and bamboo shoots. Stir gently, taking care not to break up the tofu or noodles. Reduce the heat to low, cover and cook for about 15 minutes until the vegetables are soft. Garnish with the coriander and serve in the claypot.

Mustard Greens with Garlic
cai xao toi

SOMETIMES THE BEST way to cook is the simplest way. In this recipe, you can use any Asian greens, such as Chinese mustard, Chinese broccoli, bok choy or water spinach. Serve this with roast chicken, steamed fish or claypot rice dishes.

> *Serves 4 as a side dish*
> **325 g (11 oz) Chinese mustard greens or another Asian green**
> **2 tablespoons vegetable oil**
> **5 garlic cloves, minced**
> **2 tablespoons oyster sauce or mushroom sauce**

- Cut off the stems of the mustard greens and cut them on the diagonal into 2.5 cm (1 inch) thick slices. Cut the leafy parts into 7.5 cm (3 inch) pieces.

- Heat the oil in a large frying pan or wok over high heat. Working quickly, add the garlic and stir until fragrant. Add the oyster sauce and mustard greens. Toss several times to coat the greens evenly in the sauce. Cook for 2 to 3 minutes until the greens are done but still green and crunchy. Remove from the heat and transfer to a serving plate.

Water Spinach with Tofu

rau muong xao

RAU MUONG, or water spinach (also known as morning glory or swamp cabbage), is a common vegetable in Vietnam. There it's harvested when the stems are still very young and tender and is stir-fried as in this recipe or simply steamed and served with a dipping sauce. During my visits to Vietnam, I often ate this vegetable for days in a row because it was such a great side dish to every meal.

Another popular way of preparing water spinach is to make 'curls' out of it. The hollow stems are split into long thin shreds. When soaked in cold water, they become crisp and crunchy and are used in salads or as garnishes for noodle soups. If you can't find water spinach, use regular spinach or substitute another leafy green. I think the flavour of this dish is even more intense when it's served cold.

> *Serves 4 as a side dish*
> **450 g (1 lb) water spinach**
> **2 tablespoons vegetable oil**
> **1 tablespoon chopped garlic**
> **1 teaspoon chopped fresh**
>   **Thai bird's eye chillies (optional)**
> **2 teaspoons fermented whole soya beans (see page 260)**
>   **or soy sauce**
> **Salt to taste**
> **175 g (6 oz) tofu, seared (see page 215) and cut into 1 cm**
>   **(½ inch) cubes**

- Trim and discard the chewy parts of the water spinach stems, 2.5 to 7.5 cm (1 to 3 inches) from the bottom. Cut the stems and leaves into 7.5 cm (3 inch) pieces.

- Heat the oil in a large frying pan over high heat. Add the garlic, chillies, if using, and fermented soya beans and stir for about 30 seconds until very fragrant. Add the water spinach and salt and cook for 2 to 3 minutes until tender. If the pan gets too dry, add 2 to 4 tablespoons water. Add the tofu, toss and transfer to a serving dish.

Twice-cooked Aubergine with Garlic and Basil

ca tim xao rau que

TO ME, there's something particularly enticing about the smokiness of aubergines cooked over a very hot fire. When I first had this dish in Hanoi, I was very impressed. Unlike many mushy aubergine dishes, this one stays firm and delicious, even after the aubergine has been stir-fried over high heat. I make this several ways, sometimes just with aubergine and at other times embellished with prawns and pork. Either way, it is satisfying, especially if you are able to find sweet, firm aubergines.

Serves 4 as a side dish
Vegetable oil
325 g (11 oz) Asian aubergine, preferably the small dark-purple variety, cut on the diagonal into 1.5 cm (⅗ inch) thick slices

2 garlic cloves, chopped

1 shallot, thinly sliced

3 Thai bird's eye chillies or 1 serrano chilli, chopped, or to taste

30 g (1 oz) Asian basil leaves, roughly torn

175 g (6 oz) tofu, drained and cut into 1.5 cm (⅔ inch) cubes

1½ tablespoons mushroom sauce

1 tablespoon soy sauce

75 ml (3 fl oz) water

- Heat 2 tablespoons oil in a frying pan over high heat and swirl to coat the entire surface. Add the aubergine slices in one layer (work in batches if necessary) and sear briefly for about 1 to 2 minutes total on both sides. Do not cook completely. Drain on paper towels and keep warm. Repeat with the remaining aubergine, adding more oil as necessary.

- Heat 2 tablespoons oil in a pan over high heat. Add the garlic, shallot, chillies, one third of the basil, tofu, mushroom sauce and soy sauce and stir gently for about 2 minutes until fragrant. Add the water and continue to cook for another 3 to 4 minutes until the sauce is slightly reduced.

- Add the aubergine slices and the remaining basil leaves and stir until the vegetables are thoroughly hot. Quickly transfer to a platter and serve immediately.

Loofah Squash with Mushrooms

muop xao

LOOFAH SQUASH (also known as silk squash or Chinese okra) is similar to courgette but has a slightly sweeter, earthy flavour. It resembles a long cucumber covered with ridges from one end to the other. Belonging to the same family as the vegetable used to make bath sponges, the edible loofah is harvested very young, long before those tough fibres develop.

In Vietnam, loofah squash, winter melon, fuzzy melon and kabocha squash (see Glossary page 261) are among the many vegetables used in stir-fries and soups. You can use any one of them in this recipe.

Serves 4 as a side dish
700 g (1½ lb) loofah squash
2 tablespoons vegetable oil
1 shallot, sliced
2 garlic cloves, minced
90 g (3½ oz) white mushrooms, cleaned and halved or quartered
1 teaspoon soy sauce
1 tablespoon vegetarian mushroom oyster sauce
2 spring onions, cut into thin rings
5 sprigs of coriander, cut into 5 cm (2 inch) lengths

• Cut each loofah squash crossways into 2 pieces for easier handling. Cut off the ridges and peel, taking care not to cut too deeply because most of the flavour is just under the skin. Cut on the diagonal into 2 cm (¾ inch) thick pieces.

- Heat the oil in a large frying pan over high heat. Add the shallot and garlic and stir for about 20 seconds until fragrant. Add the mushrooms, soy sauce and mushroom sauce and stir for 30 seconds. Add the squash and reduce the heat slightly. Cover and cook for 3 to 4 minutes until the squash is just softened. Stir in the spring onions and transfer to a serving dish. Garnish with the coriander sprigs and serve.

Chopstick Beans in Garlic
dau dua xao

THE VIETNAMESE CALL yard long beans *dau dua* (chopstick beans) for good reason. They're best when they're skinny (the width of a chopstick) and tender. In recent years I've seen other varieties in the West, such as purple and black, but the green ones are still the best. Use yard long beans as you would regular green beans. They're great in curries and stir-fries, or blanched and added to salads.

The traditional recipe calls for eggs and fish sauce, but if you want to make it vegan omit them both and add 2 teaspoons soy sauce.

Serves 4 as a side dish
2 tablespoons vegetable oil
1 garlic clove, chopped
1 egg, beaten
2 teaspoons fish sauce
1 teaspoon sugar

**450 g (1 lb) yard long beans, ends trimmed, cut into 7.5 to
  10 cm (3 to 4 inch) pieces, blanched in boiling water for
  4 minutes, rinsed in cold water and drained**
60 ml (2 fl oz) water
Pinch of salt
5 sprigs of coriander, cut into 5 cm (2 inch) lengths

- Heat the oil in a large pan over moderate heat. Add the garlic and stir
  for about 20 seconds until fragrant. Add the egg, fish sauce and sugar
  and stir a few times. Add the yard long beans, water and salt. Reduce
  the heat slightly, then cover and cook for about 4 to 5 minutes until
  done. Transfer to a serving plate, garnish with the coriander and serve.

Desserts and Sweet Drinks

CHI TU (Fourth Sister) is moving as fast as she can, filling up one bowl after another while her customers eagerly wait. It's hard to tell she's selling desserts because her stand looks no different from the savoury food stalls here at the Ben Thanh Market in Saigon. There are no signs of cakes or sweets, just big metal pots. Instead of holding soup or savoury dishes, they're filled to the rim with warm *che* (sweet puddings). '*Ngon lam em*,' she yells, telling me how delicious her pudding with fresh maize is. In fact, everything looks enticing – the young, green sticky rice pudding with taro root and coconut milk, the banana and tapioca stew and the mung bean pudding.

Chi Tu even has *che troi nuoc* (sweet dumplings in ginger broth), a dessert that my sister Denise and I used to love to eat as kids. Late at night, we would wait outside our front door for our favourite dessert vendor to come and serve us little bowls of this dessert. The dumplings were soft and warm and the mung bean filling inside was rich and creamy. Nothing could have prepared us better for a good night's sleep.

Like that vendor, Chi Tu serves most of her puddings at room temperature, although some can also be served hot or with ice. When served cold, they're mixed with coconut milk and ice and sometimes with tapioca strands. If you visit a *pho* shop, for example, you'll probably see diners finishing their noodle soups with tall glasses of red beans or white beans in sweetened coconut milk and crushed ice.

Besides puddings, the Vietnamese eat a lot of *banh* (cakes). Unlike the Western-style leavened breads and cakes, they're made with sticky rice or rice flour or tapioca starch and stuffed with ripe bananas, mung bean paste or shredded coconut, then steamed. Wrapped with banana or other leaves, they come in various sizes and shapes. Some are loaves, which can be sliced, and others are individual portion packages and triangles. Tea, the most common beverage, is often served with these *banh*.

Thanks to the French influence, our dessert repertoire also includes European-style cakes, pastries, breads and ice cream, although these items generally are served only on special occasions. Vietnamese coffee, another legacy from the French colonial days, is extremely popular and, because it's so rich and sweet, is certainly a dessert option.

Despite the variety of desserts available, the Vietnamese do not, except for special occasions, eat sweets right after a meal. Instead, we prefer to snack on them throughout the day and late at night.

You can serve the recipes in this chapter either way. To finish a meal, fresh fruit (such as ripe mangoes) or ice cream or sorbet are always good choices. If you're looking for something more traditional, try a pudding like Grandmother's Banana Stew with Tapioca Pearls (page 249). You can serve a small bowl right after dinner, or do what the Vietnamese would do – serve it a little later, when you have more of an appetite and the energy to truly enjoy it.

Sweet Dumplings in Ginger Broth

che troi nuoc

AT OUR HOME, my mother always prepared this dessert at Tet (Vietnamese New Year) and placed it on the ancestor worship altar as part of the celebration ritual. The dumplings are made with mung bean paste wrapped in sticky rice flour dough, then simmered in a ginger-infused broth. As a child, I especially loved the little 'pearls' made from leftover dough.

This calls for both glutinous, or sticky, rice flour and regular rice flour, which are two distinctly different starches. Some northern cooks prefer to use only the sticky rice flour, although I think it makes the dumplings a bit too chewy. The mung beans called for here are the dried skinless, split variety.

Serves 6

For the dumplings:
125 ml (4 fl oz) unsweetened coconut milk
60 ml (2 fl oz) water
Pinch of salt
90 g (3½ oz) dried split mung beans, soaked in warm water
    for 30 minutes and drained
235 g (8 oz) glutinous rice flour
175 g (6 oz) rice flour
250 ml (8 fl oz) hot water

For the broth:
225 g (8 oz) light brown sugar
5 cm (2 inch) piece of ginger, peeled and bruised with the
    flat side of a knife
625 ml (20 fl oz) hot water
3 tablespoons white sesame seeds, lightly toasted

- Make the dumplings: Place the coconut milk, water and the salt in a saucepan and bring to the boil. Add the mung beans and reduce the heat to low. While stirring occasionally, simmer for almost 15 minutes until most of the liquid has evaporated and the mung beans are soft. Remove from the heat. Whisk the beans until they're smooth. Set aside to cool.

- Shape the mung bean paste into 12 little balls about 1.5 cm (⅔ inch) in diameter. Cover and refrigerate until ready to use. (The balls are easier to handle later, when they're cold.)

- Place the glutinous rice flour and regular rice flour in a bowl. Stir in the hot water, a little at a time. Mix until the dough is well blended and sticky. Knead the dough for about 2 to 3 minutes. (The dough will be dense and stiff.) Place in a bowl, cover and let it rest while you prepare the broth.

- Make the broth: Combine the sugar, ginger and the hot water in a large saucepan. Bring to the boil and reduce the heat to very low.

- Roll the dough into a log about 6 cm (2½ inches) in diameter. Using a knife, cut it into 5 mm (¼ inch) thick slices. Flatten each piece so it's thin and wide enough to wrap around one of the balls of the filling. Place a mung bean ball in the centre and fold and seal the edges. With wet hands, roll the dumplings until they're smooth and round. Flatten the dumplings very slightly by pressing them between your palms. Make all the dumplings this way and set them aside until ready to cook. Roll leftover dough into pearl-sized balls.

- Bring a pot of water to the boil and add the dumplings and pearls. Cook for about 10 to 12 minutes until they are translucent and rise to the surface. Raise the heat under the ginger broth to medium. Using a slotted spoon, transfer the cooked dumplings and pearls to the ginger broth. Simmer for 10 minutes. To serve, place 2 dumplings and some pearls in a small bowl and ladle some broth on top. Garnish with the toasted sesame seeds and serve warm.

Vietnamese Fried Bananas with Ice Cream
chuoi chien voi kem

FRIED BANANAS ARE eaten all over Asia, either as a snack by themselves or a little more embellished as in this recipe. For variations, try using different types of bananas, such as the dwarf or saba variety that's becoming increasingly available at Asian stores. This recipe is best if made just minutes before serving.

Serves 4
85 g (3 oz) plain flour, sifted
3 tablespoons potato flour or cornflour
½ teaspoon baking powder
3 tablespoons sugar
170 ml (5½ fl oz) water

3 ripe but firm bananas
Vegetable oil for frying
3 tablespoons icing sugar for garnish
570 ml (1 pint) coconut or vanilla ice cream (optional)

- Combine the flour, potato flour, baking powder, sugar and water and stir well. Refrigerate for 30 minutes.

- Peel the bananas and cut them in half lengthways. Cut in half crossways. Set aside until ready to use. If serving ice cream, have the chilled bowls ready.

- Heat 5 cm (2 inches) of oil in a heavy frying pan to about 190°C (375°F). Dredge the bananas in the flour mixture, then carefully slip them into the hot oil. Using chopsticks or tongs, turn the bananas once and fry for 3 to 4 minutes until golden. (Do not crowd the pan.) Drain the bananas on paper towels.

- To serve, place 3 banana pieces on each plate, sprinkle with icing sugar and serve with a small scoop of ice cream, if desired.

Sticky Rice with Mung Beans and Fresh Coconut

xoi dau xanh dua

MY FAVOURITE STICKY rice vendor in Saigon is indeed a true master chef. For the past thirty years, she has been coming to the same street corner to sell her fabulous *xoi* (sticky rice) to the many customers who stop by on their way to work each morning. Although a popular breakfast item, it's also eaten as a sweet during other times of the day. Traditionally *xoi* is served on a banana leaf with a variety of toppings, including this one with mung bean paste, shredded coconut and toasted sesame seeds.

For this recipe, you'll need a steamer and the long-grain sticky rice (sold as sweet or glutinous rice) from Thailand, not the short-grain variety that's more common in Japanese and Chinese recipes.

Serves 4 to 6

90 g (3½ oz) split and husked mung beans, soaked for 2 hours and drained

2 fresh or frozen pandanus leaves, tied into a small bundle and lightly bruised with the flat side of a knife (see page 245)

200 g (7 oz) sticky rice or sweet (glutinous) rice, soaked overnight, drained

75 ml (3 fl oz) unsweetened coconut milk

7 tablespoons sugar

2 tablespoons white sesame seeds, lightly toasted in a dry pan

40 g (1½ oz) chopped Roasted Peanuts (see page 34)

½ teaspoon salt

30 g (1 oz) freshly grated coconut (page 158) or store-bought coconut flakes

- Place the mung beans and 125 ml (4 fl oz) water in a small saucepan over moderate heat. Bring to the boil. Reduce the heat and simmer for about 20 minutes until the beans are soft. Add a little more water if the pan gets dry. Using the back of a spoon, mash the beans until smooth and creamy. Set aside.

- Fill the bottom of a steamer pan one-third full of water and bring to the boil. Add the pandanus leaves to the water. Line the steamer rack with a damp, double-layered piece of muslin. Place the sticky rice on top, making sure to spread it out so that it cooks evenly. Cover and steam for about 20 minutes until the rice is cooked but still firm.

- While the rice is steaming, combine the coconut milk and 4 tablespoons of the sugar in a small saucepan and heat just until the sugar is dissolved. Remove from heat and set aside.

- Transfer the cooked sticky rice to a bowl. Add the coconut milk and stir gently with a fork or chopsticks.

- Combine the sesame seeds, peanuts, salt and the remaining 3 tablespoons sugar in a small bowl. To serve, transfer about half a cup of sticky rice to each plate. Dab 1 tablespoon mung bean paste on top, then sprinkle with the shredded coconut and sesame seed mixture. Serve warm or at room temperature with the remaining sesame seed mixture on the side.

Iced Red Bean Pudding
with Coconut Milk
che dau do lanh

MY SISTER DENISE and I used to run to our favourite dessert vendor after school and gulp down one of these before going home. Part drink, part dessert, this delightful pudding is particularly satisfying on long hot days and nights – whether in Vietnam or in the West. The soft red beans are bathed in a sweet coconut milk with chewy tapioca strands and shaved ice.

To enjoy this dessert, first stir the ingredients together, then use a long spoon to drink and eat. It can be made with different combinations such as mung beans, shredded seaweed, shredded agar-agar (a natural gelatin made from seaweed) and lotus seeds. If you prefer, you can also serve this hot. For a Vietnamese, a glass of *che dau do* after a bowl of *pho* constitutes a truly happy meal.

> **Serves 6 to 8**
> **110 g (4 oz) dried small red beans (adzuki), soaked overnight, drained and rinsed**
> **¼ teaspoon bicarbonate of soda (optional)**
> **8 to 9 tablespoons tapioca strands (see page 267), soaked in cold water for 30 minutes and drained**
> **375 ml (12 fl oz) unsweetened coconut milk**
> **2 fresh or frozen pandanus leaves, folded into a short bundle and bruised with the flat side of a knife (see opposite) or ½ teaspoon vanilla extract**
> **45 g (2 oz) palm sugar or cane sugar**
> **3 tablespoons granulated sugar**
> **Pinch of salt**
> **Shaved or crushed ice**

- Combine the beans and 1 litre (1¾ pints) water in a saucepan and bring to the boil. Reduce the heat to low and simmer for about 1 hour until the beans are soft. If they're not soft by then, speed them along by adding the sodium bicarbonate. Set aside to cool, then refrigerate until cold.

- While the beans are cooking, combine the tapioca strands and 500 ml (16 fl oz) water in a small pan. Cover and cook over moderate heat for about 20 minutes until the strands are soft. Drain.

- Combine the tapioca strands, coconut milk, pandanus leaves, palm sugar, sugar and salt in a medium pan and bring to the boil. Stir to dissolve the sugar. Remove from the heat and set aside to cool. Chill.

- To serve, divide the beans and some of the cooking liquid among 6 to 8 tall cocktail glasses. Top with the coconut milk mixture and a heaped mound of shaved ice each. Serve with long dessert spoons.

Pandanus Leaf

IN VIETNAM, the desserts are not only sweet but very aromatic, thanks to *la dua* (pandanus leaf), the vanilla of Asia. Also known as screw pine, it's used extensively to flavour puddings, cakes, sticky rice and sweet beverages. At the markets in Vietnam the vendor who sells coconuts also sells pandanus. The two ingredients are made for each other! The long, narrow green leaves, which resemble the leaves of a day lily, are tied together, then bruised with a knife before being added to the cooking liquids.

In the West pandanus leaves are available frozen and, sometimes, fresh. If you're lucky enough to find them fresh, buy extra and freeze them for later use. Pandanus extract is a poor substitute, so it's best to use banana extract or vanilla extract if you can't find the real thing.

To make pandanus juice, pulverize the leaves (with a mortar and pestle or fruit blender), adding a little water to ease the job. Strain before using. One leaf will make about 1½ tablespoons juice.

Crème Caramel

IN SAIGON, it's rather stylish to go to a French café and enjoy a strong cup of coffee and a *crème caramel*, or flan. The traditional method calls for steaming the custard in a Chinese steamer, but I prefer the flavour of baked custard. This recipe calls for six 175 g (6 oz) ramekins but if you like, you can also make it in a flan dish and bake it for about 1½ hours.

Serves 6
375 g (12 oz) sugar
125 ml (4 fl oz) water
3 eggs
3 egg yolks
570 ml (1 pint) milk
175 ml (6 fl oz) cream
¼ teaspoon salt
1 teaspoon vanilla extract

- Preheat the oven to 170°C/325°F/Gas Mark 3.

- Combine 250 g (8 oz) of the sugar and the water in a small saucepan and bring it to the boil. Reduce the heat slightly and let the mixture boil for about 10 to 12 minutes until it starts to bubble and turn brown but not black. Stir a few times so the edges don't become scorched. Remove from the heat and using a long-handled spoon, pour 2 to 3 tablespoons of the caramel into 6 ramekins. (Work fast before the caramel cools and sets.) Carefully tilt the ramekins so the bottoms are completely covered with caramel. Set aside.

- In a bowl, whisk the eggs and egg yolks together until well blended. In a heavy-bottomed saucepan, heat the milk, cream, remaining sugar and salt over moderate heat. While stirring continuously, scald the milk until the sugar is dissolved. Remove from the heat and stir in the vanilla.

- While whisking, gradually add all the hot milk to the eggs. Strain the custard into a bowl and divide it among the ramekins. Place the ramekins in a baking tray filled halfway with hot water. Bake for about 45 minutes until the tops of the custards are firm around the edges but slightly soft in the centre. Remove the ramekins from the water bath and chill for at least 4 hours. To unmould the custard, run a knife along the edge of the ramekin and invert onto a dish.

Coconut Sticky
Rice Pudding with Taro
che khoai mon

YOU CAN ALWAYS tell where the dessert vendors sit at the market near my grandmother's house. It's where the schoolchildren congregate, peering excitedly at the big pots of *che*. This dish is typical of those served there. It calls for the sticky rice to be simmered with a root vegetable such as taro or yucca, with legumes such as black beans, red beans or black-eyed peas or with fresh maize. Except for the maize, all legumes must be boiled before being added to the sticky rice. You can serve this dessert warm or at room temperature.

Serves 6 to 8
875 ml (28 fl oz) water
65 g (2¼ oz) glutinous rice (see Glossary page 264), rinsed

**225 g (8 oz) taro (see below), peeled, cut into 1.5 cm
   (⅔ inch) cubes and rinsed
90 g (3½ oz) sugar, or to taste
Pinch of salt
400 g (14 oz) can unsweetened coconut milk, not shaken
1 teaspoon cornflour
1 tablespoon pandanus juice (see page 245) or ½ teaspoon
   vanilla extract**

- Place the water in a medium pan and bring to the boil. Add the glutinous rice and bring it to a second boil. Reduce the heat to low, then simmer for about 10 minutes until the rice is almost soft.

- Add the taro, sugar and salt. Cook for about 15 minutes until the taro is soft but not mushy.

- Scoop about half a cup of the thick cream from the surface of the coconut milk and place in a small saucepan. Stir in the cornflour, then bring the sauce to the boil. Remove from the heat and set aside.

- Add the remaining coconut milk and pandanus juice to the sticky rice and gently stir to blend. The pudding should be slightly thick, and the grains should be soft but still maintain their shape. Transfer the pudding to individual small bowls. Drizzle the coconut cream on top and serve.

Taro Root

KHOAI MON, or taro, is used like a potato in Vietnam. It's mashed or shredded and added to soups and spring roll fillings or sliced and used in simmered dishes. There are two varieties: one is a large brown-skinned tuber about 25.5 cm (10 inches) long and 13 cm (5 inches) wide, and the other is a shaggy egg-shaped root. The flesh ranges from light cream with flecks to pale lavender. Raw taro root is said to cause itchiness in some people, so you may want to use rubber gloves when handling it.

Taro is also delicious in soups, curries and desserts. It has a creamy texture and a delicate nutty flavour similar to young coconut. The Vietnamese also like to cook with the sponge-like stems of a different kind of taro, one that does not produce a tuber. Called *bac ha*, they add texture to soups and braised dishes.

Grandmother's Banana Stew with Tapioca Pearls
chuoi chung

ONE OF MY grandmother's favourites, this recipe has also become a big hit among friends to whom I've introduced it. In Vietnam, this dessert is made with the dwarf banana – a fat, stubby variety commonly used for puddings and cakes. It's starchier and won't collapse into mush when cooked. This modified recipe calls for regular bananas, which are sweeter and more fragrant, although very fragile. The tapioca pearls are available at Asian stores. They're slightly larger than the instant tapioca found at regular supermarkets. For an interesting variation, substitute the bananas with cooked chunks of kabocha squash (see Glossary page 261).

Serves 6
750 ml (24 fl oz) water
6 tablespoons tapioca pearls, 1 mm (⅟₁₆ inch) wide
250 ml (8 fl oz) unsweetened coconut milk
90 g (3½ oz) sugar, or to taste
Pinch of salt
3 ripe but firm bananas
2 tablespoons chopped Roasted Peanuts (see page 34)

- Bring the water to a rolling boil in a medium saucepan over high heat. Add the tapioca pearls and stir to separate. Reduce the heat to low and simmer for about 20 minutes until the tapioca becomes translucent. Add the coconut milk, sugar and salt and stir well.

- Five minutes before the end of the cooking time, peel the bananas and cut them in half lengthways. Cut each piece again into 4 pieces. Add them to the pan and cook until just soft. At this point the tapioca pearls should be clear and cooked.

- Remove from the heat and transfer to individual dessert bowls. Garnish with the peanuts and serve hot or at room temperature. (The pudding will thicken as it cools.)

Fresh Coconut Ice Cream
kem dua

WHAT CAN BE better than finishing off a meal with fresh coconut ice cream? This recipe will be even more memorable if you go to the small trouble of finding a fresh coconut and grating the flesh yourself. Fortunately, in recent years, fresh coconuts have become available at some supermarkets. When purchasing a coconut, pick out one that is heavy and with 'eyes' that are fresh-looking and intact.

Makes 1.2 litres (2 pints)
500 ml (16 fl oz) unsweetened coconut milk
1 tablespoon tapioca starch or cornflour
250 ml (8 fl oz) milk
250 ml (8 fl oz) cream
160 g (5 oz) sugar
Pinch of salt
**60 g (2½ oz) freshly grated coconut (see page 158) or 35 g
    (1½ oz) store-bought unsweetened coconut flakes,
    lightly toasted in a dry pan**
4 tablespoons chopped Roasted Peanuts (see page 34)

- Combine the coconut milk, tapioca starch, milk and cream in a heavy medium saucepan. Heat over medium heat until the mixture starts to bubble around the edges and reaches 80°C (175°F). Stir in the sugar and salt. Remove from the heat. Strain through a fine-mesh sieve into a bowl and set aside to cool. Refrigerate overnight or for at least 4 hours.

- Add the grated coconut to the coconut milk mixture, transfer to an ice-cream maker and freeze according to the manufacturer's instructions. Serve the ice cream in small bowls and garnish with a sprinkling of the peanuts.

Lychee Sorbet
kem trai vai

IF THERE IS one fruit that seems to survive canning, it is the lychee. Sweet, juicy and intensely aromatic, it is a beloved fruit in Asia and is enjoyed fresh, canned and dried. Here its fragrant flavours are well captured in the form of a sorbet. The flavour dissipates after a week so it's best to eat it soon after it's made.

Makes 900 ml (1½ pints)
**5 x 625 g (20 oz) cans lychees in heavy syrup, drained,
   juice reserved**
90 g (3½ oz) sugar
2 tablespoons fresh lemon juice

- Measure 75 ml (3 fl oz) of the lychee syrup and set aside. Drain the lychees. (Save the extra syrup to flavour iced tea or to drink.)

- Combine the 75 ml (3 fl oz) reserved syrup and sugar in a small saucepan and heat until the sugar dissolves. Remove from the heat and set aside until ready to use.

- Place the lychees in a fruit blender and process as fine as possible. Add the syrup mixture and lemon juice and process for 1 minute. Strain the mixture through a fine-mesh sieve into a bowl. Using the back of a spoon, mash the fruit to extract as much juice as possible. Cover the lychee mixture and refrigerate for at least 4 hours. Transfer to an ice-cream maker and freeze according to the manufacturer's instructions.

Warm Soya Milk with Pandanus Leaf
sua dau nanh

I GREW UP on soya milk, but never thought of making it fresh until I started going back to Vietnam. There, fresh soya milk is sold at the markets and on street corners early in the morning and late at night. Sometimes I can walk into a market and just sniff my way to a soya milk vendor. I definitely have a nose for *sua dau nanh*, especially if it's been scented with pandanus leaf.

Since my trips to Vietnam, and after reading reports about the health benefits of soya beans, I have been making soya milk on a regular basis. It's a little time-consuming but well worth the effort. The difference between fresh soya milk and the commercial product is like the difference between canned orange juice and freshly squeezed. Although some Asian stores now carry fresh soya milk, it, too, isn't the same as homemade. Often it's watered down and is too sweet for my taste.

To make this recipe, you can use a blender or food processor. But if you want fresh soya milk on a daily basis as I do, you might want to get a soy extracting machine. It extracts and strains the milk, so all you have to do is boil it. To me, nothing is more soothing late at night than a bowl of warm soya milk.

Makes 1.75 litres (3 pints)
450 g (1 lb) dried soya beans, soaked overnight and drained
2 litres (3½ pints) water

**2 pandanus leaves (see page 245), folded and tied in a
    bundle and slightly bruised with the flat side of a knife
    or 1 teaspoon vanilla extract
3 tablespoons sugar, or to taste**

- Divide the soya beans into 4 batches. Place the first batch in the blender and add about 500 ml (16 fl oz) water. Process for about 10 seconds until the soya beans are broken down and the milk is thick and almost smooth. Transfer to a large bowl. Repeat with the remaining soya beans and water, taking care to not overfill the blender. Transfer all the pulverized soya beans and any remaining water to the bowl.

- Strain the soya milk mixture by pouring it through a fine-mesh sieve into a large pot. Using a spoon or spatula, scrape against the sieve to extract as much water as possible. Discard the solids. Repeat until the soya milk is all strained. Then rinse the sieve, line it with a piece of muslin and strain the soya milk again. Twist the ends of the muslin together and squeeze to extract the liquid. Discard any remaining solids.

- Place the pot over moderate heat and bring to a slow boil. Add the pandanus leaves and sugar. Stir to prevent the bottom from burning. When the milk starts to bubble, reduce the heat to low and simmer for 10 minutes. Serve the soya milk hot or cold. If you need to store it in the refrigerator, make sure it's completely cool before chilling it. Fresh soya milk should be enjoyed within 2 days.

Iced Pandanus Tea
nuoc la dua

THIS IS NOT a Vietnamese recipe, but it's a drink I grew up with during my childhood years in Thailand and it's too exceptional to be left out. You can serve this straight, as indicated here, or you can use it to flavour iced tea. If you're lucky enough to find fresh pandanus, float a few leaves in the pitcher or glass.

Makes about 10 servings

110 g (4 oz) packet of frozen pandanus leaves, chopped into 2.5 cm (1 inch) lengths

2.5 litres (4½ pints) water

125 g (4½ oz) sugar, or to taste

900 ml (1½ pints) crushed ice

- Place the chopped pandanus leaves and 250 ml (8 fl oz) of the water in a blender. Blend for about 1 minute until the leaves are broken down. (If necessary, add more water.) Transfer to a large bowl and add the remaining water. Strain the liquid through a sieve lined with a double layer of muslin into a pot. Add the sugar and bring the mixture to the boil. Remove from the heat and chill. To serve, fill a tall glass with ice and pour the pandanus tea over it.

Vietnamese Coffee
café sua da

IN VIETNAM, stories abound about coffee roasters who add secret ingredients to their blend – salt, spice, roasted maize, butter and even fish sauce! To make authentic Vietnamese coffee, use a very dark French roast and brew it in a special individual filter that sits on top of the cup. The slow-drip brewing process is what gives Vietnamese coffee its characteristic flavour. If you don't have a Vietnamese metal coffee filter, use a plastic drip filter, although the flavour – not to mention the ritual – isn't quite the same.

Serves 4
250 ml (8 fl oz) dark French roast coffee, medium grind
125 ml (4 fl oz) condensed milk
750 ml (25 fl oz) boiling water
1 litre (1¾ pints) ice

- Divide the coffee grounds evenly among 4 individual filters. Place the inner screen on the coffee but do not pack it down. Place 2 heaped tablespoons condensed milk in each of the 4 coffee cups. Set the individual filters on top. Pour 2 to 3 tablespoons boiling water into each filter and let the grounds expand for 2 minutes.

- Fill the filter with boiling water all the way to the rim once. The water should slowly drip through the filter, about 3 to 4 drops at a time. (If it drips much faster than that, the grounds are too large.) The brewing should take 4 to 5 minutes.

- Fill 4 tall glasses with ice. Stir the coffee well so the condensed milk is dissolved and blended. Pour over the ice and serve with a tall spoon.

Glossary

THIS GLOSSARY HIGHLIGHTS common ingredients used in Vietnamese cuisine. Many of the essential items are discussed in greater detail in the previous chapters. Herbs, which the Vietnamese eat in huge quantities, almost as vegetables, are highlighted in a separate section on page 39 in the chapter on Sauces, Condiments and Herbs.

Annatto seeds *(hot dieu)*: In Vietnam, the rust-red seeds of the annatto tree are often used to colour soups and stews. The seeds are fried in oil, then allowed to steep. Once the seeds are removed, the oil is used to make the aromatic base of braised or simmered dishes like *thit bo kho* (Beef Stew with Star Anise and Basil, see page 178).

Bamboo shoots *(mang)*: The young shoots of the bamboo tree, they're usually harvested when they're about the size of a fist. The smaller they are, the more tender. (Bamboo shoots are often referred to as the winter or spring shoot, the former being more tender.) To prepare fresh bamboo shoots, cut and discard the tough, hairy outer layers. The inner core should be sliced and boiled for 15 minutes or longer. Canned bamboo shoots are widely available and are sold as whole shoots or tips, or as strips and slices. The latter works well for curries. For stir-fries, I like to buy the whole tips and cut them to the desired shape and thickness. Always blanch canned bamboo shoots to remove any tinny flavour they may have.

Banana blossom, banana flower *(bap chuoi)*: The deep purple flower of the banana tree is eaten as a vegetable throughout Asia. It's usually sliced thin and soaked in acidic water to prevent it from turning black. Banana blossom is served raw in salads, as in Banana Blossom Salad with Chicken (see page 88), although in some recipes the tiny fruits are boiled beforehand.

Banana leaves *(la chuoi)*: The clingfilm and aluminium foil of Asia, banana leaves are used to wrap both savoury foods and desserts before steaming or grilling. In Thailand, they are used to make little moulds, trays and bowls for desserts. In Vietnam, they're used to wrap sausages, sticky rice and desserts, even becoming plates from which to serve sticky rice. The broad centre rib is removed and used as a spoon. You can find frozen banana leaves in 450 g (1 lb) packages. To use, thaw and wipe clean. Do not wash under running water because the leaves tear easily. Remove the rib before wrapping food. For grilling or steaming foods, especially those that are saucy, it's best to use a double thickness.

Bean sauce *(tuong)*: Made from puréed fermented soya beans, this condiment seasons stir-fries and dipping sauces. In Vietnam, the traditional sauce for *goi cuon* (salad rolls) is made with this condiment blended with sticky rice, coconut milk, chillies and sugar. In the United States and elsewhere hoisin (a mixture of soya beans, salt, sugar, five-spice powder and other spices and additives) has become the standard dipping sauce for salad rolls and for the meat toppings in *pho* (Vietnamese Rice Noodle Soup with Beef, see page 50).

Bean threads/cellophane noodles *(bun tau)*: Also known as glass noodles, these thin, transparent and wiry noodles are made from mung bean starch. They become soft, plump and clear when cooked. They're used in soups, salads, stir-fries and fillings. They should be soaked in water for 30 minutes before using. (For more information, see page 125.)

Bitter melon *(hu qua)*: This bitter relative of the cucumber is an unusual-looking vegetable, with warty bumps and ridges running from one end to the other. Considered highly nutritious, it is thinly sliced and stir-fried, or stuffed and braised, or added to soups. The seeds and the whitish-to-pinkish skin that surrounds them should be removed as both are quite bitter.

Black mushroom *(nam huong kho)*: Also known as Chinese black mushrooms or dried shiitake mushrooms, these fungi are prized for their rich, meaty flavour and texture. Available in different grades and prices, the most flavourful are those with deep fissures on the caps. To use, soften in hot water for 30 minutes or longer. Remove and discard the rubbery stems. Black mushrooms can be added to soups, stews, stir-fries and fillings.

Chilli paste, ground *(tuong ot toi)*: Made with coarsely ground (unseeded) red chillies, garlic and vinegar, this versatile paste is a table condiment as well as a seasoning. The Vietnamese like to add a little dab of it to their *nuoc cham* dipping sauce. It is also an essential flavouring in Vietnamese stir-fries (along with oil and garlic).

Chilli sauce, Sriracha sauce *(tuong ot)*: Similar in appearance to Tabasco, this bright-red fiery sauce is a smooth purée of seeded red chillies, vinegar, garlic and sugar. Packaged in glass or plastic squeeze bottles, it is a favourite condiment for Vietnamese *pho*, used as a dipping sauce for the meat toppings and to season the noodle broth itself. It's also popular as a dipping sauce for seafood and grilled meats.

Chilli, Thai bird's eye *(ot hiem)*: Although commonly referred to as Thai bird's eye chillies, the Vietnamese also love this special variety of fresh chillies. Slender and tiny, about 2.5 cm (1 inch) long, they're extremely hot and flavourful. They're wonderful when crushed and added to dipping sauces and stir-fries. Thai bird's eye chillies are available fresh, dried and pickled and may be green or red.

Coconut milk *(nuoc dua)*: Unsweetened coconut milk is the cream and butter of Southeast Asian cooking. It is made by soaking grated mature coconut flesh with hot water and then squeezing the coconut to extract the liquid. (For information on how to prepare fresh coconut milk, see page 158.) *Nuoc dua* is an important ingredient in curries, soups and desserts. In the West, the canned products are easily available although fresh coconuts are now also showing up at more supermarkets.

Fermented black beans *(tau xi)*: Fermented black beans are used in stir-fry dishes of Chinese origin. Also called preserved black beans, these dried loose beans are sold in plastic bags or in paper cartons. You can rinse them briefly to remove some of the salt, or use them as is.

Fermented soya beans *(tuong hot)*: Made from fermented whole soya beans (not to be confused with fermented *black* beans), this salty condiment is packed in small jars or long-neckED bottles and is labelled as salted beans, bean sauce or sweet bean sauce. All refer to the same product. It is an important seasoning ingredient in many Chinese-style dishes. The Vietnamese use this condiment to season steamed fish and to make dipping sauces such as Vietnamese Bean Dipping Sauce (see page 25).

Fish sauce *(nuoc mam)*: The quintessential seasoning in Vietnamese cooking, fish sauce is used in practically every savoury dish and dipping sauce. It is the clear, amber-coloured liquid drained from fish fermented in brine. It is pungent but the odour quickly dissipates with cooking. In addition to providing flavour, fish sauce is rich in proteins and vitamins otherwise lacking in the Vietnamese diet. It will last indefinitely. (For more information, see page 21.)

Five-spice powder *(ngu vi huong)*: Five-spice powder is a traditional Chinese spice blend that can be made with more than five spices. This fragrant brown powder is principally made with star anise and cinnamon and several other ingredients such as Szechuan peppercorns, clove and fennel. It's often used to season roasted and braised meats, especially chicken and duck.

Galangal *(cu rieng)*: This knobby rhizome is used in the same way as its cousin, the common ginger. Particularly important in Thai cuisine, it's often sliced and added to soups and used to make curry pastes. In Vietnamese cooking, it shows up only in some northern specialities such as *cha ca Hanoi* (Hanoi Grilled Fish with Rice Noodles and Fresh Herbs, see page 147) and in dishes made with dog meat and other exotic meats.

Hoisin sauce *(sot hoisin)*: A versatile condiment made from soya bean purée, sugar, five-spice powder and other spices, this brown sauce is used primarily in dipping sauces, marinades and stir-fries. You can make a particularly delicious dipping sauce by mixing hoisin sauce with onions, garlic, chillies, vinegar and crushed peanuts. This product is sold in tins or small jars.

Jícama *(cu san)*: Jícama is used extensively in Vietnam in stir-fries, salads, fillings and soups. It resembles a large turnip and has a delicate taste with a pleasant crunchy texture similar to a water chestnut. Fresh jícama is heavy, full of liquid and free of blemishes. To use, peel and cut into the desired shape and size.

Kabocha squash *(bi ro)*: Also known as Japanese squash, this small, about 20 cm (8 inches) in diameter, squat pumpkin-shaped vegetable has dark green skin with yellow spots and faint green lines. Its delicious and creamy flesh is used in a variety of recipes, including braised dishes, curries, soups and even desserts.

Lemongrass *(xa)*: A staple herb in Vietnamese cooking, this woody, fibrous stalk is finely chopped and used to make marinades or left in larger pieces to infuse soups and curries with its wonderful flavour. It imparts a delightful citrusy taste to grilled meats and stir-fries. (See page 42.)

Lily buds *(kim cham)*: Also known as 'golden needles', lily buds are small, thin (imagine a dried bean sprout) and light golden in colour. Available in 225 g (8 oz) packages, these dried delicacies should be pliable when you buy them, not dark brown and stiff. Soak the buds in warm water for about 30 minutes before using, then tie each into a knot to keep it from fraying while cooking. Lily buds have an interesting earthy flavour that blends perfectly with soy sauce, bamboo shoots and dried black mushrooms.

Loofah squash *(muop)*: My favourite of the Asian squash family, this sweet, spongy, mild-tasting vegetable is used in stir-fries and soups. Similar to a long cucumber but covered with ridges and dark-green skin, loofah squash is generally harvested when it's about a foot long. To use, peel the skin, slice and cook as you would courgettes.

Lotus stems *(ngo sen)*: In Vietnam, every part of the lotus is used or eaten, including the long stems that connect the main part of the plant to the flowers and leaves. Vietnamese cooks like to peel these stems and add them to soups and salads. In the West, lotus stems are available in jars in brine and are labelled 'lotus rootlets'. Lotus root can be substituted for lotus stems. (See page 95.)

Mung beans *(dau xanh)*: The same beans used to grow bean sprouts, mung beans are prized in Vietnamese cooking. Sold husked or unhusked, they generally are soaked in warm water before cooking. Mung beans are used to enrich savoury dishes such as Sizzling Saigon Crêpes (page 131) and desserts such as puddings and iced drinks.

Pandanus leaf *(la dua)*: Also known as screw pine, this long, pleated, smooth pointed leaf is the vanilla of Southeast Asia. It appears in many desserts, from puddings and steamed cakes to iced drinks and soya milk.

It is often folded and bruised, then steeped in coconut milk or syrup to extract its earthy vanilla aroma. Pandanus is available frozen and occasionally fresh. Substitute banana, jasmine or vanilla extract. (See page 245.)

Papaya, green *(du du xanh)*: When a recipe calls for this ingredient, it refers to the large green variety sold at Asian stores, not the unripe version of smaller papayas found in some supermarkets. In Vietnam, green papaya is shredded and eaten raw in salads with lots of fresh herbs, such as *rau ram*, Vietnamese coriander.

Peanuts *(dau phong)*: Peanuts are used extensively in Vietnamese cooking, primarily as a garnish. Roasted and chopped, they are used to garnish *bun* and other Vietnamese rice noodle dishes, as well as salads and desserts. Boiled peanuts are also eaten as snacks.

Potato flour *(bot khoai)*: In Vietnam, potato flour is used as a binder in meatballs, pâtés and *goi lua*, the sausage wrapped in banana leaves that is used in sandwiches. In some instances potato flour is mixed with rice flour batter to make a firmer dough.

Preserved cabbage *(cai man)*: Preserved cabbage is a popular garnish for soups such as *hu tieu My Tho* and noodle dishes of Chinese origin. Often labelled as 'Tianjin preserved vegetables', it is sold in earthenware pots or in plastic jars. Preserved cabbage is very salty, so use it sparingly.

Rice *(gao thom)*: The Vietnamese prefer the long-grain jasmine rice, which is eaten at almost every meal unless a noodle soup is served. Rice should be washed until the water runs clear. Although each batch is different, the standard ratio of 1 part rice to 1½ parts water should yield a good pot of rice. (See page 153 for how to cook perfect rice.)

Rice flour *(bot gao)*: This starch figures prominently in Vietnamese cooking. Most dumplings, cakes and noodles are made from rice flour. When purchasing this product, do not confuse it with glutinous rice flour (sweet rice flour), which is very different. For recipes in this book, use the Thai rice flour sold in 450 g (1 lb) bags at Asian stores.

Rice noodles: Rice noodles are a staple food in Vietnamese cuisine. The most commonly used noodles are *banh pho* (rice sticks), *bun* (rice vermicelli) and *banh hoi* (tiny sheets of woven noodles). Rice noodles are more fragile than pasta and generally require less cooking time. (See page 124.)

Rice papers, dried *(banh trang)*: Another staple in the Vietnamese kitchen, these dried, transparent, rice-flour sheets are used to wrap *cha gio*, or spring rolls, and *goi cuon*, or salad rolls. They are available in several shapes (round, triangular and square) and sizes. Rice paper should be soaked for about 10 seconds in hot water until it softens and becomes pliable before being used. (See page 108.)

Rock sugar *(duong phen)*: Also known as lump sugar, rock sugar is a solidified mixture of refined and unrefined cane sugar and honey. The Vietnamese prefer this sugar in *pho* and in other savoury dishes in which a touch of sweetness is desired. Rock sugar is also believed to keep meats firm and shiny.

Sesame seeds *(hot me)*: Hulled white sesame seeds are used extensively in Vietnamese sweets. They are often toasted and sprinkled on banana stews and puddings with coconut sauce. Mixed with roasted peanuts and salt, they are a common topping for steamed sticky rice.

Shrimp, dried *(tom kho)*: Dried shrimp are used much like dried fish, to flavour stocks, stews and stir-fries. They are available in different sizes, with the larger ones being more expensive. High-quality dried shrimp are pink and should yield slightly to the touch. Do not buy those that are rock hard. Pungent and salty, dried shrimp are used in small amounts. Vietnamese cooks like to add them to salad rolls or pound them into a paste for seasoning dumpling soups.

Shrimp paste, shrimp sauce *(ruoc)*: This pungent paste is made from fermented shrimp and salt. Sold in jars, tubs and dried cakes, shrimp paste keeps indefinitely, like fish sauce. In Thailand, a similar but firmer product (*kapi*) is used in curry pastes and dipping sauces. The Vietnamese equivalent is wet and sold as shrimp sauce. It is also used to add savouriness to noodle broths and to make dipping sauces.

Spring roll wrappers *(banh trang bot mi)*: Made from wheat flour, these wrappers are often used for wrapping *cha gio*. Although not quite as tasty as rice paper, these wrappers are easier to use and cook up golden and crisp. Available in 20 cm (8 inch) squares, they can be found in the frozen foods section of Asian stores. Before use, they're first thawed and separated into single sheets.

Squid, dried *(muc kho)*: In Asia, dried squid is appreciated both for its intensely fishy flavour and for its chewy texture. At the beaches in Vietnam, dried squid is roasted over hot coals, and then run through a hand-cranked press. The teeth of the press flatten the squid, tenderizing it at the same time. To eat, one tears off a piece and dips it into *tuong ot*, or Sriracha-style chilli sauce. Besides eating it as a snack, dried squid can be reconstituted and used in stir-fry dishes and seafood soups. To flavour stocks for noodle soups, lightly toast the squid in a dry frying pan and add to the pot. Sometimes labelled as dried cuttlefish, dried squid is packaged in plastic bags. Once opened, the bag should be sealed tightly so the strong odour doesn't overwhelm the kitchen.

Star anise *(hoi)*: This beautiful eight-pointed spice pod lends a sweet liquorice flavour to stews and soups, such as *pho*. It's best to add star anise towards the end of the cooking time as the wonderful aroma subsides with prolonged simmering.

Starfruit *(khe)*: Also called carambola, this star-shaped fruit is juicy and reminiscent of Asian pear with floral undertones. In Vietnam, ripe ones are eaten as snacks and the sour green fruits are sliced thin and used in table salads. Starfruit is a tasty accompaniment to grilled meats.

Straw mushrooms *(nam rom)*: Small and with oval caps, these mild-tasting, greyish-black mushrooms are preferred in Vietnamese cooking. Because they're harvested before the caps are open, the Vietnamese also call them *nam bup*, or bulb mushrooms. Outside of Asia, they are available canned.

Sugarcane *(mia)*: In Vietnam, sugarcane is often peeled and cut into 2.5 cm (1 inch) rounds, then skewered on a bundle of bamboo sticks. To enjoy, one pulls off a piece and chews it until all the juice is sucked out. The very fibrous and stringy flesh is then discarded. Another way of using sugarcane is as a skewer onto which a prawn paste is moulded and then grilled, as in Grilled Prawn Paste on Sugarcane (see page 142). The sugarcane imparts a sweet, delicate flavour to the prawns. Sugarcane may be pressed to make sugarcane juice or it may be refined into sugar. In the West, sugarcane is available tinned and sometimes fresh. For skewers, the tinned product works well.

Tamarind *(me)*: Tamarind is the sour-tasting pod of the tamarind tree. The pods are originally green but eventually turn dark brown. The pulp inside, which is similar to dried prunes in colour and texture, is used to flavour soups and salads. In the West, tamarind pulp is packaged in compressed blocks. To use, soften the pulp in warm water for about 20 minutes, then push through a sieve. Occasionally you may be able to find fresh tamarind pods at Asian stores.

Tapioca *(bot ban)*: Made from the cassava root, tapioca is used as a thickener in desserts such as Grandmother's Banana Stew with Tapioca Pearls (see page 249). In Asia, this product is usually referred to as tapioca pearls and generally comes in two sizes – small (about 1 mm/$^1/_{16}$-inch pellets) or the larger pearl-like size. Tapioca strands or noodles must be soaked in water for 30 minutes before using, but the small pearls can be added directly to boiling water.

Tapioca starch *(bot nang)*: Made from the pulverized cassava root, this starch is used to make desserts and dumplings. When used in combination with other flours, it enhances the pliability and chewiness of the dough.

Taro *(khoai mon)*: Taro is used much like potato. It is a starchy root, with a creamy texture and a sweet, nutty flavour. The two common varieties are the large barrel-shaped tubers with cream-coloured flesh and pink fibres, and the smaller egg-shaped tubers with purplish flesh. The larger variety is firmer; the smaller one is softer, creamier and more flavourful. In Vietnam and Thailand taro is used in soups and desserts. Some varieties will discolour after peeling so it's best to submerge the root in water if not used immediately.

Taro stems *(bac ha)*: In Vietnam, the stem of a variety of taro called *Colocasia gigantea* is used in soups. It looks identical to the stem of the regular taro – long, thick and sponge-like. Taro is often sold in long stalks, about 30 to 50 cm (12 to 20 inches). To use, peel the skin (as you would rhubarb) and cut on the diagonal into thin slices. It doesn't have any flavour, but is appreciated for its sponge-like sauce-absorbing feature.

Toasted rice powder *(thinh)*: Toasted rice is used to give gritty texture to dishes such as *bi*, shredded pork, and helps bind meats such as those used in sausages. *Thinh* is made by soaking rice in water, toasting, then grinding it into a powder. Either regular or glutinous rice can be used, but the latter will produce a coarser powder. You can also buy *thinh* in small plastic bags at Asian stores.

Tofu *(dau hu)*: Also known as bean curd, tofu is made by combining soya bean milk and a coagulant such as gypsum powder. The curds are pressed together to form cakes. Tofu is delicate-tasting, but it can absorb flavours and spices quite well, as in the Spicy Lemongrass Tofu (see page 222). (See also page 215.)

Turmeric *(bot nghe)*: Ground turmeric is used extensively in Vietnamese cooking, for both flavour and colour. It's a common ingredient in marinades and in rice-flour batters. In its fresh form, turmeric is like ginger, a knobby root with small fingers. It has dark-brown skin with ring-like markings. The flesh is bright orange, and when added to curries, soups, stews or rice dishes, it turns them brilliant yellow.

Vietnamese coffee *(café phe sua)*: A distinctively Vietnamese-French beverage, this thick, strong coffee drink is made by brewing French-dark roast coffee through an individual filter. It is served with condensed milk and can be enjoyed hot or with crushed ice (see page 256). If you can't find the special filters, use a regular plastic filter but follow the directions carefully for Vietnamese coffee.

Water spinach *(rau muong)*: Also called swamp cabbage or morning glory, this leafy green vegetable has crunchy hollow stems and arrowhead-shaped leaves. In Asia, it is generally grown in swamps and ponds. The Vietnamese like to make 'curls' out of the stems to use in salads and soups. *Rau muong* is used in simple stir-fries with garlic.

Wood-ear mushrooms *(nam meo)*: Also known as cloud ear and tree-ear mushrooms, these dried fungi don't have much flavour but are prized for their crunchy and slightly gelatinous texture. Once soaked in water, wood-ear mushrooms swell to many times their original size and become frilly clumps of rubbery tissue similar to seaweed. The two-toned larger mushrooms (black on top and tan on the bottom) can be tough and need to be sliced before using. The small black variety is better because it's tender yet still crunchy. Rinse these fungi well as they can be gritty. In Vietnam, these mushrooms are used in spring roll stuffings and in many vegetarian dishes.

Yard long beans *(dau dua)*: Also known as long beans or chopstick beans, these leggy beans, usually 30 cm (12 inches) or longer, are delicious in stir-fries, soups, curries and even salads. When buying this legume, look for young, thin pencil-like beans. There are several varieties: dark green, light green and, in recent years, purple. To use, cut into 5 to 7.5 cm (2 to 3 inch) lengths.

Menu Suggestions

WITH THE EXCEPTION of the dinner-party menu, the following menu suggestions are designed to capture the essential spirit of *New Flavours of the Vietnamese Table*: good, wholesome Vietnamese foods served in a casual manner. These are only suggestions, so feel free to mix, match and improvise. For beverages, try serving beer, iced tea, iced pandanus tea or water scented with sprigs of mint or lemon balm. For wine, try Viognier, Riesling, Roussanne, Gewürztraminer and Pinot Gris.

CELEBRATING PHO

Rice Paper-wrapped Salad Rolls with Prawns and Pork

Vietnamese Beef Noodle Soup

Iced Red Bean Pudding with Coconut Milk or
Vietnamese Coffee

NOODLES WITH FRIENDS

Grilled Prawn Paste on Sugarcane

Hanoi Rice Noodles with Grilled Pork or
Lemongrass Beef on Cool Noodles

Iced Pandanus Tea

FUN STREET-FOOD FARE

Crispy Spring Rolls

Rice Rolls with Prawns and Wood-ear Mushrooms or Sizzling Saigon Crêpes

Grandmother's Banana Stew with Tapioca Pearls

A VEGETARIAN FEAST

Salad Rolls with Jícama, Peanuts and Basil

Spicy Lemongrass Tofu

Claypot Rice with Ginger and Five Spices

Chopstick Beans with Garlic

Warm Soya Milk with Pandanus Leaf

A HOME-COOKED DINNER

Aunt Tam's Pork in Claypot

Sweet-and-sour Prawn Soup with Fresh Herbs

Table Salad

Shaking Beef

Roasted Aubergines with Spring Onion Oil

Steamed Rice

LOVING CRAB

Salt-and-pepper Crab with Ginger

Chopstick Beans with Garlic

Cucumber Salad

Steamed Rice

Lychee Sorbet

A VIETNAMESE DINNER PARTY

Mustard Leaf-wrapped Salad Rolls

Banana Blossom Salad with Chicken

Sea Bass with Lily Buds, Mushrooms and Cellophane Noodles

Caramelized Garlic Prawns

Water Spinach with Tofu

Steamed Rice

Crème Caramel or Fresh Fruit

Index